Theorising Learning to 1
Higher Education

Theorising Learning to Teach in Higher Education provides both lecturers embarking on a career in higher education and established members of staff with the capacity to improve their teaching. The process of learning to teach, and the associated field of professional academic development for teaching, is absolutely central to higher education. Offering innovative alternatives to some of the dominant work on teaching theory, this volume explores three significant approaches in detail: critical and social realist, social practice and sociomaterial approaches, which are divided into four sections:

- Sociomaterialism
- Practice theories
- Critical and social realism
- Crossover perspectives.

Readers will benefit from discussions on the role and place of theory in the process of learning to teach, whilst international case studies demonstrate the kinds of insights and recommendations that could emanate from the three approaches examined, drawing together contributions from Europe, Africa and Australasia.

Both challenging and enlightening, this book argues the need for theory in order to advance scholarship in the field and achieve goals related to social justice in higher education systems across the world. It draws attention to newly emerging theoretical perspectives and relatively underused perspectives to demonstrate the need for theory in relation to learning to teach.

This book will appeal to academics interested in how they come to learn to teach, to administrators and academic developers responsible for professional development strategies at universities and masters and PhD level students researching professional development in higher education.

Brenda Leibowitz is Chair of Teaching and Learning in the Education Faculty at the University of Johannesburg, South Africa.

Vivienne Bozalek is Professor of Social Work and Director of Teaching and Learning at the University of the Western Cape (UWC), South Africa.

Peter Kahn is Director of Studies for the online professional doctorate (EdD) in Higher Education at the University of Liverpool, UK.

The Society for Research into Higher Education (SRHE) is an independent and financially self-supporting international learned Society. It is concerned to advance understanding of higher education, especially through the insights, perspectives and knowledge offered by systematic research and scholarship.

The Society's primary role is to improve the quality of higher education through facilitating knowledge exchange, discourse and publication of research. SRHE members are worldwide and the Society is an NGO in operational relations with UNESCO.

The Society has a wide set of aims and objectives. Amongst its many activities the Society:

● is a specialist publisher of higher education research, journals and books, amongst them Studies in Higher Education, Higher Education Quarterly, Research into Higher Education Abstracts and a long running monograph book series.

The Society also publishes a number of in-house guides and produces a specialist series "Issues in Postgraduate Education".

● funds and supports a large number of special interest networks for researchers and practitioners working in higher education from every discipline. These networks are open to all and offer a range of topical seminars, workshops and other events throughout the year ensuring the Society is in touch with all current research knowledge.

● runs the largest annual UK-based higher education research conference and parallel conference for postgraduate and newer researchers. This is attended by researchers from over 35 countries and showcases current research across every aspect of higher education.

SRHE *Society for Research into Higher Education*
Advancing knowledge Informing policy Enhancing practice

73 Collier Street
London N1 9BE
United Kingdom

T +44 (0)20 7427 2350
F +44 (0)20 7278 1135
E srheoffice@srhe.ac.uk

www.srhe.ac.uk

Director: Helen Perkins
Registered Charity No. 313850
Company No. 00868820
Limited by Guarantee
Registered office as above

Society for Research into Higher Education (SRHE) series

Series Editors: Jennifer M. Case, University of Cape Town
Jeroen Huisman, University of Ghent

Published titles:

Intellectual Leadership in Higher Education: Renewing the Role of the University Professor
Bruce Macfarlane

Strategic Curriculum Change: Global Trends in Universities
Paul Blackmore and Camille B. Kandiko

Reconstructing Identities in Higher Education: The Rise of 'Third Space' Professionals
Celia Whitchurch

The University in Dissent: Scholarship in the Corporate University
Gary Rolfe

Everything for Sale?: The Marketisation of UK Higher Education
Roger Brown with Helen Carasso

Literacy in the Digital University: Critical Perspectives on Learning, Scholarship and Technology
Robin Goodfellow and Mary R. Lea

Researching Student Learning in Higher Education: A Social Realist Approach
Jennifer M. Case

Women Leaders in Higher Education: Shattering the myths
Tanya Fitzgerald

Writing in Social Spaces: A social processes approach to academic writing
Rowena Murray

Digital Technology and the Contemporary University: Degrees of digitization
Neil Selwyn

Stepping up to the Second Year at University: Academic, Psychological and Social Dimensions
Edited by Clare Milsom, Martyn Stewart, Mantz Yorke and Elena Zaitseva

Culture, Capitals and Graduate Futures
Ciaran Burke

Researching Higher Education: International perspectives on theory, policy and practice
Edited by Jennifer M. Case and Jeroen Huisman

Freedom to Learn: The threat to student academic freedom and why it needs to be reclaimed
Bruce Macfarlane

Student Politics and Protest: International Perspectives
Rachel Brooks

Theorising Learning to Teach in Higher Education
Edited by Brenda Leibowitz, Vivienne Bozalek and Peter Kahn

Theorising Learning to Teach in Higher Education

Edited by Brenda Leibowitz, Vivienne Bozalek and Peter Kahn

LONDON AND NEW YORK

First published 2017
by Routledge
2 Park Square, Milton Park, Abingdon, Oxon OX14 4RN

and by Routledge
711 Third Avenue, New York, NY 10017

Routledge is an imprint of the Taylor & Francis Group, an informa business

British Library Cataloguing in Publication Data
A catalogue record for this book is available from the British Library

Library of Congress Cataloging in Publication Data
A catalog record for this book has been requested

ISBN: 978-1-138-67726-5 (hbk)
ISBN: 978-1-138-67727-2 (pbk)
ISBN: 978-1-315-55960-5 (ebk)

Typeset in Galliard
by Saxon Graphics Ltd, Derby

MIX
Paper from
responsible sources
FSC
www.fsc.org   FSC® C013056

Printed and bound in Great Britain by
TJ International Ltd, Padstow, Cornwall

This book is dedicated to Wendy McMillan – in fond memory

Contents

Illustrations

Figures

Tables

(Use of table 3.1 – permission granted by David Cooper.)

Contributors

Paul Ashwin is Professor of Higher Education and Head of Department at the Department of Educational Research, Lancaster University, UK. Paul's research focuses on teaching – learning and knowledge – curriculum practices in higher education and their relations to higher education policies. Paul's book *Analysing Teaching–Learning Interactions in Higher Education* (2009, Continuum) critically examined different approaches to conceptualising teaching–learning interactions in higher education. He is the lead author of *Reflective Teaching in Higher Education* (2015, Bloomsbury), which is designed for all of those working in higher education who are interested in further developing research-informed approaches to university teaching.

Simon Barrie is the inaugural Pro Vice-Chancellor Learning Transformations at Western Sydney University, Australia. He is responsible for the leadership of strategic educational innovation and collaboration designed to shape the university's commitment to ensuring its students fulfill their potential as influential global citizen-scholars in a new technology-enabled world. His expertise is in engaging university communities to deliver new ways to enact the 'idea of the university' in a rapidly changing world. Simon has worked in the field of higher education for 25 years and is an award-winning teacher with an international reputation for his research on the transformative potential of higher education. He has led major national research and development projects to support Australian universities to renew their educational programmes to meet the needs of a new generation of learners. Prior to joining Western Sydney, Simon was Director of Teaching and Learning at the University of Sydney.

David Boud is Professor and Foundation Director of the Centre for Research in Assessment and Digital Learning, Deakin University, Melbourne and Research Professor in the Institute of Work-Based Learning, Middlesex University, London. He is also Emeritus Professor at the University of

Technology Sydney and an Australian Learning and Teaching Senior Fellow (National Teaching Fellow).

Vivienne Bozalek is a Professor of Social Work and the Director of Teaching and Learning at the University of the Western Cape. She holds a PhD from Utrecht University. Her research interests and publications include the political ethics of care and social justice, posthumanism and feminist new materialisms, innovative pedagogical practices in higher education, and post-qualitative and participatory methodologies. She has co-edited three books – one entitled *Community, Self and Identity: Educating South African Students for Citizenship* with Brenda Leibowitz, Ronelle Carolissen and other colleagues, another volume entitled *Discerning Hope in Educational Practices* with Brenda Leibowitz, Ronelle Carolissen and Megan Boler and a third entitled *Activity Theory, Authentic Learning and Emerging Technologies* with Jan Herrington, Joanne Hardman, Dick Ng'ambi and Denise Wood.

Angela Brew is a Professorial Fellow, Macquarie University, Australia. She is an Australian Learning and Teaching Senior National Teaching Fellow, an elected Fellow of the UK's Society for Research into Higher Education (SRHE) and a Life Member of the Higher Education Research and Development Society of Australasia (HERDSA). Her research is focused on the nature of research and its relation to teaching, learning and scholarship, models of research-led teaching and undergraduate research.

Sue Clegg is Emeritus Professor of Higher Education Research at Leeds Beckett University. She was a Mellon Visiting Scholar at the University of Cape Town in 2014. Her research draws on critical realism and feminist theory. She has been involved in theorising the nature of curriculum and researching extracurricular activity and the formation and recognition of social and cultural capital. She is currently working on the significance of powerful knowledge in higher education and its implications for theorising equity and diversity. She was editor of *Teaching in Higher Education* from 2006 to 2014. She plays a major role in the Society for Research into Higher Education and chairs their Publications Committee.

Anne Edwards is a Fellow of St Hilda's College Oxford and Professor Emerita at the University of Oxford, where she was Director of the Department of Education and co-founder of the Oxford Centre for Sociocultural and Activity Theory Research. She has worked as a teacher and researcher in higher education for 40 years, in both colleges and universities. She is a former President of the British Educational Research Association and a Visiting Professor at the University of Oslo. She has written extensively on learning in schools, universities and workplaces and holds honorary doctorates from the Universities of Oslo and Helsinki for her research on learning in and across practices.

Richard Edwards is Professor of Education in the Faculty of Social Sciences at the University of Stirling, UK. He has researched and written extensively on many aspects of education and lifelong learning, informed by post-structuralist and sociomaterialist theories (for a complete list of publications including many downloadable through the university's repository, see rms.stir.ac.uk/converis-stirling/person/11979). His most recent research is in two areas: exploring the hidden curriculum of algorithms and code in contexts of emerging infrastructures of digital higher education and their possible implications for curriculum and pedagogy; and examining the learning of people participating in citizen science projects.

Tara Fenwick is Professor of Education at the University of Stirling in the UK, and Director of ProPEL, international network for research in Professional Practice, Education and Learning, www.propel.stir.ac.uk. Her research focuses on understanding learning and practice in the changing complexities of professional work. Recent books include *Professional Responsibility and Professionalism: A Sociomaterial Examination* (2016, Routledge), *Reconceptualising Professional Learning: Sociomaterial Knowledges and Practices* (with M. Nerland, 2014, Routledge), *Professional Learning in Changing Contexts* (with M. Nerland, 2013, Routledge), *Emerging Approaches for Educational Research: Tracing the Sociomaterial* (with R. Edwards and P. Sawchuk, 2011, Routledge), and *Actor Network Theory in Education* (with R. Edwards, 2010, Routledge).

James Garraway is acting director of the Fundani Centre for Higher Education at the Cape Peninsula University of Technology in South Africa. He teaches on the regional GCert. equivalent in South Africa as well as on other informal regional and institutional academic development courses. He is particularly interested in boundary-crossing issues as students move into and out of the university system as well as ways to re-imagine the professional curriculum. His particular research interest currently is ways in which to apply activity theory to boundary-crossing and student learning within the university.

Lesley Gourlay is Head of the Department of Culture, Communication & Media, and a Reader in Education and Technology at UCL Institute of Education. Her background is in Applied Linguistics, and her current research interests include critical perspectives on student engagement in higher education, focusing on meaning-making, textual practices, digital literacies and multimodality. Her recent publications have focused on the relationships between sociomaterial perspectives and practices in higher education, with an emphasis on the role of textuality and meaning-making. She is a member of the Executive Editorial Board of the journal *Teaching in Higher Education*.

John Hannon is a Senior Lecturer in educational development at La Trobe University in Melbourne, Australia. He researches work, teaching and learning practices with emerging technologies, supervises research students and teaches on postgraduate courses in higher education. He has published extensively and internationally on educational technologies, academic development, professional practice, open education practices and intercultural communication, and has two awards for his publications. His current research focuses on academic work and teaching practices with the emergence of digital literacies in higher education contexts. In this research John draws on sociomaterial approaches to study the configurations and enactments of work and teaching practices. His research activity includes funded research into embedding digital literacies into curriculum and interdisciplinary teaching.

Peter Kahn is Director of Studies for the EdD in Higher Education at the University of Liverpool. His research interests centre on the application of perspectives from critical realism and realist social theory to the study of higher education. He is a National Teaching Fellowship holder in the UK, and a Principal Fellow of the Higher Education Academy.

Brenda Leibowitz is Chair: Teaching and Learning in the Education Faculty at the University of Johannesburg. Her key role at the university is to support the scholarship of teaching and learning amongst academics. She has been the convenor of the Southern African Universities Learning and Teaching (SAULT) Forum from 2014. She is team leader for a national NRF funded project, 'Interplay of structure, culture and agency: A study on professional development in higher education' and runs an interdisciplinary research project at the University of Johannesburg: 'SOTL @ UJ – Towards a Socially Just Pedagogy'. Her research interests include professional academic development, the scholarship of teaching and learning, language and academic literacy and social justice in higher education.

Marie Manidis has taught in secondary, vocational and higher education sectors with a teaching career spanning over 30 years and three countries. She has also undertaken a number of educational and curriculum-based research projects in these sectors. While at the University of Technology Sydney, she has taught in a range of areas including curriculum design and planning, language assessment, professional practice, research design, cultural diversity in the workplace and organisational workplace learning. Marie is currently a Postdoctoral Research Fellow investigating the first-year learning of international masters and doctoral research candidates. Her current interests are in the learning of social, organisational and professional practices in the health and academic sectors. In these areas Marie has published/presented papers in a number of domestic and international journals and conferences.

Martin Oliver is Professor of Education and Technology at the UCL Institute of Education, where he is also Head of the Centre for Doctoral Education. His research draws on the history and philosophy of technology, and explores issues of design, use and experience, primarily in the context of higher education. Recent publications have drawn on sociomaterial perspectives to investigate digital literacies; the curriculum; and infrastructures of studying.

Tai Peseta is a Senior Lecturer in the Education Innovation Team (formerly, Institute for Teaching and Learning) at the University of Sydney, Australia. Her research interests include doctoral education and curriculum, meso-level learning and teaching change, professional development of university teaching, and the scholarship of academic development. She is currently Points for Debate editor, *Higher Education Research and Development* (HERD journal), and is involved in two externally funded research projects: 'Reframing the PhD for Australia's future universities' (Australian Office for Learning and Teaching), and 'Challenges of access and equity: the higher education curriculum answers back' (World-wide Universities Network). She is a co-editor of the collection: *Identity Work in the Contemporary University: Exploring an Uneasy Profession* (2015, Sense).

Chris Winberg holds the South African National Research Foundation Chair in Work-integrated Learning and leads the Work-integrated Learning Research Unit in the Education Faculty of the Cape Peninsula University of Technology in Cape Town, South Africa. Chris' research focus is professional and vocational education (with a particular focus on engineering education), the professional development of university teachers and technical communication. She obtained a PhD in Applied Linguistics from the University of Cape Town and lectured in applied linguistics and language education at the University of Cape Town, the University of the Western Cape and at the University of Stockholm in Sweden. From 2010–2012, she was chairperson of the South African Association for Applied Linguistics. Chris was the director of the Fundani Centre for Higher Education Development at the Cape Peninsula University of Technology from 2011–2015, where she was responsible for supporting curriculum renewal, academic staff development, and for promoting educational research.

Keiko Yasukawa has been teaching and researching in Australian universities for over 30 years, initially in mathematics (where she gained her PhD) then more recently in adult education. Her research in recent years has focused on theorisations of critical mathematics and numeracy; adult literacy and numeracy pedagogy, practices and policy; and pedagogy and policies in vocational education and training. She is currently a lecturer in education at the University of Technology Sydney, where for many years she coordinated and taught in pre- and in-service teacher education programmes for adult literacy and numeracy, and vocational education and training teachers. Keiko is the lead editor of *Literacy and Numeracy Studies: An international journal in the education and training of adults.*

Preface

This book has come about due to the commitment and passion of large numbers of university teachers, researchers and academic developers in different parts of the world who desire to see teaching and learning flourish. As editors of this volume, we are aware that we all benefit from reading each other's scholarly contributions and books. We wanted to contribute to this scholarship with our particular thesis: that teaching is vitally important, learning to teach is vitally important, and theorising learning to teach is, indeed, extremely valuable and important.

This volume is in part the result of a six-year long study on the influence of institutional contexts on academics' decisions to participate in professional development activities in South Africa. In a project funded by the South African National Research Foundation, 18 academic developers from eight universities in varied geographical and socio-economic settings came together to investigate how contextual features such as: provision of resources and classroom facilities; policies on teaching and learning; interpersonal relationships amongst staff in faculties; leadership; provision of moral and material support for the professional development or professional learning of academics with regard to the teaching role, all influence academics' participation in professional development activities. The research project is called 'The interplay of structure, culture and agency: A study on the professional development of academics'. Towards the end of the second phase of the project, two of the researchers, Brenda Leibowitz and Vivienne Bozalek, wanted to explore the issue of theorising learning to teach at a meta-level, and to consider questions such as: What are the challenges and opportunities provided by different social theories? Does it matter a great deal what theory one uses to investigate a phenomenon such as learning to teach? And can one combine two or more theories from different philosophical and ontological orientations as a conceptual framework on which to base a study? At the same time, we wanted to share with a larger public, with the use of particular examples, the affordances of several lesser known theoretical approaches, which we had been exploring: sociomaterialism, practice-based theory and critical and social realism. Our project was informed by a critical and social realist perspective, but loosely so. There was an agreement amongst the team that individuals or sub-groups were free to apply other theoretical frameworks to analyse the data.

It was at this point that we made contact with our third editor, Peter Kahn, who has had a more concerted focus on the use of critical and social realist ideas in research on teaching and learning. He came out to South Africa and engaged fruitfully with the research team, a visit during which the idea of this book was conceived. John Hannon, a contributor to Chapter 13, also joined us in South Africa at a national colloquium we held, on contextual approaches to academic development. His interest in sociomaterialism gave a different flavour to our deliberations. We were fortunate that there were people on three continents who were enthusiastic to contribute to the topic of professional learning, in relation to the topics we were exploring. The result is this edited volume. Three (and a third) of the chapters in the book are based on data collected as part of the 'Interplay of structure, culture and agency' research project. We thank and acknowledge the rest of the research team for their participation and insights that have nourished our writing and deliberations.

We would in particular like to acknowledge the role played by the co-writer of Chapter 3, Wendy McMillan. We wish to dedicate this edited collection to Wendy, who was part of the National Research Foundation project on Culture, Structure and Agency, but who sadly passed away in December 2015. She was a great enthusiast for the project and dedicated many hours to the collection and analysis of data, as well as co-writing the University of the Western Cape (UWC)'s institutional report. She contributed to this edited collection by painstakingly reading through the data on interviews with vice-chancellors as well as reading the work of Karen Barad, even though her health was failing towards the end of her life. Her enthusiastic and painstaking contributions to this book and the project as a whole are acknowledged and continue in many forms after her physical passing. Wendy McMillan was an educational specialist in the Faculty of Dentistry, University of the Western Cape (UWC). She won two national awards for teaching and learning and was recognised for her contributions to the scholarship of teaching and learning in health sciences and more generally.

We celebrate the life of Wendy McMillan, as well as the creativity and dedication of academics all over the world. We also honour the scholars and researchers of learning to teach, onto whose scholarly edifice we add our own modest contribution.

Brenda Leibowitz, Vivienne Bozalek and Peter Kahn

Introduction

Brenda Leibowitz, Vivienne Bozalek and Peter Kahn

This book is an exploration of theorising learning to teach in higher education and the associated field of academic development. Our aim is to support those who are learning to teach, and those who conduct research on teaching and learning. We argue that research within this field benefits from an engagement with social and educational theories that assist with the pursuit of social justice in higher education. We do this by providing introductions to three theoretical approaches: sociomaterialism, practice-based approaches, and critical and social realism. We also provide case studies based on these three approaches, as well as 'crossover' cases, which use more than one theory simultaneously.

Why is theorising learning to teach so important?

For academics

Theorising learning to teach is valuable for academics, who are concerned with learning and development. Learning to teach is facilitated by opening up spaces where new conversations can be held across differences, and taken-for-granted assumptions can be interrogated (Bozalek 2011). Teaching in higher education has become more complex and challenging (Teichler 2006) with changing technologies, shifting worlds of work, and new and exciting teaching and learning approaches. But in many countries regimes of quality assurance, monitoring schemes and performance enhancement schemes deprive academics of a sense of commitment, intrinsic motivation and vocation. Theorising how we learn to teach can not only allow one to draw attention to the values and ethics that are inherently at stake in higher education, it can also provide insight into how we are positioned in the world and into the contributions we can make through our actions.

Theorising learning to teach provides a powerful means to extend insight into one's growth and development. It should help us to consider how to learn more, what steps to take, which constraints to avoid and which to attempt to overcome, and so on. Theorising can also help to consider teaching in relation to matters of ethics and values. Theory can provide a more substantive basis for criticality. Theorising should help to consider the purpose of what we do and the premises on which we base our decisions, in order that we teach for transformation in and through education (Kreber 2013). Being armed with expansive theories of how we learn, which we have interrogated in the light of our own experiences and reflections, should also help us to develop greater understanding and interest in how our students learn.

For academic developers

The habit of theorising about learning to teach is vital for those whose professional practice involves supporting the learning to teach of others – known variously as 'academic development', 'professional development' or 'faculty development' (Leibowitz, 2014) and more recently, 'teaching and learning' (Bozalek & Dison 2013). Theorising learning to teach is the form of expertise one requires in order to provide guidance to administrators and academics and to strengthen one's own sense of authority and identity. In many parts of the world academic developers are positioned as 'between', 'marginal' or 'liminal' (Green & Little 2013). The lack of appreciation of academics for the work of academic developers and vice versa was noted in the UK context by Healey and Jenkins in 2003, and this group frequently suffers at the mercy of policy regimes and organisational restructuring, as was pointed out in Australia by Palmer et al. (2011).

Theorising learning to teach allows for a more critical and careful underpinning of the professional advice academic developers provide. For example, learning to teach in higher education is regarded by many as a process that occurs naturally, on-the-job, by learning from more experienced academics and by interacting with students. In other instances it is viewed increasingly as something one learns via a formal programme, for example a certificate or diploma programme that takes place part-time over two years. These programmes are most common in Europe. In those settings where formal programmes to learn to teach are encouraged, there are often additional funding or teaching excellence schemes, as well as quality regimes, which, rather than suggest that an academic needs to be taught to teach, imply that one should be encouraged and motivated or monitored and policed to do so. Then there are those who believe that to support the professional learning of academics, one needs to pay attention to productive interpersonal relationships, career-path opportunities and positive material conditions which would both enable and motivate lecturers to learn. These views are all based on theories about how adult educators learn, whether these theories are implicit or explicit. At points one theory is favoured, and at points another. How do academic developers decide how to go about their work, and how do they decide how to advise senior administrators what change and enhancement strategies to devise, if they have not theorised how academics as adults learn to teach? For example, if the issue is seen as being located in the individual, as it is in certain theories, then learning to teach would involve changes either in the individual lecturer and what he or she does, or in the individual student – a remedial approach so that they can 'get up to speed'. However if the theory is relational – it is the whole assemblage which becomes important, including human and non-human entities. Furthermore, how do academics provide professional advice if they have not theorised a related phenomenon, how academics change? We agree with Trowler, Saunders and Bamber (2009, p. 7) that 'change agents should have an explicit theory of change if they want to increase their chances of success'.

For academic developers who see themselves as activists or lobbyists, there is a need for theorising that takes into account matters of institutional context as well as socio-political and material conditions. For instance, is there one strategy to support the professional learning of academics that would apply in the same way in a highly competitive, research-oriented and well-resourced university that attracts students from top-performing schools internationally, as in a university in a materially impoverished setting with students who come from low-performing schools? Similarly, is there one strategy to support academic development in an institution where there is an extremely authoritarian and top-down form of management, as in an institution where structures of management are relatively flat? And what of universities in contexts of conflict – between students and staff, or religious groupings or even genders? What theoretical positions facilitate our support for academics to learn to teach in these different settings?

For researchers

A final group that would benefit from theorising learning to teach are researchers and senior students in the field of professional academic development. In the current era there are very few educational journal reviewers or doctoral examiners who would view a study on learning to teach as adequate if it were not based on a conceptual framework that will allow the researcher to analyse the data, or if it were not informed by theories that the research would like to confirm or develop in some way. As Ashwin (2009) demonstrates, the theoretical lens one adopts has a crucial bearing on the way one then views teaching and learning, and on the outcomes of the research. Kahn (2015) argues further that one's theoretical stance has significant implications for how research methodology is framed, with implications for the values that one's research promotes.

There are many descriptive accounts, and a smaller, but still daunting number of theories about how professionals learn. Many of these have been applied to the learning of academics as teachers: from the 'how to' lists, to the psychological theories of the 1980s onwards (for example of Prosser & Trigwell 1999), the emphasis on reflection in and on action (Schön 1983), on critical reflection in transformation theory (Mezirow 1991), on situated learning and communities of practice (Wenger 1998), constructivist approaches, and many more. Given this wealth of theorisations to draw upon, one can quite easily become overwhelmed, or alternatively shy away from the more challenging theories. We argue that the solution is not to avoid, but to take the time to explore different theoretical approaches, and to work with those which are most illuminating, most helpful in terms of research design, most likely to lead to useful suggestions for a way forward, and most enjoyable to engage with. We also advocate working with theories that shed light on pressing matters that affect our time, that provide solutions to current and possible future problems, and that provide a clear sense of the purpose of teaching and learning in higher education. In this book we provide some interesting studies of higher education researchers, academic developers and academics all working with theories on learning to teach. In this way we seek to illustrate some of the benefits and illuminative power theories on learning to teach may have. We also provide some examples of researchers 'crossing over' from one theory to another, as a means to stimulate further reflection on the nature of theory and particular theories.

Motivation for our choice of approaches

Because we are interested in the idea of 'theorising' rather in advancing one particular theory, we have intentionally created a volume in which three theoretical perspectives lie side by side. We consciously chose three which are less mainstream in the scholarly literature on teaching and learning, to provide some exposure to them, but in addition, because we believe they have significant explanatory power. One of the appeals of the three theories for us as editors is that all three deal with issues of ethics and facilitate considerations of values and social justice.

In the next section we provide a brief explanation of the three theoretical approaches.

The three theoretical approaches

Sociomaterialism prioritises the material – holding that 'matter matters' – and is not docile or passive, but is capable of making itself intelligible. Sociomaterialism does not privilege or centre humans above non-humans, but sees them on an ontologically similar plane. Furthermore, sociomaterialism is based on a relational ontology, where individual or discrete entities are not seen to pre-exist relationships – rather they are constituted through relationships, as is agency. Karen Barad (2007) refers to this as 'entanglement' while Deleuze and Guattari (1987) refer to it as 'assemblages'. Sociomaterialism rejects humanism's dualistic and hierarchical taxonomies, or representational thought, arguing instead for a flat ontology beyond dualisms, hierarchies and stable, closed or essentialised meanings (MacLure 2013). Thus discourse and matter are regarded as being mutually constituted – material-discursive – in sociomaterialism. Sociomaterialism proposes that the university teacher or researcher is part of the world, rather than ontologically separate and exterior to it, which has implications for critique, intentionality and reflexive practice, all of which assume a position of exteriority or distance, as elaborated in the first section of this book.

Practice-based approaches cover a broad range of theories about learning, as is discussed in the opening chapter in the second part of this volume, which illuminates these approaches. Within these approaches, learning is seen as contextual, social and ongoing, with individuals learning (Hager, Lee & Reich 2012) or even forming an identity (Dreier, 1999) via participation. Fenwick and Nerland (2014, p. 3) describe the centrality of practices in learning thus: 'practices, both as an enactment of and a medium for learning, have been argued to weave knowing together with action, conversation and affect in purposeful and regularised orderings of human activity'. Practices are 'embodied', thus not purely cognitive. Practice-based theories emphasise the contextual, the action-based, the experiential, the relational, the social as well as the material. Professional learning, from this point of view, takes into account the way that doings and understandings are repeated and organised not only by the lecturer, but also by features of the context, including how others teach and understand their teaching. Supporting lecturers to learn to teach requires attention to the practices themselves, thus not solely to lecturers as individuals.

The final cluster of theories that is covered by the book is critical and social realism. This paradigm operates in the first instance as a broad philosophical stance, offering an alternative standpoint to both positivist and postmodern notions of the social world. In this view, education is not simply about that which can be measured and nor can it simply be reduced to the experiences of knowers. The field stems most directly from the work of Roy Bhaskar on the philosophy of science during the 1970s. Bhaskar (1979) argued that social reality is constituted by causal tendencies that give rise to the actual events that we experience, even if it remains the case that our knowledge of the different strata that are apparent in this account are fallible. The world is held to exist in a way that remains connected to our human constructions of it. The field offers scope to facilitate non-reductionist analysis of the relations between environments for learning, knowledge and the interior worlds of teachers and learners. A range of theorists are more or less closely associated with this paradigm including Archer (1996), Lawson (2006) and, to a lesser extent, Bernstein (2000). The emphasis on explanatory critique in the field is designed in part to help contribute towards emancipatory action.

Structure of the book

The book is divided into four parts, including one on each of the theoretical stances. Since the book is intended for readers from a wide variety of disciplinary orientations, we have included a chapter that provides an introduction to each of the theories. The parts contain several additional chapters that further elaborate on the theories or show what they can offer for researching learning to teach. The fourth part, containing 'crossover' approaches, tackles by example some of the meta-questions raised in this introduction about choosing theoretical approaches. They feature some of the advantages of the different theories and the feasibility of using them within research studies together.

A note on the varied approaches in the book: readers will notice that there are a variety of styles, influenced by authors' personal preferences and the theoretical orientation being discussed. Some chapters are discursive, whereas others offer advice for learning to teach, professional academic development or for research in this area. A further outcome of the exploration of varied conceptual approaches is that there are terms used across the book in different ways. The usage of the terms 'agency' or 'reflection' provide examples of this. This will become apparent in the chapters themselves. Most importantly, readers will notice that not all authors within a part interpret a theory in exactly the same way, which is a significant point: theories are not unitary bodies of thought, but more like clusters of consonant ideas that build upon one another.

Part I: Sociomaterialism

Part I starts with an introductory chapter on sociomaterialism. This chapter is useful for the reader who knows little about sociomaterialism and its relation to learning to teach in higher education, as it provides an accessible introduction to understanding this framework by elaborating on shared notions informing sociomaterial practices, as well as some differences. Tara Fenwick and Richard Edwards consider how sociomaterialism could inform practices of learning to teach in relation to criticality and social justice. The chapter also uses the work of Bruno Latour (2004) to critique critique – from the viewpoint of social justice, and Fenwick and Edwards explore the implications of this critique for critical higher education pedagogies. This critique of critique is taken further in the third chapter in this part by Vivienne Bozalek and Wendy McMillan, who propose a diffractive methodology, from a new materialist perspective, in lieu of critique. A diffractive methodology is used in this chapter to examine the details of transcribed interview data of South African vice-chancellors in a respectful and care-full manner, reading one text through another in an attempt to create something new and develop inventive provocations (Barad 2007). Using Barad's (2014) and MacLure's (2013) notions of curiosity, surprise and wonder, Bozalek and McMillan focus on one of the interviews with the vice-chancellors, which appealed as a 'hot spot' or 'data that glowed' (MacLure, 2013) in relation to social justice and inequalities regarding learning to teach in South Africa.

The second chapter of this section on sociomaterialism by Lesley Gourlay and Martin Oliver provides a practical example of how sociomaterialism can be used in academic development by focusing on the entanglements of students and their knowledge practices with print-based and digital technologies. The authors show how sociomaterialism might be fruitful as an approach as it pays attention to a more situated stance to academic development. They illustrate the importance of networks and entanglements by referring to a set of academic development materials developed as part of a UK government-funded JISC 'Developing Digital Literacies' research project. These materials, based on themes arising from an analysis of students' multimodal journal data, use ethnographic links to students' networked, situated sociomaterial practice, rather than relying on or being structured by more abstract categorisation.

The fourth chapter, by Richard Edwards and Tara Fenwick, provides another example of sociomaterialism and its application to knowledge infrastructures and how they are made to work in higher education. This is a relatively new, emerging area of investigation in higher education, which has to date focused largely on learning analytics in a rather enthusiastic manner for learning to teach, without much hesitation about the pitfalls of these, from the perspective of equity and justice. The chapter explores some of the challenges and possibilities of digital analytics and visualisations, and their implications for learning to teach in higher education.

Part II: Practice theories

Part II on practice begins with an introduction to the field by David Boud and Angela Brew, who summarise key tenets of the literature on practice, and the implications for theorising learning, change and teaching. They conclude with two important implications from practice theory: that learning is not based on a deficit notion of lecturers' learning and that responsibility for learning is shared. In the second chapter in the section Marie Manidis and Keiko Yasukawa illustrate central themes within practice theory, namely, that learning is situated and that it comprises an ecology of overlapping practices. Keiko's approach to teaching, and the manner in which she and Marie document this, provide an illustration of the richness suggested by this way of understanding teaching and learning. In the third chapter in this section Tai Peseta and Simon Barrie turn the gaze from lecturers to academic developers, and how they are inducted into the profession. Practice-based approaches are not a tight, homogenous field. Whilst Manidis and Yasukawa surface a concept allied to that of practice, that of 'metapractices', Peseta and Barrie illustrate a term linked to the theory, that of 'stewardship', which they believe will enrich theories on practice in higher education. They argue for the idea of caring for the field of academic development, and for those who enter it, via on-the-job and judiciously selected contextual mechanisms. Anne Edwards rounds off this section by considering the contribution of practice via an emphasis on the learning of the student, and what this might mean for learning to teach. Her closing chapter for this part draws from one of the theoretical contributions to practice theories: cultural historical activity theory, derived from the work of Lev Vygotsky. Edwards' chapter provides a useful bridge to the final part, on critical and social realism, as it focuses on concepts from practice, such as the social situation of development, and it discusses an idea which is foundational to the work of social realist, Margaret Archer – that of agency.

Part III: Critical and social realism

The field of critical realism is well known for the density of its specialist lexicon. Technical terms abound in texts that are linked to the field. The first chapter in Part III thus provides an introduction that is both accessible and closely argued.

It also demonstrates why the field provides us with resources to think about learning to teach and higher education at large. This chapter comes from Sue Clegg, one of the earliest researchers to apply critical and social realist perspectives to the study of higher education (Clegg 2005). In the next chapter, Peter Kahn argues that the constraints and enablements of the context within which teaching occurs, as well as the possibilities and limitations of agency, need to inform professional development practice for the emergence of high quality education. Drawing on perspectives from Archer, this chapter focuses on scope for agency when teaching is set within a particularly challenging context. It shows how the context of a particular higher education system impacts on teaching and learning practice, and on the professional development of academic staff in their teaching role. This part concludes with a chapter by Chris Winberg, which looks at how both teaching and the process of learning to teach occurs on a collective basis. In this it shares an emphasis that is common to other parts of the book. However, this chapter offers a distinctive account in exploring the role that individual and collective reflexivity, central themes of realist social theory (Archer 2007), nonetheless play in shaping teaching.

Part IV: Crossover perspectives

The final part of the book is focused on crossover perspectives aligned to the three main theoretical paradigms. This part opens with a chapter by Brenda Leibowitz that addresses a range of questions of relevance to the academic wishing to think more deeply about their professional learning, the academic developer seeking to develop a professional practice based on engagement with theory, and the researcher intent on investigating this field. Does it matter which theories one adopts? Can one use theories with very different philosophical bases in combination? On what basis does one choose a theoretical framework? She offers an exploration of these questions that is both autobiographical and discursive, based on a project that involved 18 academic developers from across South Africa. She considers what the different theoretical stances highlighted by the book illuminate about the process of learning to teach, whether in their philosophical foundations, or the advantages and limitations they pose for developing precepts for practice. The chapter by John Hannon, James Garraway, Tai Peseta and Chris Winberg stems from an international project that looked at workgroups linked to a programme of professional development on university teaching and learning. The account draws on the three main theoretical perspectives to explore how academic knowledge and practices are negotiated and produced. In looking at how workgroups operate, it considers how the positions taken by the theories illuminate various aspects of learning to teach. Their analysis considers also how one's theoretical stance influences the methodology and conclusions of one's research.

The concluding chapter by Paul Ashwin explores what is highlighted by the different accounts of learning to teach in higher education and what remains hidden. Based on this analysis, he considers the implications for future research, practices and policies related to learning to teach in higher education, and makes the important point that the introduction or adoption of 'new' theories should not erase the significance or prior theories. Rather, they should build on what came before.

References

Archer, M. S. (1996), *Culture and agency: The place of culture in social theory*, Cambridge University Press, Cambridge.

Archer, M. S. (2007), *Making our way through the world: Human reflexivity and social mobility*, Cambridge University Press, Cambridge.

Ashwin, P. (2009), *Analysing teaching-learning interactions in higher education: Accounting for structure and agency*, Continuum, London.

Barad, K. (2007), *Meeting the universe halfway: Quantum physics and the entanglement of matter and meaning*, Duke University Press, Durham.

Barad, K. (2014), 'On touching – the inhuman that therefore I am (v1.1)', in S. Witzgall & K. Stakemeier (eds), *Power of material/politics of materiality*, Diaphanes eText, Zurich-Berlin.

Bernstein, B. (2000), *Pedagogy, symbolic control and identity: Theory, research, critique*, Rowan & Littlefield, Oxford.

Bhaskar, R. (1979), *The possibility of naturalism: A philosophical critique of contemporary human science*, Harvester Press, Brighton.

Bozalek, V. (2011), 'Acknowledging privilege through encounters with difference: Participatory learning and action techniques for decolonizing technologies in Southern contexts', *International Journal of Social Research Methodology*, vol. 4, no. 6, pp. 465–80.

Bozalek, V. & Dison, A. (2013), 'Using the human capabilities approach as a normative framework to evaluate institutional teaching and learning interventions at UWC', *South African Journal of Higher Education*, vol. 27, no. 2, pp. 383–400.

Clegg, S. (2005), 'Theorising the mundane: The significance of agency', *International Studies in the Sociology of Education*, vol. 15, no. 2, pp. 149–64.

Deleuze, G. & Guattari, F. (1987), *A thousand plateaus: Capitalism and schizophrenia*, (trans. and foreword B. Massumi), University of Minnesota Press, Minneapolis.

Dreier, O. (1999), 'Personal trajectories of participation across contexts of social practice', *Outlines*, vol. 1, no. 1, pp. 5–32.

Fenwick, T. & Nerland, M. (2014), 'Editors' introduction' to *Reconceptualising professional learning: Sociomaterial knowledges, practices and responsibilities*, Routledge, London.

Green, D. A. & Little, D. (2013), 'Academic development on the margins', *Studies in Higher Education*, vol. 38, no. 4, pp. 523–37.

Hager, P., Lee, A. & Reich, A. (2012), *Practice, learning and change: Practice-theory perspectives on professional learning*, Springer, Dordrecht.

Healey, M. & Jenkins, A. (2003). 'Discipline-based educational development', in: H. Eggins & R. MacDdonald (eds), *The scholarship of academic development*, Buckingham, SRHE and OUP.

Kahn, P. (2015), 'Critical perspectives on methodology in pedagogic research', *Teaching in Higher Education*, vol. 20, no. 4, pp. 442–54.

Kreber, C. (2013), *Authenticity in and through teaching in higher education: The transformative potential of the scholarship of teaching*, Routledge, London.

Latour, B. (2004), 'Why has critique run out of steam? From matters of fact to matters of concern', *Critical Inquiry*, vol. 30, pp. 225–48.

Lawson, T. (2006), *Economics and reality*, Routledge, London.

Leibowitz, B. (2014), 'Reflections on academic development: What's in a name?' *International Journal for Academic Development*, vol. 19, no. 4, pp. 357–60.

MacLure, M. (2013), 'Classification or wonder? Coding as an analytic practice in qualitative research', in R. Coleman & J. Ringrose (eds), *Deleuze and research methodologies*, Edinburgh University Press, Edinburgh.

Mezirow, J. (1991), *Transformative dimensions of adult learning*, Jossey Bass, San Francisco.

Palmer, S., Holt, D. & Challis, D. (2011), 'Strategic leadership of teaching and learning centres: From reality to ideal', *Higher Education Research & Development*, vol. 30, no. 6, pp. 807–21.

Prosser, M. & Trigwell, K. (1999), *Understanding learning and teaching: The experience in higher education*, Oxford University Press, Buckingham.

Schön, D. (1983), *The reflective practitioner: How professionals think in action*, Basic Books, New York.

Teichler, U. (2006), *Changing structures of the higher education systems: The increasing complexity of underlying forces*, ingentaconnect.com

Trowler, P., Saunders, M. & Bamber, V. (2009), 'Introduction: Continuities, enhancement and higher education', in V. Bamber, P. Trowler, M. Saunders & P. Knight (eds) *Enhancing learning, teaching, assessment and curriculum in higher education*, Oxford University Press, Maidenhead.

Wenger, E. (1998), *Communities of practice: Learning, meaning and identity*, Cambridge University Press, Cambridge.

Part I

Sociomaterialism

Sociomaterialism

Chapter 1

How sociomaterial approaches could support higher education as a critical practice

Tara Fenwick and Richard Edwards

Introduction

In higher education, as elsewhere, sociomaterial approaches focus not on an individual learner or an individual's skills, but on the collective, where this embraces the human and non-human. In this collective, we need to recognise the ways that materiality of all kinds – both the human and non-human – actively enable, influence and constrain what people think and do, the patterns in which they move, and the consequences of their activities. 'Stuff' matters, and it is matter. Knowing and capability are not generated and controlled only through humans. They are more-than-human, produced at least partly through the ways things work on, with and through humans' perceptions, emotions, practices and judgements (e.g. Nespor 1994, Edwards 2011, Fenwick & Edwards 2014).

Yet materials are often missing from accounts of higher education, and specifically in programmes and events that focus on learning to teach in higher education. Materials tend to be accepted simply as part of the backdrop for human action, overlooked because of a preoccupation with consciousness and cognition, or relegated to brute tools subordinated to human intention and design. Clearly, in higher education, a range of materials shape practice and pedagogy: textbooks and tests, digital broadband and databases, grassy commons and car parks, locked doors and passwords, dust and bodies, etc. These things each embed histories as well as values, and are deeply bound in the politics of what it becomes permissable to know and to do. As such, they raise questions for how we approach teaching and how we understand our own pedagogic practices.

However, a sociomaterial approach is not characterised by an enumeration of objects. The emphasis is not just on acknowledging all these things, but on analysing webs of relations – the entanglements of material with social forces. These entanglements bring forth what appear to be particular separate objects, communities, or spaces. For instance, while most educators appreciate the importance of their environments of practice, these environments actually are comprised of a myriad of specific relations among technological, affective, natural, manufactured, symbolic and bodily sociomaterial dynamics. Human thought, intention and feeling are woven into these dynamics – neither subordinate to them, but not governing them, either. These relations and the particular ways that they exert influence to enable or constrain ideas and actions are too often washed into vague references to big categories: cultures and structures, like racism or curriculum. While such categories may be useful shorthand descriptions to refer to broad patterns, they tend to reassert the centrality of human activity, meanings and identities – even when writers think to add 'ecological' considerations to their analysis to remind us of contextual issues affecting human activity.

The main problem is when such big categories become identifiable, commonplace, even inevitable entities to organise the flux of existence. Wielding such categories to understand the complexities of what becomes enacted in higher education teaching and learning, we can quickly lose the capacity to discern critical nuances that make all the difference. How do particular human and non-human things assemble and change one another to produce important (problematic or desirable) effects, in terms of whatever educative purpose is adopted? Or even, what new purposes are being suggested through these relations? How are capacities produced (as a collective phenomenon)? What constraints or exclusions are generated through certain sociomaterial relations? What new productive possibilities are emerging that could be amplified? While such questions are significant for all educational practices, they are especially important where there are explicit attempts to develop a higher education to support justice and equity rather than simply reproduce existing hierarchies and inequalities. Yet how frequently do we address such questions when learning to teach?

This chapter offers a brief, introductory account of sociomaterial understandings and how these might both inform our pedagogies as well as, in the spirit of this volume, support higher education as a critical and just practice.[1] It is in four parts. First, we introduce some shared ideas informing a variety of sociomaterial approaches and some of their differences. Second, drawing specifically upon the work of Bruno Latour (2004), we outline an approach to critique derived from actor-network theory and some of the implications for higher education as a just practice. Third, given that criticality is often perceived to be a key purpose of higher education, we will explore the implications of sociomateriality for critical higher education pedagogies. Finally, we draw out some general points and issues for further consideration. The argument is suggestive rather than exhaustive. For fuller discussion and illustrations, see Fenwick and Edwards (2010), Fenwick et al. 2011 and Fenwick and Landri (2014).

Sociomateriality – it's matter that matters

By sociomateriality we refer to a broad arena of academic endeavour which is seeking to revalue and reconceive the role of matter and material relations in human practices. Sociomaterial approaches help to make visible the material dynamics in practice situations – the moving relationships among bodies, substances, objects, technologies and settings as well as symbols and desires, human interactions and emotions. A sociomaterial approach treats the material and the social as mutually implicated in bringing forth everyday action and knowledge. The emphasis shifts away from preoccupations with language, communication, discourses and identity. Instead, materiality is foregrounded as a critical force in relation with the social. It is in the relations among both material and social forces that everyday practices are produced. Capacity is thus viewed as distributed; agency is not a capacity inherent in human actors alone, but in their relations within the more-than-human.

For us, sociomateriality embraces certain strands of work in, for instance, actor-network theory (ANT) and its many 'post' ANT performances, posthumanism, new materialism, practice-based theories, spatial theory, non-representational theory and complexity theory. In referring to a range of different academic endeavours like this, we recognise the need to keep open their points of difference as well as their affinities. Although they are all distinct and have important differences, we could argue that they share at least three broad overlapping common elements.

First, they do not erase human activity, but help to highlight the ways materiality enables, expresses, shapes and extends it. In higher education, we often focus on cognition, meaning-making, dialogue and reflection. We tend to lose sight of how physical settings shape the possible meanings and solutions, how tools embed knowledges and elicit particular ways of using them, and how particular bodies evoke particular forms of dialogue. We also tend to focus on individual human beings as though they act separately from the material objects, technologies and settings that penetrate us and one another, 'intra-acting' to bring forth what appear to be solid separate things (Barad 2007).

One example of this can be seen in our own studies of simulation education involving mannequins (e.g. SimMan®) and simulated hospital wards, tutors' instructions from the side, and video cameras through which students' performance is observed and assessed. Students' activity and knowledge is brought forth in material spaces that are simultaneously pedagogical, pretend-real medicine, and real materials entangled with what students do:

> For many students entering the SimMan® scenario with the acute trauma, an initial difficulty is simply entering and engaging with the built simulated environment. It is foreign, they appear initially awkward, as though suddenly conscious of their bodies and hands as intruders in this space. One performs a rectal examination but forgets a glove. When SimMan® 'vomits' (gagging sounds from the room speaker), the tutor is side-coaching – Get your hands in there! Really get into his mouth!
>
> In the multi ward scenario the student doctor enters a cubicle, the patient is sitting in the bedside chair. The student draws near to take the history and sits on the bed, a cardinal error which he realises immediately but then seems unable to correct. He is also aware that he may now have failed the simulation. Yet he feels stuck there, unsure how to change the arrangements or conclude the session effectively. As one tutor explains, students find it

difficult to respond proactively to the environment – they react as though other people and events are doing things to them.

(from Fenwick & Abrandt Dahlgren 2015, p. 362)

Second, phenomena are taken to be gatherings of heterogeneous natural, technical, human and non-human elements. What appears to be an independent 'object', such as the mannequin students practice on, is not a static thing with inherent properties that sprang into being. Rather, it has been brought about through a history of negotiations, which generated its design and accumulated uses. If we examine the SimMan® mannequin now, in a particular situation, we realise that it is not separate from the particular ways in which it is being used. It is performed into being in this gathering of human and non-human dynamics – it is an *effect* of these sociomaterial relations. Researchers examine these gatherings, asking how and why some elements become combined, some become included and others excluded, and most importantly, how elements change as they come together, as they intra-act. Everything – such as standards of teaching practice, disciplinary identities, laboratory skills as well as objects and environments – is performed into existence in webs of relations. Materials are enacted, not inert. They *act*, together with other types of things and forces, to exclude, invite, and regulate activity. This is not arguing that objects have agency (the capacity to act). Any educational practice, even one as commonplace as lecturing, is a collective sociomaterial enactment, not a question solely of an individual's cognitive and practical skills, as anyone whose computer has crashed in the middle of a presentation will testify.

Third, many sociomaterial perspectives accept uncertainty as an operating principle in everyday life, as well as in the knowledge, tools, environments and identities that are continually produced within it. Uncertainty is not just ambiguity: it means that chance and emergence are always operating in the unfolding configurations, which continually open a multiplicity of possibilities. Unpredictable novel patterns are always emerging. Sociomaterial theories offer specific analytic tools that can examine much more precisely just how these new assemblages, or combinations of things, are emerging, why they come together to produce and mobilise particular effects, and when they do not.

Within these broad common elements, there are very different approaches and views among sociomaterial perspectives. Here we provide a very brief introduction to four that are influential within the discussion of different aspects of higher education pedagogy – actor-network theory (ANT), complexity theory, practice theory and new materialisms.

ANT is a methodology, not a theory, emerging from poststructural orientations and STS (Science and Technology Studies). It treats human and non-human elements as co-contributors to networks, which assemble and reassemble to generate the things of the world (e.g. Latour 2005). When anyone speaks of a system or 'structure', like capitalism or racism, ANT asks, how has it been compiled? Where is it? What is holding it together? ANT traces how these assemblages are made and sustained, how they order behaviours as well as space and objects, but also how they can be unmade. ANT therefore is very good at examining taken-for-granted practices, such as curriculum implementation or assessment practices (e.g. Nespor 1994; Sørenson 2009; Edwards 2011).

Complexity theory offers a range of approaches emerging chiefly from evolutionary biology and physics, cybernetics and general systems theories. Most view phenomena, events and actors as mutually dependent and mutually constitutive, emerging together in unpredictable, dynamic patterns. Emergence occurs through myriad interactions among diverse elements: these are non-linear and freely forming, have some overlap and a few simple constraining rules, but crucially have bottom-up organisation and multiple feedback loops. Complexity theorists in education such as Davis and Sumara (2006) and Osberg and Biesta (2007) are particularly interested in how to introduce these dynamics of emergence, nested systems, and self-organisation into classrooms, as well as how to help students learn to negotiate the dynamic complexity of life.It is important to mention the growing higher education interest in 'practice theory'. This often works from conceptions of 'knowing-in-practice', where knowing is a continuous enactment performed through assemblages that are taken to be more-than-human (e.g. Hager et al. 2012, Nicolini 2012). A wide range of research using these theories is tracing practice in different organisations. Studies might ask, how do different groups negotiate ways to work together when each is shaped by very different logics, instruments, material procedures, etc? Or, how does the introduction of a new technology reshape not only how people work and learn, but also their relations with others, their identities, and their knowledge?

Finally, an important branch of studies that is gaining widespread influence in educational research is calling itself 'new materialisms' to differentiate their approach from historical materialism rooted in Marxist conceptions (e.g. Coole & Frost 2010, Dolphijn & van der Tuin 2012, Lenz Taguchi 2010). These are particularly interested in bodily meshings with materials of all kinds, and often work from ideas of philosopher Gilles Deleuze of process ontology and continuous 'becoming', or Karen Barad's vocabulary of 'intra-acting' to examine how particular social and material forces bring forth very different ways of being. Many chapters of this book develop these ideas in detail so we will not dwell on them here.

In general, sociomaterial approaches help us to examine established practices that have become taken for granted and entrenched: blackboxes, in Latour's (2005) words. Examples in higher education might include systems of establishing student records or timetables, spaces such as VLEs (virtual learning environments), lecture theatres, slide presentation software, and so forth. For higher education pedagogy, sociomaterial approaches offer resources to open the material relations holding such practices in place, and the ways in which many forms of inequity may be enacted through them. Concurrently, sociomaterial sensibilities attune to the unpredictability as well as the patterns that offer new possibilities, as well as the emergent effects of any attempts to change practices. Increasingly, some higher education researchers in developing countries, and particularly those focused on technology-enhanced learning, are turning to sociomaterial approaches to provide better – more nuanced – understandings of the complexities involved in the inextricable entanglements of diverse people and beliefs, policies and politics, technologies and environments (Quimno et al. 2013). Sociomaterial approaches offer methods by which to recognise and trace the multifarious struggles, negotiations and accommodations whose effects constitute the 'things' in education, whether one's focus is upon teaching and learning, identities and recognition, participation and access, research and the politics of knowledge, or freedom and justice. Rather than such concepts be taken as foundational categories, or objects with properties, they can be explored as themselves effects of heterogeneous relations. The concepts can also help us to open up the black boxes of the purposes of higher education and here we come to the discussion of criticality and pedagogy.

Materiality, criticality and justice

Sociomaterial approaches could be viewed as apolitical, disinterested in issues of power and inequality, better at providing description more than prescription. However, we argue that they offer alternative ways of framing these issues, different approaches to criticality and critique and thus address existing inequities and injustices, which have interesting possibilities for pedagogy (Postma 2014, Edwards & Fenwick 2015). To explore this issue, we focus on the work of Latour (2004, 2005) and his argument that established practices of critique in the social sciences, in particular those influenced by the work of Bourdieu, have run out of steam. If higher education pedagogy aims to develop criticality in certain of its practices, and Latour is correct, then his observations need to be considered, not least if we utilise those approaches to critique to promote different, more just forms of practice. This is a position also argued persuasively, if from different theoretical framings, by, for instance, Boltanski and Thevenot (2006) and Braidotti (2013). 'The critique of critique objects to the now dominant forms of social and cultural criticism for their denunciative mode of critique' (Folkers 2016, p. 4). The high-level argument is that good critique needs to be affirmative and experimental and not simply an unveiling of power relations and what is wrong. Critique needs to be working *through* practices and not simply *about* them, from which arise implications for higher education pedagogy, who and the ways in which people are engaged as 'students' and the forms of studentship and criticality to which they are enrolled.

Many critical educationalists have worked hard to reveal the machinations of capitalism, interrupt knowledge that is commonly described as received thinking or supporting false inevitabilities, or expose the power flows that are claimed to produce domination or limit subjectivities. Yet educational practices have more or less successfully avoided changing the existing reproductions of power and inequalities despite these critiques. Talking and writing *about* power, inequity and injustice have made certain things visible, but the practices emerging in enacting that visibility have not significantly changed the issues critiqued, as they tend to be framed within a representational epistemological stance (Hacking 1983). Inequalities continue to be supported through higher educational practices, despite, or maybe in part because of, those established practices of critique.

Latour (2004) comments on the way the critic can unveil the truth to others by identifying the agents through which power is exercised behind their backs. Here, the logic of critique is about taking apart, separating out and unveiling what lies behind actors to explain their position and actions:

> This time it is the poor bloke, again taken aback, whose behavior is now 'explained' by the powerful effects of indisputable matters of fact: 'You, ordinary fetishists, believe you are free but, in reality, you are acted on by forces you are not conscious of. Look at them, look, you blind idiot' (and here you insert whichever pet facts the social scientists fancy to work with, taking them from economic infrastructure, fields of discourse, social domination, race, class, and gender, maybe throwing in some neurobiology, evolutionary psychology, whatever, provided they act as indisputable facts whose origin, fabrication, mode of development are left unexamined).
>
> (Latour 2004, p. 238)

For Latour, these social substitutes do not explain, but themselves need exploring, as the social alone cannot be taken as foundational. He is arguing that explanations relying upon taken-for-granted social categories substitute the invisible and hidden for the visible. The politics – and we would suggest higher education practice – emerging from this form of social explanatory critique is limited, a commentary on how most actors are dupes of some order or other that is beyond them. It is the critic that is always right and able to see what is invisible to others. This suggests that the forms of criticality emerging from such approaches simply reinforce the injustices and inequities that they unveil, because the general populace is caught in forms of 'false consciousness' and addressing such situations requires more than enlightenment and the assumptions of human agency and exceptionalism upon which they are based. In other words, such traditional forms of critique are not able to mobilise the actor-networks through which issues can be addressed more fully.

From within ANT, Latour offers an alternative approach for criticality:

> The critic is not the one who debunks, but the one who assembles. The critic is not the one who lifts the rugs from under the feet of the naive believers, but the one who offers the participants arenas in which to gather. The critic is not the one who alternates haphazardly between antifetishism and positivism like the drunk iconoclast drawn by Goya, but the one for whom, if something is constructed, then it means it is fragile, and thus in great need of care and caution.
>
> (Latour 2004, p. 246)

These practices of assembling are not to be encompassed through traditional forms of higher education practice, that separate out some student groups from others and from non-students, that separate out knowing-in-practice into different disciplinary framings, that focus on the cognitive and the literary at the expense of other forms of becoming, that separate out the human from the non-human, and the mind from the body, and that separate the social from the material. In this framing, to focus on a socially just higher education is already to limit what can be achieved, as the social as a separate domain of life is only one aspect of the practices of inequity and injustice. It is for such reasons that Latour has been critical of parts of the environmental movement for separating nature from society, as for him it is through their differing assemblings that environmental problems have been generated and from which the possibilities for sustainability emerge. Similarly, the sociomaterial assemblings through which inequity and injustice are enacted in higher education as part of wider practices can only be addressed by developing alternative assemblings of the human and non-human rather than through a focus on *social* justice as a separate domain. Assembling to experiment in ways of being takes precedence over separating and explaining. This entails very different forms of higher education and pedagogic practices than the ones with which we are perhaps more familiar.

There is an invitation, openness and hospitality in such practices that some might find unsatisfactory. To offer critique might be argued to make a stand, to have a standpoint, to emancipate ourselves from something. For Latour, the danger of such enactments is that they can result in too hasty separations and closures, turning matters of concern into matters of fact under hegemonic social explanations that reproduce inequalities. His empirical approach is focused on keeping open the controversies, or at least slowing down the process of resolving controversies about that of which the world is made, to resist available explanatory categories and examine more closely the controversies and uncertainties about how resources and agency are distributed, the kinds of agencies that are enacted in different sociomaterial formations, and the ways that actors contextualise one another. The effort of analysis, for Latour (2005, p. 261), should be 'to highlight the stabilising mechanisms so that the premature transformation of matters of concern into matters of fact is counteracted'. These are places for trials and experiments. The question then for educationalists, is what in our practices of critique do we attach or gather and how can we attach better to have impact upon inequities and injustices through our pedagogic practices? This is a pedagogy of attachment and experimentation, attuning to the material relations among human and non-human dynamics that can constitute inequities as well as offer entry points for transformative change.

Critical sociomaterial pedagogy

Moving these ideas forward into concrete suggestions for higher education pedagogy when learning to teach is a challenge, partly because the whole orientation of sociomaterial approaches is to question and unsettle as well as to experiment. These are about understanding how the world is non-coherent – materially and discursively heterogeneous – whereas pedagogy inherently often tries to impose coherence. Further, a critical orientation is interested in investigating, even countering, inequalities and exclusions as well as monolithic certainties and authorities. Addressing what might seem like competing concerns and also being able to challenge the increasing weight of standardisation, audit and accountability in relation to teaching and learning is challenging.

In fact, there are many examples from educators working and writing about their work in the difficult spaces of these critical sociomaterial pedagogies. People like Helen Verran, Dianne Mulcahy, Hillevi Lenz Taguchi, Heesoon Bai, in addition to the examples below and many others we have written about extensively (see Fenwick & Edwards 2010, Fenwick et al. 2011, Fenwick 2016). Across them, there seem to be shared commitments to appreciating at least three things: disruption and keeping open matters of concern; emergence with its attendant activities of attunement and experimentation; and difference or heterogeneity, involving the ontological politics of multiple material worlds.

One example is Fountain (1999), one of the first educators who developed curricula integrating ideas inspired by ANT. She challenges conventional science knowledge that privileges detached, scientific reasoning which fails to recognise the complex interpenetration of the various factors which make up these issues. Her alternative strategies are designed to move pedagogy from (re)presentations of facts to practices of critical experimenting and intervening. For example, instead of simply applying scientific formulas, students are encouraged to map the associations that are employed to produce and to represent these particular scientific explanations, and then to examine the associations in higher education that enable or constrain particular points of view. Students also seek the associations that do not appear, the things that are not mentioned or are discredited, the things that are not yet imagined but that may be at work, as well as those things and people that have been rallied and mobilised to enact and authorise particular concepts. These kinds of pedagogies, contends Fountain (1999, p. 339), can move education 'from a rhetoric of conclusions towards a rhetoric of contentions'. Here education is in part about engaging with the infrastructures of authority in knowledge practices.

On a similar tack, Gough (2004) suggests a pedagogy of interference, actively engaging students in inventing or imagining new ways to experiment with the real – knowledge – and make it move. Informed by actor-network tactics, Gough engages students in mapping the seemingly infinite networks, objects, and coded technologies among things and people that hold together any mundane everyday task in a particular moment, such as making a cup of coffee or obtaining an article from the library. But the main lessons, for Gough, come when students go beyond tracing existing networks of the 'real' to interfere with these networks and imagine new associations. Gough suggests engaging students in critically subverting fixed knowledges like science texts, inventing cyborg fabulations that gather stories, facts and materials in unexpected configurations, and generally to open spaces of ambiguity.

Many experiments are underway in higher education to engage students in these critical practices, and to attune students to the sociomaterial dynamics influencing them and others in everyday intra-actions (e.g. Fenwick 2015a & b). While these examples may appear to be somewhat removed from the immediate practical concerns of many, they are offered here in a spirit of opening new ideas and approaches that reach beyond familiar discourses and models of pedagogy.

For instance, in the UK and perhaps elsewhere, digital skills are increasingly prominent in curricular wishlists for students, and digital technologies are ubiquitous environments mediating higher education and students' everyday lives and future employment practices. Pedagogies that experiment with and through these technologies, therefore, are useful entry points to teach the sorts of critical capabilities that help students to de-naturalise their worlds – to keep open the controversies and disrupt the stabilising mechanisms. One place for students to begin disrupting their relations with digital media is by critically examining the regulatory codes and openings built into the software itself. These create technological infrastructures of everyday life, or 'code/space' as Kitchin and Dodge (2011) describe it. Code doesn't just mediate existing social forms, it acts – it does things – and it interpolates, mixes with and ultimately produces collective political, economic and cultural life (Williamson 2013), in ways that are fundamentally changing higher education and communication. Existing histories of social media already can be seen to influence particular forms of participation, problem-solving, or resistance. Facebook algorithms and routines, for instance, shape the content and style of exchange, and the nature of what is taken for knowledge. Patterns of 'friending', favouriting, following, trending have become normalised (Van Dijk 2013). These sociomaterial processes are bound to affect how students, their peers and educators, engage online.

For instance, Bayne (2010) engages students in critically experimenting with those 'uncanny' elisions between presence/absence and here/there that they experience through the multiple synchronicities of virtual engagement. This approach of 'productive disruption' (Bayne 2010) encourages students to reconfigure their natural sense of the 'strange' and their participation in distributed agency. Students can learn not only to disrupt and actively resist the perpetuation of material inequities through human-non-human intra-actions, but also to attune to those surprising possibilities that emerge for creativity, sustainable ecologies and hope.

Elsewhere, Somerville (2013) has argued that the goals of education for sustainability cannot be realised using the same ways of being and knowing with which we currently operate. One major challenge for educators lies in somehow connecting multiple interests – industrial, biopolitical, governmental, scientific, local community and environmental – working through fundamental difference among their (sociomaterial) systems of knowledge. She describes in detail one initiative to promote learning of ecological sustainability that clearly demonstrates the difficulties of bridging different material worlds.

The project, involving art and storytelling to link academics and higher education students with Aboriginal communities, focused on the rapidly disappearing Murray–Darling Basin river system (MDB), a prominent Australian example of the global crisis in water shortage. Perspectives among government, local towns, businesses, environmental groups, and the many Aboriginal peoples affected by the MDB are sharply divided. Somerville, with her colleagues and students, partnered with Aboriginal communities and artists to share knowledge and collectively learn new approaches to respond to the MDB crisis. Using an arts-based approach, the initiative sought to both bridge these knowledges and to mobilise new knowledge. Paintings and other art pieces were produced to represent the specific Aboriginal knowledges of MDB history and relations with local communities, and were presented to groups along with accompanying oral stories. Community audiences were invited to engage with the complex, layered meanings embedded in the artworks and stories in a process facilitated to invite new discoveries. Somerville (2013) describes the overall approach as pedagogical, teaching in the space between the different worlds of indigenous and non-indigenous knowings to explore how knowledge can travel between them.

Learning difference, then, involves students recalling and sharing deep personal embodied experiences of their 'country'. Art-making is one approach, having students make and share idiographic maps or drawings of significant elements of their own place memories and sense of place. Another starting point is objects brought by students, or photos of objects, representing important personal place elements. Through storytelling, students seek to identify not the similarities among them, but one another's different material worlds – and the distinct knowledges they each bring from these worlds. From here, students can be invited to discuss a shared issue, perhaps framing a problem of practice and seeking a solution, or responding to a multi-stakeholder controversy such as hydraulic fracking, or co-productive placemaking. Students can also undertake case-based projects in multi-disciplinary gatherings, such as architecture, civil engineering and urban planning to examine issues of child protection, and so forth. If possible, students might become actively involved in, or at least visit, a multi-stakeholder community consultation meeting, such as a controversial initiative to address threats to ecological sustainability. Or, a classroom recreation of such a consultation might begin by having students research the different participants – how they live in particular materialities, and what knowledge they bring from those worlds – then attempt to role-play a dialogue that gathers these productively.

The point in all such activities is to slow down the rush to frame and solve the problem, by first concentrating on coming to gather and engage with each other's sense of place – the deep differences in how each are located materially and historically – and to understand and connect the different knowledges that each brings from their location. The central challenge is to engage meanings and histories across different material worlds in ways that do not appropriate or dismiss the other's world of being. Anthropologist Mol (2002) writes about these practices of moving across different worlds as ontological politics, patching together different knowledge systems in a juxtaposition that may feel incoherent. For Somerville (2013), in the pedagogical undertaking to share water knowledge across diverse cultural groups of students, artists, bureaucrats and scientists, the challenge is to enter another's material world, and seek the flows between it and other worlds. For both, difference is taken seriously as a difficult and deeply material encounter. Difference is not to be resolved in these crossings, but to be honoured on its own terms as a profound experience that cannot be known prior to engagement.

These examples are intended to be illustrative, not prescriptive. Higher education is unlikely to be well served by stuffing more topics into its curricula. The point here has been to illuminate different ways of engaging students to support different forms of critical practice based upon experimentation and intervention, not to propose more projects and learning activities to liven up the classroom. The emphasis has been on reconsidering the content and approaches of pedagogy in terms of the dynamics of sociomateriality and criticality based upon supporting engagement with matters of concern. The examples outlined illuminate some of these dynamics and their negotiations: disruption and keeping open matters of concern; emergence with its attendant activities of attunement and experimentation; and difference involving the ontological politics of multiple material worlds.

Thinking across our own studies as well as the sorts of examples and literature outlined here, we have elsewhere proposed that in a sociomaterial key, learning might be understood in terms such as these (Fenwick 2015 a, b, Fenwick et al. 2011):

- attending to minor, even mundane, fluctuations and uncanny slips;
- attuning to emerging ideas and action possibilities – the intra-actions of ongoing mattering processes;
- noticing one's own and others' effects on what is emerging in terms of sustainability, equity and justice;
- tinkering amidst uncertainty to seek more productive alternatives; and
- interrupting blackboxes of practice to hold open their controversies and disturbances.

Likewise, critical sociomaterial pedagogy in higher education might begin by introducing activities that appreciate and stimulate the disruption, emergence, and difference that enable these sorts of learning processes.

Conclusion

Overall, we have suggested that sociomaterial approaches highlight the precarious links and contingent entanglements of human and non-human elements that bring forth knowledge systems. Knowledge is not a body or an authority, but an effect: it is performed into existence in practice, in all the webs of relations that are worked at, around and against constantly. These are precarious because they are filled with ongoing controversy, or matters of concern, despite the press to tighten them into matters of fact. They also require a great deal of work and bolstering from other allied networks to survive. When learning to teach in higher education, this entails envisioning one's own practices as a form of knowing in practice and not simply the transmission or facilitation of ideas. It involves engendering matters of concern through intervening and experimenting. It requires relating different material resources and relationships. Bringing what is often taken for granted into the arena of that to be negotiated and decided requires a broader pedagogic envisioning than that which is often expected by institutions, colleagues or students. This involves risk-taking and responsibility.

Sociomaterial approaches trace the process through which diverse elements become combined into knowledge networks, and how some networks stabilise, extend, enrol others and circulate to exert power, while others dissolve, distort, mutate or become appropriated. This can be particularly useful in higher education where highly entrenched knowledges of discipline and pedagogy jostle with fragmented mobile virtual worlds, markets and employability demands, league tables, the requirements for public engagement and other systems attempting to enrol and calculate processes of teaching and learning.

Rather than limiting knowledge to human consciousness and endeavours, a sociomaterial analysis also helps illustrate the more-than-human assemblings that perform knowledge in higher education: the coded software infrastructures and electronic records, buildings and timetables, historic discursive-material practices, and myriad apparatuses – method assemblages – that bring forth and sometimes reify particular ideas and activities, including specific practices of criticality. These assemble different sociomaterial worlds, not just different worldviews. The question is not simply which knowledge is most valuable, which is simply transmitted, but rather, what knowledges are circulating here, how are they being constituted and extended, what work are they performing, and what (desirable or undesirable) consequences of regulation and possibility are they producing? The focus is on inquiring rather than acquiring.

If we follow Latour and others who recognise the networks and materials at play, knowledge cannot be viewed as coherent, transcendent, generalisable, unproblematic or inherently powerful. The preceding examples and studies show that knowledge and the real emerge together. If we wish to experiment with these ways of engaging, then there are many possibilities for higher education curriculum and pedagogy and for developing a criticality which is not the preserve of the critic in pursuing the more-than-human and an affirmative higher education to address sociomaterial inequities and injustices. The risk in terms of learning to teach in such ways can be great, but also so can the effects.

Note

1   The chapter draws from material previously published in Fenwick 2015 (a, b) and Edwards and Fenwick (2015).

References

Barad, K. (2007), *Meeting the universe half-way*, Duke University Press, Durham, NC.

Bayne, S. (2010), 'Academetron, automaton, phantom: Uncanny digital pedagogies', *London Review of Education*, vol. 8, no. 1, pp. 5–13.

Boltanski, L. & Thevenot, L. (2006), *On justification: Economies of worth*, Princeton University Press, Princeton, NJ.

Braidotti, R. (2013), *The posthuman*, Polity Press, Cambridge.

Coole, D. & Frost, D. (2010), 'Introducing the new materialisms', in D. Coole & S. Frost. (eds), *New materialisms: Ontology, agency, and politics*, Duke University Press, Durham.

Davis, B. & Sumara, D. J. (2006), *Complexity and education: Inquiries into learning, teaching and research*, Erlbaum, Mahwah, NJ.

Dolphijn R. & van der Tuin, I. (eds) (2012), *New materialism: Interviews & cartographies*, Open Humanities Press, University of Michigan.

Edwards, R. (2011), 'Translating the prescribed into the enacted curriculum in school and college', *Education Philosophy and Theory*, vol. 43, no. S1, pp. 38–54.

Edwards, R .& Fenwick, T. (2015), 'Critique and politics: A sociomaterialist intervention', *Educational Philosophy and Theory*, vol. 47, nos. 13–14, pp. 1385–1404.

Fenwick, T. (2015a), 'Sociomateriality and learning: A critical approach', in D. Scott & E. Hargreaves (eds), *Sage handbook of learning*, Sage, London.

Fenwick, T. (2015b), 'What *matters* in sociomateriality: Towards a critical posthuman pedagogy in management education', in T. Beyes, M. Parker & C. Steyaert (eds), *The Routledge companion to the humanities and social sciences in management education*, Routledge, London.

Fenwick, T. (2016), *Professionalism and professional responsibility: A sociomaterial examination*, Routledge, London.

Fenwick, T. & Abrandt Dahlgren, M. (2015), 'Towards sociomaterial approaches in simulation education: Lessons from complexity theory', *Medical Education*, vol. 49, no. 4, pp. 359–67.

Fenwick, T. & Edwards, R. (2010), *Actor-network theory in education*, Routledge, London.

Fenwick, T. & Edwards, R. (2014), 'Networks of knowledge, matters of learning, and criticality in higher education', *Higher Education*, vol. 67, no. 1, pp. 35–50.

Fenwick, T. & Landri, P. (eds) (2014), *Materialities, textures and pedagogies*, Routledge, London.

Fenwick, T., Edwards, R., & Sawchuk, P. (2011), *Emerging approaches to educational research: Tracing the socio-material*, Routledge, London.

Folkers, A. (2016), 'Daring the truth: Foucault, parrhesia and the genealogy of critique', *Theory, Culture & Society*, vol. 33, no. 1, pp. 3–28.

Fountain, R. (1999), 'Socio-scientific issue via actor-network theory', *Journal of Curriculum Studies*, vol. 31, no. 3, pp. 339–58.

Gough, N. (2004), 'RhizomANTically becoming-cyborg: Performing posthuman pedagogies', *Educational Philosophy and Theory*, vol. 36, no. 3, pp. 253–65.

Hacking, I. (1983), *Representing and intervening: Introductory topics in the philosophy of natural sciences*, Cambridge University Press, Cambridge.

Hager, P., Lee, A. & Reich, A. (2012), *Practice, learning and change*, Springer, Dordrecht.

Kitchin, R. & Dodge, M. (2011), *Code/space: Software and everyday life*, MIT Press, Cambridge, MA.

Latour, B. (2004), 'Why has critique run out of steam? From matters of fact to matters of concern', *Critical Inquiry*, vol. 30, pp. 225–48.

Latour, B. (2005), *Reassembling the social*, Oxford University Press, Oxford.

Lenz Taguchi, H. (2010), *Going beyond the theory-practice divide in early childhood education: Introducing an intra-active pedagogy*, Routledge, London.

Mol, A-M. (2002), *The body multiple*, Duke University Press, Durham.

Nespor, J. (1994), *Knowledge in motion*, Falmer Press, London.

Nicolini, D. (2012), *Practice theory, work, and organisation*, Oxford University Press, Oxford.

Osberg D. & Biesta, G. (2007), 'Beyond presence: Epistemological and pedagogical implications of strong emergence', *Interchange*, vol. 38, no. 1, pp. 31–51.

Postma, D. (2014), 'Education as sociomaterial critique', in T. Fenwick & P. Landri (eds), *Materialities, textures and pedagogies*, Routledge, London.

Quimno, V., Imran, A. & Turner, T. (2013), 'Introducing a sociomaterial perspective to investigate e-learning for higher educational institutions in developing countries', paper presented to the 24th Australasian Conference on Information Systems (ACIS), 4–6 December.

Somerville, M. (2013), *Water in a dry land: Place learning through art and story*, Routledge, New York.

Sørensen, E. (2009), *The materiality of learning*, Cambridge, Cambridge University Press.

Van Dijk, J. (2013), *The culture of connectivity: A critical history of social media*, Oxford University Press, Oxford.

Williamson, B. (2013), 'Code acts: How computer code configures learning', *Digital Media and Learning Research Hub*, accessed 4 February 2013, http://dmlcentral.net/blog/ben-williamson/code-acts-how-computer-code-configures-learning

Chapter 2

Reflecting on things

Sociomaterial perspectives on academic development

Lesley Gourlay and Martin Oliver

Introduction

The aims, discourse and practices of academic development in higher education rest on a series of assumptions about the nature of academic practice and student engagement, assumptions which shape its approaches to enhancement and change. In this chapter, we review and critique these, drawing on sociomaterial theory and evidence from a project that explored the academic practices of students and staff.

Academic development is an area of professional practice concerned with the support and development of academics' work; typically, there is a strong focus on the development of teaching, and academic developers are commonly responsible for threshold qualifications for academics, such as certificates in learning and teaching in higher education (Eggins & Macdonald 2003). As a form of practice, it includes direct interventions such as workshops, but also includes the creation of conditions believed to be conducive to the development of academic work as professional practice – including working with academics as they learn to juggle competing aspects of their role, creating conditions for learning within work through variety and feedback, and encouraging people to locate their practice in a conscious and deliberate way in terms of space, time, practices and social groups (Boud & Brew 2013).

Although there are strong critical undercurrents within academic development, the field has been dominated by somewhat abstract formulations, such as 'active learning', 'student-centeredness' and 'learning styles'. We argue that these constructs, whilst well-intentioned, can come to represent unchallenged orthodoxies which are ideologically as opposed to empirically based. One result of this has been a relative lack of attention to disciplinarity, the situated nature of academic practice and the wide variations in the academy in terms of how knowledge is constructed, shared and developed. A further outcome, which is less recognised in the literature, is a lack of attention to the sociomaterial and embodied nature of academic practice.

In order to ground this critique in specific examples, we focus on a common technique within academic development: asking academics to reflect on their experiences. This technique of 'reflective practice' has become a core element of academic development practice, and holds a central position in how participant progress is assessed. This approach is intended to form a link between theory and practice through the discussion of specific academic contexts. However, it has been critiqued as having become part of an educational orthodoxy (Clegg 2000), which academics have learnt to subvert in order to 'play the game' by using it to demonstrate a positive orientation to 'active learning', and other such generic constructs (Macfarlane & Gourlay 2009). As Warhurst (2008) argues, reflection needs to recognise how teaching and learning is situated, and how it benefits from interactions with students by revealing their reactions to specific practices. Although reflective practice may appear to be strongly anchored in the day-to-day, we argue that an explicit or implicit focus on framing constructs such as 'active learning' or 'student-centredness' may render the reflection less meaningful. We also argue that the deployment of a sociomaterial, fine-grained ethnographic perspective may serve to strengthen the insights and depth of reflection, by focusing in greater detail on what students actually do.

To summarise, in this chapter, we present an alternative perspective on student engagement, proposing a close-up analysis of how students engage day-to-day with knowledge practices in complex networks, enrolling non-human actors while engaging with both print-based and digital technologies. We argue that academic development as a field would benefit from greater attention to these networks, and that by doing so the student would no longer be conceived of as a somewhat free-floating subject, or flattened into a (value-laden) category such as 'engaged', 'disengaged', 'deep' or 'surface' learner, or 'digital native'. We will illustrate this with reference to a set of academic development materials developed as part of a UK government-funded Joint Information Services Committee (JISC) 'Developing Digital Literacies' research project. These materials, based on themes arising from an analysis of students' multimodal journal data, seek to maintain an ethnographic link to students' networked, situated sociomaterial practice, rather than relying on or being structured by more abstract categorisation. We conclude with a discussion of how this perspective can be incorporated into reflective practice, leading to a more situated stance towards academic development.

Ideologies in academic development

Arguably, contemporary academic development has been founded on a series of constructs addressing the nature of teaching and learning in higher education, and also pertaining to the subject positions of students and academic staff. This has been driven, at least in part, by policies based on the ideology of 'student as consumer' – an idea that has shaped policies, been taken up by popular media and led to a new industry in 'market comparisons' internationally, including the UK, the US, Australia, Canada and parts of Scandinavia (Barefoot et al. 2016). This has led, for example, to the proliferation of student experience surveys, such as the National Survey of Student Engagement in the US, the Australasian Survey of Student Experience and the National Student Survey in the UK. The political consequences of this idea, in the way that it reframes the relationship between universities and society, is what makes it ideological: it has consequences for the relative power of different social groups, but often remains implicit within policy work, its taken-for-granted positioning making it difficult to critique, or even to explore empirically.

Laudably, the field has also been driven by a set of values that has placed the student at the centre of attention, seeking to take account of their perspectives and experiences. It has also been driven by a desire to move away from a lecture-based pedagogy, which has often been perceived as a 'teacher-centred', and by extension is assumed to be insensitive to the diversity of student needs and to the challenges that they face as learners. In response, constructs such as 'active learning' and 'student-centredness' have gained currency, alongside an emphasis on course design based on 'learning outcomes', as opposed to content.

This has gained wide support via bodies such as the UK Higher Education Academy, as can be seen in the current HEA United Kingdom Engagement Survey (HEA 2016), and this perspective has also been taken up by equivalent government bodies internationally. New lecturers in the UK are generally expected to complete a course that focuses on these aspects of academic work, typically taking the form of a PgCert programme on teaching and learning, or on academic practice. These courses vary, and clearly critical and contrasting perspectives may be included, but typically these draw primarily on research into student learning in higher education which has been critiqued for focusing on a relatively small group of dominant concepts (e.g. Haggis 2009). These constructs tend to be introduced to new lecturers as principles that should guide their practice as educators, as appropriate to their context. As a result, the content of the courses tends to centre on the concepts mentioned above, such as a strong focus on the importance of 'deep learning' and the encouragement of active 'student engagement'. Whilst such concepts have been critiqued in the educational literature for being over-simplistic (e.g. Webb 1997, Haggis 2003), they still dominate academic development, and enjoy considerable support and funding, forming the cornerstone of how not only individuals but also higher education institutions are assessed. This is visible in the kinds of questions asked within student satisfaction surveys, which are based on notions of 'student engagement'; they also increasingly influence how teaching is evaluated, as can be seen in the current proposals in the UK, set out in the 2015 Green Paper on higher education (BIS 2015), which seeks to introduce a teaching excellence framework (TEF) to the UK sector. As such, these concepts have an increasing level of constitutive and also normative influence over the sector and the expectations placed on it in terms of higher educational knowledge practices. Due to these recent changes, it can be argued that the role of academic development is becoming more strategic and far-reaching, as the potential beneficiaries of these developmental activities are no longer simply the students, but also the HEI itself, whose financial independence and reputation is increasingly bound up in the perceived 'success' evaluated by these teaching and student satisfaction assessment exercises conducted at a national level.

It might be argued that this is a positive development, bringing to the fore the needs and rights of the students which – it is often argued in academic development contexts – have long taken second place to the demonstration of excellence in research. However, as educational practice becomes more central to how we perceive the success of a university, it is all the more imperative that the measures of 'success' that are used represent a nuanced and credible account of the lived experience of students and academic staff, as opposed to being based on questionable and over-simplistic ideologies which do not stand up to critical scrutiny or provide meaningful purchase on our understanding of contemporary educational process.

The relatively weak evidence base for these concepts is one reason to question their dominance. A further flaw lies in the attempt at a generic application of relatively crude concepts across a very broad set of disciplines and contexts, each of which has a distinct history and set of epistemological values and practices which may vary greatly in terms of what is seen as knowledge, expertise and the legitimate expression of disciplinarity. A common theme in academic development circles centres on academic staff and their apparent 'resistance' to such attempts to inculcate these values and practices (e.g. Di Napoli & Clement 2014). However, it might be observed that often this scepticism is based on a recognition of these two weaknesses – a lack of evidence on which to base the guiding principles, and a perceived lack of relevance to the context at hand, and might therefore be understood as a resistance to specific ideologies, rather than to academic development *per se*.

A further shortcoming in these accounts is that what constitutes 'good' educational practice – in addition to the relatively abstract nature of the concepts being deployed – is the emphasis on a somewhat aspirational and ideological discourse of student agency and cognition – the ideas that students are free to act, in an unproblematic way. The construct of 'student engagement'– while appearing to place students centre stage – arguably encourages a very narrow band of behaviour – in particular observable, interactive practices which conform to a specific set of ideas about what constitutes a 'good student' (Gourlay 2015b). Inherent in this construct are value-laden notions of 'active' versus 'passive' which may in fact serve to invalidate the practices of students who do not exhibit valorised behaviours, due to personal preference or indeed educational or cultural background. This may lead to a devaluing of practices which are not amenable to observation, or may be read as 'passive', such as reticent participation in class, or 'invisible' solitary study practices. A further result of this focus on 'active learning' is an emphasis on desired qualities of the individual student, such as determination, motivation and confidence. While these are clearly important, there is a risk emphasising these personal qualities may lead to an overly individualistic and somewhat abstracted conception of practice that assumes agency lies primarily in the individual. Additionally, it could be argued that these are culturally specific and favour an anglophone educational culture where such attributes are prized, thus rendering 'deficient' student behaviours which are central to other educational cultures – such as silent listening, deference in class, and so on.

In contrast, an alternative sociomaterial reading of student engagement would move the focus away from these broad notions governing agency and behaviour of the individual, and instead would theorise the student first and foremost as constantly entangled in complex networks of social actors, both human and non-human. This helps to recognise the considerable variation there is in academic practices, between students, disciplines and national systems, particularly when access to technology is taken into account (Goodyear et al. 2005). This reframing would include elements which have been traditionally seen as neutral 'context' against which social action takes place – such as physical spaces and temporal frames. It would also reframe physical artefacts conventionally regarded as 'tools', such as digital devices, and elements regarded as 'information', such as texts or verbal lectures. A sociomaterial perspective (as elaborated in this volume by Fenwick and Edwards) would regard all of these elements as agentive actors in higher education knowledge practices, and as such would seek to interrogate critically conceptions of 'student engagement' or related notions such as 'active learning', which position the student as the primary or sole site of agency.

Implications for academic development

This shift has implications for academic development, whose foundational principles arguably rest on the notion of 'facilitation' of learning, which is assumed to emanate from student agency when the right conditions are provided for this to flourish. The onus in this perspective appears to be on the lecturer to provide these opportunities through a maximisation of student active participation in interactive tasks. Although this type of practice may be very valuable, what is missing from this account is a recognition of the powerful role of sociomaterial networks in these practices, and in particular the highly specific, emergent and sociomaterially-situated nature of these networks. In practical terms, this may, for example, be to do with the layout of the classroom on that particular day, or the devices and texts present during the task at hand, and how these may inhibit, influence or generate particular practices. This may also include what is materially produced by the students, such as notes or artefacts – what is made, retained or transformed materially by a task in addition to the generation of talk and cognitive activity. A sociomaterial perspective would also recognise what is *not* currently observed or physically present – networks of practice extending beyond the temporal or physical 'context' of the particular observed educational encounter – such as online networks, and practices taking place over a longer timeframe. If viewed in these terms, we argue that what is within the gift of the lecturer to 'facilitate' is subtly altered, with a more granular level of attention being brought to bear on the detail of student practice and the sociomaterial networks in which it is entangled, and also a concomitant reduction in the emphasis on individual student agency and the performance of 'engagement'.

One of the key approaches in academic development is the use of structured 'reflection' as a means of focusing on participants' own educational practice, while applying the principles discussed above. Although ostensibly personal and led by the participant on the course, this approach has been critiqued as implicitly normative and convergent (e.g. Clegg 2000, Macfarlane & Gourlay 2009). The avowed intention is to relate abstract concepts to the particular of day-to-day practice in a specific setting. However, if the emphasis is on demonstrating a commitment to 'active learning' or 'student engagement', it is likely that the account will seek to identify what would conventionally be seen as evidence of success on those terms, with markers such as high levels of verbal interaction being highlighted. As long as the reflective task is designed to exhibit these outcomes, educational process will be seen through a prism which privileges certain features of the observable flow of practice, and which elides others. What is needed to address this is a different kind of process, one that provides a more inclusive lens through which to view these processes.

In the next section, we will describe a research study which used such an alternative perspective to investigate the day-to-day study practices of a small group of postgraduate students over a one-year period, using a sociomaterial framing. We will discuss the possible implications for academic development, and will describe a set of development resources which were created on the basis of the research findings. These were designed to encourage academic staff discussion and reflection while also raising awareness of the importance of the sociomaterial in educational practices and process, as opposed to focusing on the concepts critiqued above.

Methodology

The examples presented in this chapter are drawn from data from a JISC-funded project on students' digital literacies. (Further information about this can be found in Gourlay & Oliver 2013.) This was undertaken at a UK postgraduate institution specialising in education, and consisted of three phases of empirical work (analysis of an existing survey, focus groups and longitudinal multimodal journaling plus a series of semi-structured interviews). The journaling work involved 12 students, three drawn from each of: PGCE courses (the UK qualification to teach in compulsory education), taught Masters courses, taught Masters courses studied at a distance, and doctoral students; the journaling was also undertaken by four members of academic staff over a slightly shorter period. The study received institutional ethical clearance and followed approved procedures for informed consent, including guarantees of anonymity and confidentiality, and the right to opt out at any point.

The student body at the institution is predominantly mature and postgraduate, representing diverse countries of origin and prior educational experiences. Many students combine study with work and family responsibilities, and have not studied for several years. Participants in the journaling phase of the project were invited from those who had volunteered to take part in the focus groups, to ensure that the diversity of the student body was represented, in terms of gender, age and study status (home/EU or international student; full-time or part-time).

The longitudinal multimodal journaling involved 3–4 interviews with each participant over a period of 9–12 months. (Students studying at a distance were interviewed over Skype.) All interviews were recorded and transcribed. The first interview explored students' histories of using technology in their studies. As part of this, the participants sketched maps and used these to talk through their patterns of studying, including the ways in which they studied in different locations. At this first meeting, all participants were given an iPod Touch handheld device, with which to take photos, videos, notes or other records of their study practices. Participants were encouraged to focus on their day-to-day lived activities, and the networks and material/spatial aspects of their practice, to avoid making abstractions rather than retelling the specifics of their practices (Gourlay 2010). At each subsequent interview, the discussion was structured around the data that each student chose to present to the interviewer. These images, videos and notes formed part of the data set, as did the presentations that the students made: initially, these were typically conversations around individual images, but by the end of the series of interviews, several participants produced structured presentations in which they themselves categorised data in terms of patterns or themes they identified as salient.

The analysis of the data set, together with the transcripts, images and videos, provided detailed insights into how student practices unfolded day-to-day, at a level of granularity not normally afforded by interview or questionnaire-based research into student engagement. The themes that were identified in the analysis centred on the powerfully co-constitutive nature of the sociomaterial in these practices, in particular the roles of digital devices, texts, temporal frames and material spaces as non-human actors in networks of practice (see Gourlay & Oliver 2013, Gourlay 2014, Gourlay 2015a for a fuller discussion of the results). The findings of the study undermined the view critiqued above – that the primary site for student agency resides in the cognitive or attitudinal approach of the student, and also questioned the notion that the quality of these practices is amenable to direct and unproblematic intervention on the part of the lecturer. Instead, the research results suggested that study practices are highly localised, contingent, emergent and situated.

These findings were then used as the basis for designing academic development materials. (JISC n.d.). These materials seek to build on the already established principle of reflection in academic development, but add a further dimension of explicit and structured focus on situated sociomaterial practices and networks. Participants in academic development settings are asked to undertake some of the same multimodal and non-textual data collection processes used within the project, documenting what they do in their day-to-day scholarly practices and also seeking to document precisely what their students are asked to do. Excerpts from the research data set and from other publicly available sources are used to provide illustrations and points of comparison. This is intended to show possible forms of diversity and difference in practice, as a prompt for further analysis and reflection on practices from a sociomaterial perspective.

In the following section, two examples are provided of data from the student and staff journaling, showing the themes that were developed in relation to these, and the ways in which these links were reflected in the subsequent design of the development materials.

Constitutive spaces

The use of spaces featured as a theme across the entire data set. Participants such as Juan (a male Masters student) spoke eloquently about how they associated these spaces with specific forms of work, and the connotations that they carried:

> I enjoy [...] being, sort of, in a dusty, you know, sort of, wooden shelved, kind of, old library, where it's, sort of, cosy and warm, that's, you know, I like that and that's a part of the experience of studying that I enjoy.
>
> (Juan, interview 1)

> Where I live it could be, you could be in a town sort of anywhere and you wouldn't really necessarily notice. Whereas you come in here and you come over the Waterloo Bridge and you see St Paul's and the Houses of Parliament, you know, you're in London, you're doing something again. You know, this is where people do important things and that, kind of, thing and it gives it a reality. [...] It focuses me a little bit on that.
>
> (Juan, interview 3)

These spaces had become associated with sets of practices. Drawing on a mobilities perspective (Edwards et al. 2011), this illustrates how the repetition of practices in specific locations over time results in 'sedimentation', and the creation of meanings and associations.

For some participants, the use of technology enabled them to carry out academic activities in a range of different locations – different spaces could be connected together by carrying tablets, laptops or books from one site to another. Yuki, a female Masters student, characterised this in terms of being 'less bound by place', where being 'bound' meant connecting to location-specific networks of resources and people needed to carry out their studies. Gertrude (a female academic), by contrast, drew a map (Figure 2.1) and explained how the network she had set up at home allowed considerable freedom, whereas the office computer (drawn next to a 'sad face' sticker) was connected to administrative systems but blocked the installation of software needed for academic work. The freedom and creativity she

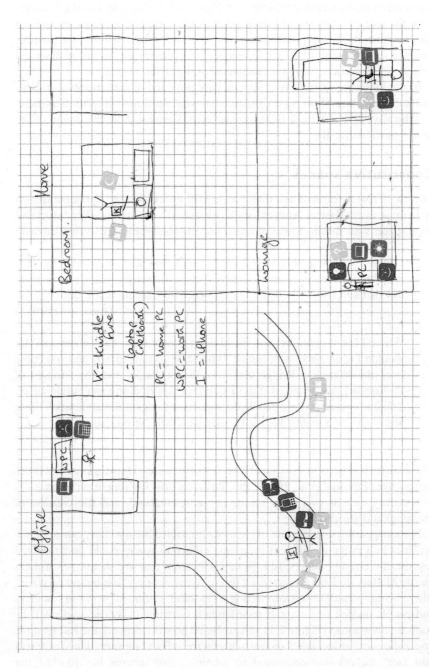

K = Kindle fire

L = Laptop (netbook)

PC = Home PC

WPC = Work PC

I = iPhone

Figure 2.1 Gertrude's map

enjoyed teaching an online course from home was a marked contrast to her experience of being blocked and frustrated, trying to do academic work in the office. She also explained how different practices were associated with different times – writing academic work at her desk in the day, writing emails on a laptop on the sofa in the evening, and reading papers on a Kindle E-reader in bed at night.

These examples illustrate the ways in which space was not merely some backdrop or container for students' practices, but was constitutive of them, and also constituted through them.

Within the project, this led to implications for institutional policies on the provision of services (such as wifi) and different kinds of space for students. To encourage academics to reflect on what the implications might be for them and for their students, the staff development materials included a series of resources and tasks intended to generate a sociomaterially-oriented form of reflection (although this term was not explicitly introduced). Participants are asked to sketch out the spaces and places where they undertake their own academic work, and to identify the network of resources that they drew on to carry that work out in these different places. They are asked to compare these with maps drawn by other participants, and shown examples of maps generated by participants in the research project, so that similarities and differences can be identified. This stimulates discussion, but grounds this in their day-to-day lived activities, and the networks and material/spatial aspects of their practice. The broader intention and subsequent discussion is focused on sensitising the participants to their students' equivalent networks and day-to-day practices, leading to a more detailed type of insight into the lived daily experiences of the students and the challenges they face. This could generate insights for the academics in terms of how to structure, guide and support study practices, reading and academic writing – all key aspects of academic performance that have arguably received less attention than classroom-based pedagogies within academic development.

Following texts

Whilst the project was initiated to study student digital literacies, participants' images and accounts were full of books, print-outs, notebooks, folders, post-it notes, pens and other conventional printed materials and artefacts, and several participants brought these materials along to the interview for additional emphasis. None of the participants appeared to view the digital/analogue as an 'either/or' binary; for all of them, digital and print texts co-existed in a complicated set of intertwined relationships. However, this complexity was only visible during the process of production; by the point of submitting work for assessment, for example, the messy interplay was hidden by the apparently simple print or digital artefact.

An obvious example of this was provide by Juan's discussion of fieldwork: his description of generating data illustrates the process of *entextualisation* (Silverstein & Urban 1996), where talk is taken from an interactional setting and made into a textual record. However, even when they were created, these texts were not stable; they were constantly reworked and recreated. There were frequent moves between digital and print versions of the text – for example, Gertrude described printing off a course outline so that she could read through it and get an overview of the course she had to teach, annotating and editing it with marker pens, then returning to the virtual learning environment to make changes to the digital version. Several participants described similar patterns when drafting work, moving iteratively between print and digital versions to refine the text. Another student teacher, Louise, described how most of the texts she used when teaching were reworkings of previous materials:

> It's mostly sources that are coming from other professional development courses that we work on, whether they're accredited or not accredited. And they're repurposed, I mean, a very small number of items can just be repurposed, they can be left as they ... as they ... as they are ... as they are whole, and used differently. Um, that's a small number, most items are edited, changed, worked into something else, um, because this is, you know, a pretty unique context that we're working with. Um, so, yes, they do have to become very bespoke for these particular students, yes.
>
> (Louise)

She described a complex process of editing, which involved sharing drafts with colleagues using the Dropbox cloud storage service, in an editing process that involved at least eight points at which what looked like a ready-to-use text was moved, edited or re-created before being made available to her students. This illustrates what Blommaert (2005, p. 46) has called *text trajectories*, whereby 'a lot of what we perform in the way of meaning-attributing practices is the *post-hoc* recontextualisation of earlier bits of text that were produced [...] in a different contextualisation process, at a different time, by different people, and for different purposes'.

Juan produced a flow chart-like map of the process of writing his dissertation, showing the spaces, services and technologies through which his text passed on the route to submission. These included movements of other text in the library, and on the library's computer; movement of electronic versions of the text onto and off a USB memory stick; the passage of ideas from written notes to a folder annotated with post-it notes and then typed to create a digital version; sharing of versions with the tutor over electronic systems and with peers in the student bar; as well as physical creation of various versions through printing it off (in a different college, where printing was cheaper); before finally printing, handing this to a company to bind the text, and then handing the bound version in to an administrator to go out for marking. No trace of this complex journey remained in the final printed and bound version that an academic then received to mark.

Revealing this complexity shows the processes of disciplinary knowledge production in a way that is rarely seen. Given how central writing remains in academic work, this has implications for the kinds of support made available to

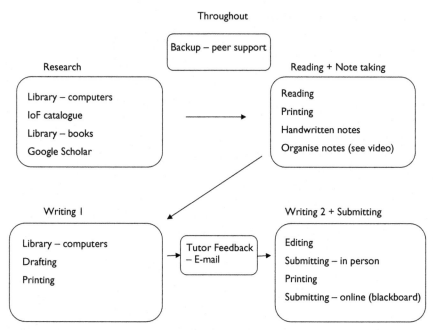

Figure 2.2 Juan's map of the process of writing a dissertation

students within the curriculum, and the opportunities provided to them to rehearse and develop these forms of practice (see, e.g., Bazerman et al. 2005, for an account of the value of writing across the curriuculum). It also offers a more nuanced account of what 'student engagement' might look like, showing how a student who may say little in class could be transforming ideas and working with a rich diversity of texts in the production of an assignment.

To encourage other academics to reflect upon these complex but normally invisible processes, this research approach was incorporated into a set of academic development materials. Participants in the academic development sessions that use these materials are asked to choose an actual text they have produced, and then to create notes and take images (or bring other artefacts) that illustrate the process of its creation, and to bring these along for discussion with peers. Images from the project data set are also provided, again to support comparisons and contrasts. To stimulate the discussion, participants are asked to think about what other texts were used to create this; how they were found, accessed and managed; when and why the work moved between different modes (image, writing, layout, speech, etc.); when it changed format (paper, post-its, word processing files, wikis, e-mails, etc); and how different versions of and revisions to the work stored, recorded and/or managed. Consistently, this prompts participants to consider the interplay between people, things and spaces, and this typically results in a deeper appreciation of the complex and negotiated practices students need to develop in order to study successfully.

Discussion and conclusions

Current orthodoxies around academic development may be well intentioned and apparently student-centred, but we contend that these broad-brush and at times ideological concepts – while apparently benign – in fact oversimplify and elide key elements of the lived experience of students and academics. In doing so, they risk distorting practice in ways that are unhelpful. Students' classroom talk (or online discussion) is important, but if this is mistaken for being the primary proxy for learning, and the only evidence that educators have of their 'engagement', this can disadvantage learners who may be just as thoughtful, and potentially just as successful, but who happen to speak less in front of the teacher. This can undermine the very values that motivated academic developers to focus on students' experiences in the first place.

Paying attention to the rich but messy lived reality of students' knowledge practices – to the sociomaterial, situated ways in which students achieve success – can help us to avoid this irony. Attending only to students' public behaviour misses the ways in which they work with people, texts, devices and so on as part of their studies, 'behind the scenes'. This can be particularly important in drawing attention back to questions of social justice: students in different countries, disciplines or even institutions have very different access to the infrastructure and technology that they need for their studies; some must go to considerable length to re-create the study environments that others take for granted, as has been shown with studies of students from disadvantaged socio-economic groups in South Africa (Czerniewicz, Williams & Brown 2009).

Drawing attention back to these overlooked elements changes how we understand students' engagement. It suggests new kinds of reflection for academics who are seeking to enhance and deepen their understanding of educational processes in ways which are sensitive to the embodied, social and material conditions of studying, and offers an opportunity for the kinds of professional learning advocated by Boud and Brew (2013). This perspective highlights and values diversity and difference, and can help to raise difficult but necessary questions about the nature of success, equity and power in a range of disciplinary and educational settings that do not start and stop with the individual student's cognition, or their spoken public performance. In practical terms, this type of focus can allow academic staff to gain insights into challenges that students may be facing in their engagement outside the classroom, in particular in relation to the selection and engagement with academic texts, and the development of academic writing. A more nuanced awareness of the complexities of study practices and the challenges faced by students in meeting the demands of coursework can support academic staff to provide greater scaffolding and guidance for students in how to approach their work outside the classroom – support and guidance which have often been regarded as 'remedial', and therefore outside of mainstream academic practice.

Specific examples of such practices are, of course, helpful in stimulating such reflection. However, individual cases cannot 'stand for' wider student experiences in a simple, unproblematic way. Rather than advocate specific materials, or codify cases into some student typology, the argument here is that academics need to pay close attention to their own practices, and to the practices of their students. This kind of process, supporting attention to the complex details of students' lives, can support a different quality of reflection, one that is better able to discern the influences of disciplinarity, the situated nature of academic practice and the varied ways in which knowledge is created within higher education.

References

Barefoot, H., Oliver, M. & Mellar, H. (2016), 'Informed choice? How the United Kingdom's key information set fails to represent pedagogy to potential students', *Quality in Higher Education*, DOI:10.1080/13538322.2016.1153899.

Bazerman, C., Little, J., Bethel, L., Chavkin, T., Fouquette, D. & Garufis, J. (2005), *Reference guide to writing across the curriculum*, Parlor Press LLC, Indiana.

BIS (2015), *Fulfilling our potential: Teaching excellence, social mobility and student choice*, Department for Business, Innovation and Skills, Sheffield. https://www.gov.uk/government/uploads/system/uploads/attachment_data/file/474227/BIS-15-623-fulfilling-our-potential-teaching-excellence-social-mobility-and-student-choice.pdf

Blommaert, J. (2005), *Discourse: A critical introduction*, Cambridge University Press, Cambridge.

Boud, D. & Brew, A. (2013), 'Reconceptualising academic work as professional practice: Implications for academic development', *International Journal for Academic Development*, vol. 18, no. 3, pp. 20–221.

Clegg, S. (2000), 'Knowing through reflective practice in higher education', *Educational Action Research*, vol. 8, no. 3, pp. 45–469.

Czerniewicz, L., Williams, K. & Brown, C. (2009), 'Students make a plan: Understanding student agency in constraining conditions', *Research in Learning Technology*, vol. 17, no. 2, pp. 7–88.

Di Napoli, R. & Clement, M. (2014), 'The agency game in academic development: Compliance and resistance', *International Journal for Academic Development*, vol. 19, no. 10, pp. 1–3.

Edwards, R., Tracy, F. & Jordan, K. (2011), 'Mobilities, moorings and boundary marking in developing semantic technologies in educational practices', *Research in Learning Technology*, vol. 19, no. 3, pp. 219–32.

Eggins, H. & Macdonald, R. (2003), *The scholarship of academic development*, Routledge, London.

Goodyear, P., Jones, C., Asensio, M., Hodgson, V. & Steeples, C. (2005), 'Networked learning in higher education: Students' expectations and experiences', *Higher Education*, vol. 50, no. 3, pp. 47–508.

Gourlay, L. (2010), 'Multimodality, visual methodologies and higher education', in M. Savin-Baden & C. Howell Major (eds), *New approaches to qualitative research*, Routledge, London.

Gourlay, L. (2014), 'Creating time: Students, technologies and temporal practices in higher education', *E-learning and Digital Media*, vol. 11, no. 2, pp.141–53.

Gourlay, L. (2015a), 'Posthuman texts: Nonhuman actors, mediators and technologies of inscription', *Social Semiotics*, vol. 25, no. 4, pp. 48–500.

Gourlay, L. (2015b), 'Student engagement' and the tyranny of participation', *Teaching in Higher Education*, vol. 20, no. 4, pp. 404–11.

Gourlay, L. & Oliver, M. (2013), 'Beyond 'the social': Digital literacies as sociomaterial practice', in R. Goodfellow & M. Lea (eds), *Literacy in the digital university: Critical perspectives on learning, scholarship and technology*, Routledge, London.

Haggis, T. (2003), 'Constructing images of ourselves? A critical investigation into "approaches to learning" research in higher education', *British Educational Research Journal*, vol. 29, no. 1, pp. 8–104.

Haggis, T. (2009), 'What have we been thinking of? A critical overview of 40 years of student learning research in higher education', *Studies in Higher Education*, vol. 34, no. 4, pp. 37–390.

Higher Education Academy (HEA) (2016), *United Kingdom Engagement Survey*, https://www.heacademy.ac.uk/research/surveys/united-kingdom-engagement-survey-ukes

Joint Information Services Committee (JISC) (n.d.) *JISC design studio*, http://jiscdesignstudio.pbworks.com/w/page/68745849/Mapping%20Spaces%2C%20Tasks%20and%20Tools

Macfarlane, B. & Gourlay, L. (2009), 'The reflection game: Enacting the penitent self', *Teaching in Higher Education*, vol. 14, no. 4, pp. 454–59.

Silverstein, M. & Urban, G. (ed.) (1996), *Natural histories of discourse*, University of Chicago Press, London.

Warhurst, R. (2008), 'Reflections on reflective learning in professional formation', *Studies in the Education of Adults*, vol. 40, no. 2, pp. 171–91.

Webb, G. (1997), 'Deconstructing deep and surface: Towards a critique of Phenomenography', *Higher Education*, vol. 33, no. 2, pp.19–212.

Chapter 3

Diffracting learning/teaching entanglements

A South African vice-chancellor's perspective

Vivienne Bozalek and Wendy McMillan

Introduction

This chapter considers data from interviews conducted with eight vice-chancellors from both historically advantaged and disadvantaged higher education institutions (HEIs) in South Africa, as part of a larger national project on professional development of teaching and learning. It hones in on one particular interview which was a 'hot spot' and which 'glowed' (MacLure 2013) during data analysis. The perspective of vice-chancellors on learning to teach is important for providing insights into the broader context in which the process of learning to teach takes place. This is because it is vice-chancellors who are affected by both past and current policies and discourses, while also being pivotal in affecting and being affected by institutional enablements and constraints regarding learning to teach. The material-discursive in terms of past and present sociopolitical discourses and policies, as well as access to resources, deeply affect learning to teach at both a systemic and institutional level. Vice-chancellors find themselves at the interface between these national and international discourses, policies, and practices as part of their specific university environments where these discourses and policies are enacted. These entanglements dynamically reconfigure learning to teach in higher education.

Before this chapter was formally written, Wendy McMillan passed away unexpectedly, on 23 December 2015. Dates had been set in January 2016 to write this chapter together and it is with great sadness that I now have to write this chapter without Wendy's vibrant physical presence – engaging, provoking, interrogating, encouraging, and always taking responsibility for keeping us on the track of writing. The ideas for this chapter come from the intensities and materialities of our meetings during 2015, the physical settings of Mont Fleur conference centre, Common Ground cafe and the University of the Western Cape Social Sciences Building, Wendy's orderly hard copies of all texts and transcripts, my MacBook Air, our verbal and written musings and contestations, which were all part of the inventive provocations and inspirations for this chapter. Wendy's careful attentiveness to fine details and doing justice to texts through doing close readings, looking for differences that matter, exemplifies Barad's diffractive methodology (Barad 2007), which is used in this chapter. All these entangled doings, beings and becomings are what made her a wonderful academic companion with whom to work. In 2015 we spent quite a few hours reading Karen Barad's work and the eight interviews of the vice-chancellors together, and this chapter builds on those discussions, although with the theft of my computer on Friday 23 October 2015 much of our initial analysis of the interviews was lost to us. Thereafter, in December 2015 we had to re-peruse all the interviews in preparation for a conference presentation on vice-chancellors' interviews at the Society for Research in Higher Education (SRHE) in December 2015, which I presented on our behalf, and a large part of this paper is based on that presentation. We alighted on one particular vice-chancellor's interview, which we read diffractively through both Barad's work and through social justice concerns in South African higher education – this for us was the data 'hot spot' which 'glowed' (MacLure 2013).

Barad's quantum physics and queer theory helps me to come to terms with the vacuum of Wendy's passing as it enables me to try to understand in/determinacy and dis/continuity of space, time and matter (spacetimemattering) and the liveliness of non/being and how 'self' and identity are queered (Barad 2012), becoming undone (Grosz 2011). This chapter also shows how, despite Wendy's physical absence while writing this, the past and future are always already there in the present and how our beings and thoughts are always already entangled with each other, helping to constitute and reconstitute the becomings of this chapter.

The focus of this chapter is on issues of social justice in teaching and learning and learning to teach in South African higher education. A feminist new materialist theoretical perspective is used to illuminate these issues through the analysis of an interview conducted with one of the eight vice-chancellors who took part in a larger study on professionalising teaching and learning, referred to in other chapters of this book. The chapter is structured in the following way: Firstly, there is a short description of the higher education landscape in the South African context focusing particularly on issues of inequity and social justice in the current context. This is followed by a description of the theoretical framework used in the chapter – new feminist materialism, then by a short section on the methodology used – feminist new materialisms – for the analysis of the data for this chapter. The data was collected as part of the larger study on which this chapter is based. Excerpts from one interview, as data which 'glowed' (MacLure 2013) are then presented and discussed in relation to issues of social justice focusing on affirmative and productive possibilities for learning to teach in South African higher education.

The continued inequalities of South African higher education

On 13 January 2016 the vice-chancellors, principals and rectors representing all 26 higher education institutions in South Africa issued a joint statement regarding their commitment to continuing widening access for quality higher education for all students and the socio-economic transformation of South African higher education institutions towards the constitution of the country (Universities South Africa 2016). This was in response to the #feesmustfall movement and student-led protests which swept through South African higher education in the latter part of 2015, disrupting examinations and the academic programmes at these institutions. The #feesmustfall movement, which is continuing action and protests into 2016, continues its focus on equitable access to higher education, especially for those students who experience race and class barriers to gaining access (Nicolson 2016). The joint statement by the vice-chancellors also calls on the state to make provision for adequate financial aid for students and for more adequate subsidisation of the higher education sector, as well as a recognition that this sector has been underfunded by the state.

These concerns, expressed by the vice-chancellors about the higher education sector as a whole, are important to note. However, the differences that exist within the higher education system *between* the institutions are not mentioned in this joint statement. This omission serves to elide the realities of continuing discrepancies that exist between institutions. Bozalek & Boughey (2012) and Cooper (2015) have written about issues of social justice affecting South African HEIs and the stark inequities that continue to exist between these institutions, following the apartheid legacy during which time many of these institutions were set up. The ways in which this is made manifest is that those institutions which were historically disadvantaged continue to struggle with paucity of funding, geopolitical positioning, human and material resources. In addition to these difficult conditions for learning to teach in these institutions, the students who apply to these institutions are generally the least academically prepared for university study, and the most economically impoverished students (see the study by Breier (2010) for example). There is thus a double dis/advantage in South African higher education. Those institutions with resources – many of them historically white institutions from the apartheid era – attract and recruit the top performing students in the system and have the resources to attract academics who are highly regarded (Boughey & McKenna 2011). They also have much lower student–staff ratios – what is known as the full-time equivalent (FTE) ratio in South Africa. Thus, despite the heady enthusiasm in which policies were developed for higher education towards the demise of apartheid in the early and mid 1990s (see the *White Paper 3: A programme for the transformation of higher education* (Department of Education 1997)), the imagined future of changed demographics and conditions of universities has not come to fruition – it was envisaged that HEIs would be less monocultural and more mixed in terms of race and class. The sobering picture of higher education is evident in the table below, which appears in Cooper's (2015) article on social justice and South African student enrolment data trends, showing the continued racialisation of higher education institutions:

Table 3.1 23 universities – full-time equivalent (FTE) student enrolments according to 'race' and year – 2008 compared to 2012

University	White		Indian		Coloured		African (S African)		Foreign & Unknown		Total	
	2008	2012	2008	2012	2008	2012	2008	2012	2008	2012	2008	2012
1 Pretoria	59%	54%	4%	4%	2%	2%	28%	32%	7%	8%	100%	100%
2 Cape Town (UCT)	39%	34%	7%	7%	15%	13%	19%	23%	20%	23%	100%	100%
3 Kwazulu-Natal (UKZN)	12%	7%	35%	29%	3%	2%	43%	56%	7%	6%	100%	100%
4 Stellenbosch	69%	68%	1%	2%	16%	15%	7%	8%	7%	8%	100%	100%
5 Witwatersrand (WITS)	30%	24%	15%	13%	3%	3%	43%	51%	9%	9%	100%	100%
6 North West (North W)	56%	47%	1%	1%	3%	3%	36%	46%	3%	3%	100%	100%
7 Johannesburg	24%	13%	5%	4%	3%	3%	64%	74%	4%	5%	100%	100%
8 South Africa (UNISA)	22%	17%	8%	7%	5%	4%	55%	64%	10%	9%	100%	100%
9 Free State	37%	33%	1%	1%	5%	5%	49%	56%	8%	6%	100%	100%
10 Nelson Mandela (NMMU)	27%	25%	2%	1%	14%	14%	47%	52%	10%	7%	100%	100%
11 Western Cape (UWC)	4%	4%	7%	5%	48%	46%	32%	36%	9%	9%	100%	100%
12 Rhodes	43%	38%	3%	3%	3%	3%	28%	33%	23%	22%	100%	100%
13 Limpopo	1%	1%	1%	1%	0%	0%	96%	96%	3%	2%	100%	100%
14 Cape Peninsula (Technology)	17%	14%	1%	1%	33%	29%	42%	48%	7%	9%	100%	100%
15 Tshwane UTechnology	9%	6%	0%	0%	1%	1%	85%	90%	4%	3%	100%	100%
16 Zululand	0%	0%	1%	0%	0%	0%	96%	99%	3%	0%	100%	100%
17 Fort Hare	5%	3%	1%	0%	2%	2%	76%	85%	16%	10%	100%	100%
18 Central UTechnology	14%	9%	0%	0%	3%	3%	77%	83%	6%	4%	100%	100%
19 Durban UTechnology	5%	3%	17%	13%	2%	2%	74%	80%	2%	2%	100%	100%
20 Vaal UTechnology	3%	2%	0%	0%	1%	2%	86%	88%	9%	8%	100%	100%
21 Venda	0%	0%	0%	0%	0%	0%	97%	93%	2%	7%	100%	100%
22 Walter Sisulu	0%	0%	0%	0%	0%	0%	98%	97%	1%	2%	100%	100%
23 Mangosuthu UTechnology	0%	0%	0%	0%	0%	0%	100%	99%	0%	1%	100%	100%
Total	23%	20%	6%	5%	6%	7%	57%	62%	6%	8%	100%	100%

Source: Cooper (2015).

The above table divides HEIs in South Africa into three groups – five upper band, seven middle band and eleven lower band categories in terms of their research intensivity, indicated by postgraduate enrolments and staff publications. Cooper (2015) also shows how the continued socio-economic and racial inequalities are masked in official categorisations of HEIs in South Africa in the above table, which shows the figures of student enrolment in 2008 and 2012 in HEIs in these bands. Bearing in mind the percentages of racial groupings in South Africa in terms of apartheid racial categorisation: (79.2% black African, 8.9% white, 8.9% coloured, 2.5% Indian or Asian, 0.5% 'other') (South Africa.info n. d.), the racialised representation of students has not altered in ways which are anticipated in the Higher Education White Paper (Department of Education 1997). As can be noted in the table, the Universities of Pretoria and Stellenbosch continue to recruit large groups of white students, while the historically black or disadvantaged institutions, mainly represented in the third band are almost all populated by black African students. It is only the Universities of Technology in the third band that continue to enrol students from other racial categories, probably because they are merged institutions which amalgamated historically advantaged and disadvantaged institutions.

Cloete (2016) points out that South Africa is the only African country with a differentiated higher education system. The inequalities between HEIs in South Africa play a vital role in the ways in which teaching and learning and learning to teach is enacted in the various universities. The student-staff ratio, geographical location of the university, students' prior school background and preparedness for tertiary education, the physical and economic resources available to the staff and students, how these institutions are perceived by the public and their entanglements produce enabling or constraining conditions for learning to teach (Bozalek & Boughey 2012, Cooper 2015).

The next section outlines the conceptual framework used to analyse the data in this chapter.

Feminist new materialisms as a conceptual framework

This chapter uses feminist new materialisms as a conceptual framework for analysis of the data. Similar configurations of this framework include sociomaterialism, material feminism, new materialism, new feminist materialism, critical posthumanism, and affect theory, which are all relational ontologies. Theorists such as Karen Barad, Rosi Braidotti, Gilles Deleuze, Felix Guattari, Donna Haraway, Myra Hird, Vicky Kirby, Bruno Latour, Brian Massumi, Isabelle Stengers and Patricia Clough, among others, have been associated with these relational ontologies. What all of these theorists and configurations of approaches have in common is a focus on matter or materiality, a relational ontology, seeing difference as affirmative, and transdisciplinarity.

A new feminist materialist perspective is a fruitful one for examining the data which are the focus of this chapter for a number of reasons. Firstly, because of its emphasis on the *material*, it enables a focus on all the aspects – human and non-human, that constitute the context in which the vice-chancellors operate and how learning to teach is affected by this. As Fenwick and Edwards point out in their framing chapter of this section of the book 'a sociomaterial analysis also helps illustrate the more-than-human assemblings that perform knowledge in higher education'. Secondly, in its relational ontology, new feminist materialism facilitates an exploration of the connections and entanglements which play out between HEIs, policies, practices, and discourses, being threaded through each other. Thirdly, new feminist materialism allows us to move beyond human intention and consciousness, focusing instead on how the material and discursive are mutually constituted as material-discursive – with neither existing outside of the other. Humans, in their intra-actions, are part of the world and its becoming, rather than in the world. Karen Barad (2007) created the neologism 'intra-action' which she distinguishes from interaction, to describe her agential realist ontology, which is premised on the notion that entities do not pre-exist relationships but come into being through relationships. Thus, rather than seeing agency as existing within individuals as separate beings, intra-action assumes that agency emerges through enactments in mutual entanglements (Barad 2007, Pacini-Ketchabaw 2012). Thus, the vice-chancellors, who are the focus of this chapter, in their intra-actions, are part of the higher education environment rather than only being influenced by it or influencing it. Fourthly, new feminist materialism in its focus on an ethico-onto-epistemological perspective regards ethics, ontology and epistemology as inseparable (Barad 2007). Thus matters of *concern* cannot be separated from matters of *fact* in considering learning to teach. The injunction that 'matter' matters means that in exploring the material, the researcher is obligated to attend to the ethical (Latour 2004). Social justice is considered to be an important part of these ethical considerations in new feminist material accounts offered by Barad, Braidotti and Haraway, to name a few of these theorists (see Bozalek in press for more details of socially just pedagogies from a posthuman perspective). Concerns with social justice are particularly pertinent in relation to learning to teach in the South African higher education landscape, where issues of inequity continue to dominate, as has been illuminated in the previous section. The fifth and final reason we offer for the usefulness of a feminist materialist position is that it allows us to move beyond the confines of critique – as Bruno Latour (2004) put it 'critique has run out of steam' – which was noted by Fenwick and Edwards in the opening chapter of this section. Barad, MacLure and Latour all pose problems regarding the practice of critique, which tends to pit one point of view against another, undermining a particular position in favour of another. In an interview with Barad by Juelskjær & Schwennesen (2012), she refers to the epistemological damage done through this conception of critique. MacLure goes as far as calling it a 'sadistic enterprise' which 'divides, categorizes, objectifies and judges' (MacLure 2013, p. 14). Critique assumes a stance which is exterior, moralising and superior rather than seeing oneself as located as part of the phenomenon being investigated – this is why Barad proposes that 'critique doesn't have the kind of political traction that is so needed' (Juelskjær & Schwennesen 2012, p. 14). In place of critique we use a diffractive methodology, which examines the details of texts such as the interview data examined in this chapter, respectfully and with care, not setting up positions in opposition to each other, but rather reading one text through another in an attempt to create something new and develop inventive provocations (Barad 2007). As Barad (2014b, p. 154) notes, 'Doing theory requires being open to the world's aliveness, allowing oneself to be lured by curiosity, surprise, and wonder'.

Interviews with vice-chancellors

The interviews with the vice-chancellors were conducted at the eight HEIs which were part of the larger national South African research project investigating professional development in teaching and learning in South Africa. Table 3.2 below provides some detail of the institutions.

Each vice-chancellor was interviewed by a project member from a neighbouring institution, generally the Director of Teaching and Learning from that institution. They were asked about their personal vision, the strengths and accomplishments of their institutions regarding teaching and learning, the goals and priorities for staff development regarding teaching and learning, what systems were in place for this, how staff respond to professional development, and the factors that enable and constrain learning to teach professional development. Who the interviewer and interviewee were, the interview questions, as well as the physical setting of the interview, all intra-act as material-discursive practices, making certain responses possible, while excluding others (Pacini-Ketchabaw 2012).

As mentioned in the section above, we used a diffractive methodology to analyse the interviews, where insights from texts are read through one another. We first read through all the interviews ourselves, then together, noting particularly how the institution, where it was placed geographically and in terms of access to resources, the staff–student ratio and the feeder schools which the students came from, impacted on learning to teach. The insights from the interviews were read through a lens of social justice regarding learning to teach. There was one interview in particular, however, which was what Maggie MacLure (2013, p. 661) calls a 'hot spot', where the data appears to glow, the detail of which 'arrests our gaze and makes us pause; the connections that start to fire up; the conversation that gets faster and more animated' (MacLure 2015, p. 662). This was one interview which confounded common sense by not falling conventionally into the stereotypes of institutional type – an interview of a vice-chancellor at a merged University of Technology, who had an *enlarged vision* of what teaching and learning professional staff development and a university might look like. This was the text which had affective resonance, beckoning us – and to which we desired to return to again and again. Reading with this text provoked

Table 3.2 Details of higher education institutions where vice-chancellors were interviewed

	Historical legacy (advantaged v. disadvantaged) (merged v. not merged)	Focus	University type	Student population	Campuses	Urban v. rural	No of students (in 2010)	Permanent staff/ student ratio (2012)	Established	Student success rate (in 2009)
1	Advantaged	Research	Traditional	Elite schools	3	Urban	25000	1:23	1829	84
2	Advantaged	Research	Traditional	Elite schools	4	Urban	27694	1:28	1881/1916	84
3	Advantaged	Research	Traditional	Elite schools	1	Rural	7274	1:21	1904	83
4	Disadvantaged	Teaching	Traditional	Disadvantaged schools	3	Urban	18031	1:32	1960	79
5	Disadvantaged Merged	Teaching	Traditional	Disadvantaged schools	3	Rural	11074	1:34	1916	79
6	Disadvantaged Merged	Teaching	Traditional	Disadvantaged schools	1	Rural	11000	1:32	1981	79
7	Advantaged and disadvantaged Merged	Teaching	University of Technology	Disadvantaged schools	8	Urban	36000	1:42	1960 and 1962	79
8	Advantaged and disadvantaged Merged	Teaching	University of Technology	Disadvantaged schools	8	Urban	23000	1:42	1956 and 1907	76

Source: Leibowitz, Bozalek, Winberg & van Schalkwyk, 2015

new ways of understanding the data of the other interviews with vice-chancellors. This new feminist materialist or diffractive reading of data is different in that the data itself becomes a constitutive force intra-acting with us in our reading these texts through the lenses of socially just pedagogies in South African higher education. Here data analysis can be regarded as 'an enactment amongst research-data-participants-theory' (Mazzei 2013). Thus the object and agencies of observation are entangled and agentic – data is not something passive or dead, but a performative agent, transforming us and influencing our own becoming as researchers, the material and human forces intra-acting with and making themselves intelligible to each other (Barad 2007). This way of looking at data is in contrast with coding of data, which reduces the complexity of details in the data, removing the researcher from the data, and creating closure and stasis through representational data categories, rather than an entanglement or becoming-with the data (MacLure 2013; Hultman & Lenz Taguchi 2010).

The next section will cover some of the insights we developed about learning to teach in South Africa through our intra-actions with South African texts on social justice and higher education and a close reading of the interview which emerged unpredictably as an intensity between us (Mazzei 2014), releasing us from the 'banality' of coding data (MacLure 2013, p.174).

The entanglement of HEIs

The first thing that glowed as a hot spot for us in the selected text of one of the vice-chancellors was the enlarged vision that was expressed in this interview, which was largely absent in other interviews with vice-chancellors. Other interviewees tended to focus exclusively on their own institutions, both in terms of their successes and constraints with regard to learning to teach in higher education. This interviewee, by contrast, had a conception of higher education as an entangled system where what is happening in one institution would inevitably mutually constitute practices of learning to teach at other institutions. While some vice-chancellors were disconcerted by their academic teaching and research staff being 'poached' by other institutions, this vice-chancellor had a much more relaxed approach. In fact, his approach veered towards what might be regarded as a 'radical openness' (Barad 2014b, p. 160), understanding that an academic who is valuable to one university would be of value to any other institution, and the whole of higher education as a system would not suffer if the person moved from one institution to another:

> And by the way, we are all part of the same system, so whether somebody is here or at HAIx, it's good for the system.

Thus his institution, which was poorly resourced and in need of good academics, would lose this academic, yet he was generous enough to see it as not a loss for his own institution, but as a circulation of expertise in higher education. In a similar vein, he showed awareness of the problems regarding the differentiated system of higher education – where some institutions are regarded as world-class and others as 'less than' – recognising that those that are recognised as 'world-class' exist at the expense of those which are less valued. These institutions are entangled, where those regarded as 'other' – the HDIs – are inextricably bound to the 'world-class' institutions. An ethical position would recognise otherness in itself – something that the other interviewees who were vice-chancellors from HAIs found difficulty in doing. As Barad (2014b, p. 162) notes:

> Entanglements are relations of obligation – being bound to the other – enfolded traces of othering. Othering, the constitution of an 'Other,' entails an indebtedness to the 'Other,' who is irreducibly and materially bound to, threaded through, the 'self' – a diffraction/dispersion of identity. 'Otherness' is an entangled relation of difference (différance). Ethicality entails noncoincidence with oneself.

The views about the higher education system and its institutions expressed in the interview that we chose from the eight vice-chancellors take as their departure point a decolonising logic, where difference or alterity is seen as affirmative rather than as lack, as foreign or as negative. As the vice-chancellor expressed it:

> My view is that we don't need world-class universities – we need a world-class university system. That actually you know, the excellence of a place like the University of X, fundamentally depends on other places functioning at a decent level because it's all about the pipeline.

The view of the HDI as an in/appropriated other (Trinh Minh-ha in Barad 2014a) provokes a rethinking of difference and relationality as difference *within* – thus those at the HAI or world-class university do not recognise the difference within. They do not see the HDI as a productive space, a space of creativity. Rather, they see it as an apartheid construction which is to be avoided or relegated to a less valued position as an institution in a differentiated system. The views of the interviewee we chose to focus on were out of the ordinary, in his specific choice to make a contribution to the in/appropriated other – in this case the merged University of Technology rather than an HAI, which he considered would not benefit to such an extent from his leadership:

> Seventy-five per cent of the students that come to our institution are first-time learners in their families, higher education learners. The majority of them come from really financially stressed families. About 40% of our students have some form of financial aid and so on. So I mean, I was just saying to the people in Nutrition a few minutes ago that if I had a choice between being here as vice-chancellor or at HAIx, I'd probably choose my

institution. Because what should I do at HAIx? You know, it's a functioning university.

He was quite open and happy to be making a contribution to his particular university, which was viewed as less than or the inappropriate/d other, and found no reason to be seeking out a more privileged space to enact his academic contributions. The choice of taking up the challenges of an HDI and a merged UoT was a deliberate choice to be in proximity with and taking forward the in/ appropriated other.

Ethics and aesthetics – a holistic approach to teaching and learning to teach

Latour's (2004), Braidotti's (2013) and Barad's (2007) notion of moving beyond critical deconstruction and critique to alternative enactments of becoming, where power is not only seen as limiting but also as affirmative, has particular relevance for the way in which the interviewee saw teaching and learning. This provides the impetus for rethinking teaching and learning as an important practice that should be nourished, grown and cared for, something that needs attentiveness to ascertain how teachers are flourishing and how courses are growing:

> and getting people to understand that we do actually *cherish* good learning and teaching, good teaching. That's the one side. The other side of course is a whole range of processes … to give us some sense of how courses are growing, you know how teachers are teaching [our emphasis added].

The interviewee was also unusual in his enlarged vision (Bozalek 2011, Young 2011) of what teaching at a University of Technology might entail and the sort of curriculum which may be possible to pursue. This was made visible in his expressed discipline in ethics and aesthetics as being important for education, rather than adhering to the expected technicist view of education in a UoT:

> you know if students are doing Engineering. Engineering might actually expect students to do a course on … I don't know … the ethics of engineering, or something on, what you call it, the place of beauty in Engineering or whatever … aesthetics of engineering.

Moving beyond binaries – teachers and learners

Moving beyond or rethinking dualisms or binary oppositions is one of the main tenets of posthumanism and new feminist materialist philosophies (Braidotti 2013).The vice-chancellor that we focused on was able to shift away from binary oppositions of teacher/learner and to view academics as learners as well as teachers.

He also envisaged academics to be lifelong learners, encouraging them to engage in continuing learning and scholarly practice, and with scholarly knowledge:

> We really have to get the academics into a mode of becoming lifelong learners themselves ... Academics as lifelong learners ... it's not simply for them to get a doctorate, but it's to say to them we want you to start learning again. We want you to start engaging with new ideas.

His approach to learning to teach illuminates lifelong learning as a process of potentialities and becomings for academics, rather than a conventional professional development approach that could be construed as more limiting and instrumentalist. Seeing academics as lifelong learners is a more ontologically powerful way of conceiving learning to teach in that it is not viewed as a once off exercise but more of a freedom to follow new ways of thinking as part of a lifelong endeavour of constant engagement.

The materiality of social justice

In feminist new materialist approaches to data analysis, matter is seen as vital and vibrant and as having agency and as being 'mutually constituted' with the discursive (Barad 2007, Lenz Taguchi 2013, Phillips & Larson 2013). With regards to social justice, learning to teach and higher education, the material and the discursive are thus imbricated in each other. It is also what the material *does* that matters rather than what it is – the energies and forces of transformation that emanate from matter (Coole 2014, Ingold 2014). It matters then that the student-staff ratio is much higher at some institutions, such as the one focused on in the interview which we were interpolated by:

> The difficulty of course is that, unlike HAIx and so on, where the staff/ student ratios are still very low ... about 1 to 17 is the kind of ratio. In certain faculties [here] it's more like 50 or something like that. So it's not an easy task to expect our staff members to complete their studies, well that's the way I'm looking at it.

Thus, the number of students to staff members directly affects the ability of academic staff in having the time to engage in other activities, such as learning to teach or pursuing other further education. However, the materiality of this is not acknowledged either by official bodies, such as Higher Education Councils, which evaluate teaching and learning at HEIs. It is also not taken into account by those in more fortunate positions with low staff-student ratios, particularly those from HAIs who may take for granted that academics could have the time to pursue opportunities which would benefit their teaching.

Funding and resources are another material reality that heavily impacts on teaching and learning to teach. Earlier on in this chapter, the issue of differentiation was alluded to. In the excerpt below, the interviewee notes that if differentiation is insisted upon for a higher education system, then at least the institutions should be given the funding that they need to operate properly:

> So there is no question about the fact that this is predominantly a teaching institution, but then it should be funded so it can do the teaching properly. We can't have students coming from dysfunctional schools, being in classes where they are one in forty and one in fifty on an average. We really have to work towards this idea that students will get personal attention ... So the differentiation debate for me is really to say that institutions, whatever they are and whatever their kind of mandate is, that they are funded properly to do what they are expected to do.

Another material aspect of South African tertiary education which has direct impact on learning to teach is the after-effects of merging institutions, which happened post-1994. Many of the merged institutions are still battling to deal with affects between the merged parties in faculties and disciplines, and with physical difficulties of coordinating efforts across geographically disparate campuses (Gachago et al. 2015). Some institutions have still not managed to develop an institutional identity with which all parties identify, and in others there remains a disparity regarding resources that are available for teaching at the various campuses (Jansen 2003, Kamsteeg 2008). The vice-chancellor in the interview we focused on was very aware of the influences of the merger of his institution on learning to teach:

> Well, I think that the merger of the two former technikons was a very difficult enterprise, and I think that we're still seeing difficulties that grew out of that. So just to say that we're at the point where even today we're dealing with what you might call post-merger issues, and there's a lot of emotion related to that. So that's something that we have to kind of really work at, and we also have to work at building a new institutional culture. So in other words, really getting people to go beyond the merger and kind of really saying, well, we are now a new institution, we are part of this new institution.

The materiality of the mergers also has affective consequences regarding identification with and belonging to the institution, sometimes taking up to ten years for people to feel that they belong (Gachago et al. 2015). These affective aspects would impact on teaching and learning and affect academics' motivation to take part in initiatives regarding learning to teach.

Conclusion

This chapter has considered an example of how new feminist materialisms can be put to use to intra-act with data from a project on learning to teach in higher education in South Africa. The focus of the chapter was specifically on issues of social justice in higher education and how the material-discursive affects learning to teach in relation to a continued situation of inequality in the country. In focusing on data that glowed (MacLure 2013) from a transcription of one of the eight vice-chancellors who were interviewed for the project, we attempted to show how a new feminist materialism facilitates a creative way of looking at data and hence, an affirmative ethics of potentiality. In contrast to providing a critique of how more conventional interviewees construed learning to teach in their institutions, focusing on an unusually open and response-able interviewee made it possible to consider creative and affirmative sensibilities with regard to the envisioning a response to continued inequalities and injustices in the higher education system. Importantly, the ways in which all higher education institutions are mutually entangled became evident in the interview, highlighting the inseparability of historically advantaged and disadvantaged institutions. Thus the image of discrete and independent institutions, as they were viewed by other interviewees, who largely focused on their own constraints and enablements, was rendered problematic in this interview. Responsibility not only for oneself, but for the other, was foregrounded in the interview. Secondly, the historically disadvantaged institution as an in/appropriate/d other, became seen as something to be valued in its alterity. Difference is then seen from an affirmative position, rather than being pathologised. The response-ability and accountability regarding what really matters, the conviction that he was making a difference to an institution that needed his leadership and his attentiveness to matter that matters all emanated from what he expressed in the interview. The dualism between teacher and learner was also challenged by the interviewee in his view of academics as lifelong learners – as partners learning alongside students. The impact of the material was also highlighted in the interview with funding, physical infrastructure, student-staff ratios and the aftermath of merging all intra-acting with and affecting learning to teach.

All in all, the interview provides an ethical response to issues of social justice and inequality which could motivate others to think more carefully about the entanglements of institutions and consider novel ways of engaging and enacting change in the material-discursive interstices of learning to teach as an educational practice in higher education.

References

Barad, K. (2007), *Meeting the universe halfway: Quantum physics and the entanglement of matter and meaning*, Duke University Press, Durham and London.

Barad, K. (2012), 'On touching – The inhuman that therefore I am', *Differences*, vol. 23, no. 3, pp. 206–23.

Barad, K. (2014a), 'Diffracting diffraction: Cutting together-apart', *Parallax*, vol. 20, no. 3, pp. 168–87.

Barad, K. (2014b), 'On touching – The inhuman that therefore I am', in S. Witzgall & K. Stakemeier (eds), *Power of material/politics of materiality*, Diaphanes eText, Zurich-Berlin.

Boughey, C. & McKenna, S. (2011), *A meta-analysis of teaching and learning at five historically disadvantaged universities*, Council on Higher Education, Pretoria.

Bozalek, V. (2011), 'Acknowledging privilege through encounters with difference: Participatory learning and action techniques for decolonising methodologies in Southern contexts', *International Journal of Social Research Methodology*, vol. 14, no. 6, pp. 469–84.

Bozalek, V. (in press), 'Socially just pedagogies', in R. Braidotti & M. Hlavajova (eds), *Posthuman glossary*, Bloomsbury, London.

Bozalek, V. & Boughey, C. (2012), '(Mis)framing Higher Education in South Africa', *Social Policy & Administration*, vol. 46, no. 6, pp. 688–703.

Braidotti, R. (2013), *The posthuman*, Polity Press, Cambridge.

Breier, M. (2010), 'Dropout or stop out at the University of the Western Cape?', in M. Letseka, M. Cosser, M. Breier & M. Visser (eds), *Student retention and graduate destination: Higher education and labour market access and success*, Human Sciences Research Council Press, Cape Town.

Cloete, N. (2016), *Free higher education. Another self-destructive South African Policy*, paper published by the Centre for Higher Education Trust (CHET) in January 2016.

Coole, D. (2014), 'New materialism: The ontology and politics of materialisation', in S. Witzgall & K. Stakemeier (eds), *Power of material/politics of materiality*, Diaphanes eText, Zurich-Berlin.

Cooper, D. (2015), 'Social justice and South African university student enrolment data by "race", 1998–2012: From "skewed revolution" to "stalled revolution"', *Higher Education Quarterly*, vol. 69, no. 3, pp. 237–62.

Department of Education (DoE) (1997), *White Paper 3: A programme for the transformation of higher education*, Department of Education, Pretoria.

Gachago, D., Sosibo, Z. & Ivala, E. N. (2015), 'Nostalgia, anxiety and gratification: Narratives of female staff in a merged higher education institution', *Alternation*, vol. 22, no. 16, pp. 19–43.

Grosz, E. (2011), *Becoming undone: Darwinian reflections on life, politics, and art*, Duke University Press, Durham.

Hultman, K. & Lenz Taguchi, H. (2010), 'Challenging anthropocentric analysis of visual data: A relational materialist methodological approach to educational research', *International Journal of Qualitative Studies in Education: QSE*, vol. 23, no. 5, pp. 525–42.

Ingold, T. (2014), 'An ecology of material', in S. Witzgall & K. Stakemeier (eds), *Power of material/politics of materiality*, Diaphanes eText, Zurich-Berlin.

Jansen, J. (2003), 'Mergers in South African higher education: Theorising change in transitional contexts', *Politikon, South African Journal of Political Studies*, vol. 30, no. 1, pp. 27–50.

Juelskjær M. & Schwennesen, N. (2012), 'Intra-active entanglements: An interview with Karen Barad', *Kvinder, Køn og Forskning*, vol. 21, nos 1–2, pp. 10–23.

Kamsteeg, F. (2008), 'In search of a merged identity: The case of multi-campus North-West University, South Africa', *TD*, vol. 4, no. 2, pp. 431–51.

Latour, B. (2004), 'Why has critique run out of steam? From matters of fact to matters of concern', *Critical Inquiry*, vol. 30, pp. 225–48.

Leibowitz, B, Bozalek, V, Winberg, C & van Schalkwyk, S 2015, 'Institutional context matters: the professional development of academics as teachers in South African higher education', *Higher Education*, vol. 69, no. 2, pp. 315 – 330.

Lenz Taguchi, H. (2013), 'Images of thinking in feminist materialisms: Ontological divergences and the production of researcher subjectivities', *International Journal of Qualitative Studies in Education: QSE*, vol. 26, no. 6, pp. 706–16.

MacLure, M. (2013), 'Classification or wonder? Coding as an analytic practice in qualitative research', in R. Coleman & J. Ringrose (eds), *Deleuze and research methodologies*, Edinburgh University Press, Edinburgh.

MacLure, M. (2015), 'The "new materialisms": A thorn in the flesh of critical qualitative inquiry?' in G. S. Cannella, M. S. Perez & P. A. Pasque (eds), *Critical qualitative inquiry: Foundations and futures*, West Coast Press, Walnut Creek, CA.

Mazzei, L. A. (2013), 'A voice without organs: Interviewing in posthumanist research', *International Journal of Qualitative Studies in Education: QSE*, vol. 26, no. 6, pp. 732–40.

Mazzei, L. A. (2014), 'Beyond an easy sense: A diffractive analysis', *Qualitative Inquiry*, vol. 20, no. 6, pp. 742–46.

Nicolson, G. (2016), 'Fees must fall: Reloaded', *Daily Maverick* 12 January 2016, accessed 13 January 2016, www.dailymaverick.co.za/article/2016-01-12-fees-must-fall-reloaded/#.VpVX5ZN96b8

Pacini-Ketchabaw, V. (2012), 'Acting with the clock: Clocking practices in early childhood', *Contemporary Issues in Early Childhood*, vol. 13, no. 2, pp. 154–60.

Phillips, K. & Larson, M. L. (2013), 'The teacher–student writing conference reimaged: Entangled becoming-writing conferencing', *Gender and Education*, vol. 25, no. 6, pp. 722–37.

South Africa.info (n. d.), accessed 14 January 2016, www.southafrica.info/about/people/population.htm#.VpYmrZN96b8

Universities South Africa (2016), *Joint statement from vice chancellors, principals and rectors of universities in South Africa*, accessed 13 January 2016, www.cut.ac.za/leadership/joint-statement-vice-chancellor-principals-rectors-universities-south-africa/

Young, I. M. (2011), *Responsibility for Justice*, Oxford University Press, Oxford.

Chapter 4

Knowledge infrastructures, digital higher education and the hidden curriculum

Richard Edwards and Tara Fenwick

Introduction

Increasingly, higher education has become entangled in digital technologies for pedagogy, research and organisational management. Often under the banners of extending opportunity, inclusion, equity, greater openness, widening participation and the more efficient organising of higher education, these technologies take many different forms and their spread and uptake are uneven around the globe. In relation to pedagogy and research, there is much discussion of their development, how best they can support academic endeavours, what skills academics need to teach using such technologies and the extent to which they provide the basis for different practices through, for instance, the uses of open educational resources or learning analytics, and/or the posing of different questions to be addressed by research. Here the technologies are positioned often as simply the manifestations and extensions of human intention and resourcefulness, as simple enablers of educational goals.

Less attention has been given to the ways in which they reconfigure the practices, management and governance of the academy through new forms of data, representation, audit, comparison and accountability or the reconfigurings of the hidden curriculum they may enact (Williamson 2014, 2015, Edwards & Carmichael 2012). The latter is particularly significant when these technologies are deployed as part of strategies to address exclusions and inequities, as they may embed different inequalities rather than overcome them. Nor have these debates significantly impacted upon the discussion of or training courses for learning to teach in higher education. Technologies tend to be presented as providing new resources or tools rather than there being deeper discussion of how they might reconfigure the possibilities for teaching and learning in more profound and perhaps problematic ways.

How to chart and make sense of this emergent world of higher education is of much concern in assessing the significance of the actualities and potentialities of digital technologies in relation to its multiple purposes. In this chapter, we draw upon certain strands of sociomaterial thinking to suggest the ways in which digital higher education is an emerging part of different 'knowledge infrastructures'

(Edwards 2010) through which data is generated, ordered, visualised and enacted. These infrastructures – embracing both the human and non-human – are producing different types of artefacts, relationships and practices, which raise significant possibilities and challenges to ways of teaching and doing academic work and its visible and hidden effects.

Drawing examples from research, the chapter will explore some of the challenges posed, identify existing trends and suggest some possibilities arising from both the spread of these technologies, but also from conceptualising higher education as integral to emerging knowledge infrastructures. In particular, we will point to the ways in which the representation of knowledge as truth is challenged by the seductive visualisations made available through digital technologies as part of the hidden curriculum of higher education. In this way, we aim to pose questions regarding the significance of academic ways of working, ways of understanding and representing knowledge through teaching and research, and the position of higher education practices as integral to the knowledge infrastructures within the increasingly digitised world. We want to suggest that in considering what is involved in teaching in higher education, we need a far more critical engagement with the question of what is required when drawing upon digital technologies.

To situate higher education as a knowledge infrastructure is to position it as one of the producers and disseminators of knowledge, recognising that it is only one form of the institutionalisation of knowledge. This is not to deny its importance and significance as a specifically educational institutional arrangement with all the associated value attributed to it. However, this should not be assumed a priori and a key challenge posed by the spread of digital technologies is precisely one of the shifting distributions of authoritative knowledge production. In other words, we cannot take the information and representations with which we interact through digital means for granted, given the work of software, hardware and data, and the automated work that goes on 'behind the screen'. It is this that we wish to explore as part of the reconfiguring of the hidden curriculum of higher education and what that means for teaching.

The hidden curriculum refers to the things that are learned by students that are not the intended outcomes of curriculum and pedagogy (e.g. Snyder 1971, Apple & King 1983). While mostly developed in relation to schooling, it has also been formulated in relation to higher and distance education (e.g. Margolis 2001, Anderson 2001). The notion of the hidden curriculum has been used as part of the critique of educational institutions as reproducing inequality. It is argued that while students may be learning particular subjects and skills at a prescribed level, at an enacted level, they learn many other things, including the possibilities they have within existing opportunity structures. Institutions might officially develop the curriculum to support the learning of all students. However, those things which are selected as part of the formal curriculum and the pedagogies through which they are taught provide hidden messages to certain types of students that education and educational advancement is not for them. The reference to curriculum in the term suggests that hidden curriculum is primarily concerned with the forms of knowledge and authoritative discourses made available in educational institutions. However, the hidden curriculum may not simply be about knowledge, but also the forms of lecturer-student and student-student interaction that are deemed allowable within the curriculum. The same is the case for the resources used in classrooms, the books, artefacts, furniture and, of course, learning technologies: all may carry hidden as well as explicit messages. In this way, individuals can become socialised into particular roles in the social order, and inequality is reproduced. From this perspective, the hidden curriculum is one of the primary educational ways through which social inequality is reproduced. The workings of the digital within such processes is of great significance. When learning to teach in higher education, we tend to focus on what is or should be made visible. Exploring what is hidden and its affects can help us understand some of the issues faced by students and our own assumptions as teachers, which influence our teaching.

The chapter is in three parts. First we will explore the notion of knowledge infrastructures, their role and how they are made to work. In particular, we focus on the work of code, ontologies and algorithms within them. This is an emerging arena for research and, to date, despite the increasing research on learning analytics, there has been little or no focus on higher education as one of these infrastructures. Such an approach provides different insights into academic practices in general, but also specifically those that attempt to address issues of equity and justice. Second, we outline some of the implications of framing academic practices in this way. In particular, we explore some of the challenges it raises in relation to the hidden curriculum and some of the limitations as well as possibilities in the use of digital analytics and visualisations. These are issues which few address in relation to their teaching, but which we suggest require greater attention. Third, we outline some broad possible implications for higher education. This situation requires further detailed empirical research. This chapter can be read as a different point of departure for research agendas in higher education teaching and academic practices rather than as presuming to represent significant conclusions.

Knowledge infrastructures

Kitchin and Dodge (2011) describe how many of the infrastructures underpinning the modern world depend on computer code for their functioning. They detail the existence of 'coded infrastructures', such as computing networks, communication and broadcast entertainment networks, transport and logistics networks, security and policing networks, and satellite-based global positioning systems. These coded infrastructures orchestrate and order many aspects of daily life and embed software code firmly within the systems that constitute contemporary societies and aspirations for developments such as 'smart cities'. Less noted, however, are the knowledge infrastructures that organise the data through which particular things are known, understood, managed and enacted and how they come to be formed. As digital data are increasingly used to 'see', 'know' and 'intervene' in worlds, the knowledge infrastructures within which such data is collected, analysed and made visible are becoming increasingly significant. Edwards et al. (2013, p. 5) refer to knowledge infrastructures as:

> ecologies, or complex adaptive systems; they consist of numerous systems, each with unique origins and goals, which are made to interoperate by means of standards, socket layers, social practices, norms, and individual behaviours that smooth out the connections among them.

Both the development of such infrastructures and their operations, uptakes and effects are beginning to be researched. This work raises important questions for both higher education pedagogy and research (cf. Williamson 2015).

The growing research on the work of software, code and algorithms (e.g. Manovich 2013, Neyland 2015, Totaro & Ninno 2016) and knowledge infrastructures (e.g. Lampland & Star 2009) have therefore the potential for providing significant resources through which to explore the embedded work of digital technologies in academic practices (Edwards 2015a). Knowledge infrastructures do not simply represent data, but select, translate and transform them and this is what we wish to suggest is part of a hidden curriculum. It is the ontologies, codes, algorithms and the linking of data in knowledge infrastructures that make things perform in particular ways and become specific actors in the enactment of higher education. The digital technologies are not, therefore, simply tools through which human intention is applied to the intended goals of, for instance, inclusion, widening participation, equity, but are fundamental to the actions to which they contribute. In using or choosing to use certain digital technologies and resources therefore we are already impacting upon what is taught and how it is taught. In relation to this, a significant role is played by forms of classification, the establishment of standards and the ontology-building associated with the development of digital databases, and the ways in which complex knowledge is represented. In higher education, how this occurs and with what effects in relation to the resources drawn upon in teaching and research is largely left unexamined, unquestioned and hidden from those using the digital technologies and resources. To classify requires as much as possible the removal of ambiguity from representation, when, of course, many knowledge claims are ambiguous and contested and it is critical engagement with them that is fundamental to educational practices.

This is important because, while access to digital resources may be attractive, their provenance and credibility are also issues to be addressed. Edwards et al. (2013, p. 10) point to some of the issues raised in the digitalisation of data in knowledge infrastructures:

first, a plethora of 'dirty' data, whose quality may be impossible for other investigators to evaluate; second, weak or non-existent guarantees of long-term persistence for many data sources; and finally, inconsistent metadata practices that may render reuse of data impossible – despite their intent to do the opposite.

In similar vein, Halford et al. (2013) explore the implications of the development of the semantic web and the promises propounded about the internet as a linked database. The big promises of open data are framed as enabling greater transparency, transcending knowledge silos and making greater advances in knowledge. These are not unimportant possibilities. However, the authors also point to some of the challenges associated with such promises, not least the naming of data entities, the structuring of data and the processing of data. To build an ontology, to name and categorise an entity in a consistent way across space and time, is not without its challenges, not least because such categories themselves might be subject to challenge. These challenges are commonly identified by those who research knowledge infrastructures, but the extent to which they are influencing the uptake of digital technologies in higher education is open to question, as is the extent to which they are part of the explicit discussion of learning to teach. As a result, Halford et al. (2013, pp. 178–79) argue that in the development of knowledge infrastructures 'making some things "known" tends to obscure other things and, indeed, ways of knowing' and that 'ontology building is not a simple or solely technical matter'. It is this obscuring in the process of making visible that points to why digital technologies need to be considered as part of the hidden curriculum of higher education when considering what and how one teaches. Totaro and Ninno (2016) argue that in part this is due to an inappropriate application of an algorithmic logic to human practices.

Ontology-building, the naming and structuring of digital data in the enactment of knowledge infrastructures, has itself become a subject of increasing research. Yet how many of us teaching in higher education are familiar with these practices or their implications? Ribes and Bowker (2009, p. 199) argue that:

> ontologies are an information technology for representing specialized knowledge in order to facilitate communication across disciplines, share data or enable collaboration. In a nutshell, they describe the sets of entities that make up the world-in-a-computer, and circumscribe the sets of relationships they can have with each other ... In the wake of ontologies the information of a domain is substantially reorganized, facilitating data exchange and reuse.

Ontologies are fundamental to the work of digital technologies in knowledge infrastructures, but how they are developed and the extent to which that process is taken for granted once they are developed is critically important in relation to the digital representations and visualisations of knowledge and their uptakes. In their study of an ontology-building process, Ribes and Bowker (2009) found the outcome was determined by the pragmatic digital requirements for the data to be machine-readable rather than for it to represent a fundamental epistemological resolution of categorisation. Thus, it is arguable that the representation of data for the purposes of digitalisation requires different qualities than those associated with existing practices in research and pedagogy. Yet this work is often hidden from those who are engaging with the data. In the practices observed by Ribes and Bowker, one critical dimension was not achieved – the representation of disagreements, uncertainties, ambiguities and ambivalences. These are qualities that it might be argued are centrally important to a worthwhile higher education. There can be a perceived authority to digital data behind which lie hidden disagreements.

These issues of inclusion, exclusion and the removal of ambiguity in developing ontologies have been highlighted in a range of studies (e.g. Randall et al. 2011). We therefore see how digital technologies raise important questions about the politics of knowledge, because 'turning everything into data, and using algorithms to analyze it, changes what it means to know something' (Manovich 2013, p. 337). This raises important concerns for lecturers or students who may still view such technologies more comfortably as benevolent and containable tools to extend participation, address exclusions and injustices or to make education more open (Edwards 2015b). When users do not question the origins or composition of such data, they are vulnerable to embedded errors and important omissions. However, the apparently neutral, inevitable format of data presentation, its visualisations and increasing interactivity, is seductive. Within the enacting of digital knowledge infrastructures, accessibility of information can take precedence over knowledge controversies. What then are some implications of this research for academic practices?

Higher education practices

There is extensive research on many aspects of digital higher education, For instance, there is burgeoning research on learning analytics and their potential to enhance provision for students (Buckingham Shum 2014, 2015, Gasevic et al. 2015). Learning analytics explore the existing use of digital technologies by students as the basis for developing different, better practices for them; precedent guides the future. Such predictive analytics are being used to explore student retention through the identification of variables that influence dropout, for example, part-time work commitments, number of classes enrolled, paper grades and available support from friends and relatives. Students are able to be assigned a dropout prediction score, which is shared with staff who can then monitor their activity and provide resources to keep them enrolled (Harris 2014). These predictive analytics are also being used for more educative purposes to improve student attainment by, for example, matching lecturers and students, reshuffling student work groups, and acting like recommender software to suggest resources and classes to individual students. This data is being cross-linked with projected labour skills demands, demographics, aptitude tests and markers of students' online engagement to determine students' employment paths and suitable curricula. There are significant efforts also to examine issues, such as how code and algorithms reflect and relate to specific understandings of pedagogy and assessment (Knight et al. 2014), to examine issues of student privacy (Prinsloo & Slade 2015) and to develop greater transparency in the use of learning analytics through the use of open source software and participatory design approaches.

At one level, this work is held to have the potential to 'personalise' learning, making it more adapted to individual student requirements, and thereby enhance people's opportunities. This assumes teachers know how to access, interpret and are able to act on such data. At another level, it might result in a person being 'trapped' by their past choices, when in education we might want to challenge and extend someone's opportunities. Here personalisation of teaching and learning seems like a constraint. In relation to wider social and predictive analytics, the latter is referred to as a 'filter bubble' (Pariser 2011), where a person has their existing preferences reinforced through the ways in which aspects of the digital knowledge infrastructure work. Similar effects could arise from the use of learning analytics. However, more positively, there are attempts to develop analytics that, for instance, identify students more at risk of failing their programmes.

Issues of decontextualisation in the development and uptake of learning analytics have been raised also as part of the critique of such approaches. For example, Laurillard (2012) argues that, because the data has been generated as by-product from a system of past interactions, it cannot be applied simplistically to a particular set of questions regarding the future. While lecturers can collaborate with learning analysts to ensure that local data is captured according to issues of most concern to them and to students to improve their own practices, the key is that academic staff, who understand the particular complexities of contexts and concerns within their field of expertise, need to still have discretion over their use.

Many therefore warn that the growth and unexamined nature of analytics, as they permeate higher education practices, are creating a particular form of rationality, and potentially a new epistemological order (Kallinikos 2010). It is such issues that have informed work to explore the hidden curriculum of the knowledge infrastructures of higher education (e.g. Edwards & Carmichael 2012). Edwards and Carmichael argue this as an addition to the work exploring the uptake of digital technologies in higher education in relation to openness and inclusion. In particular, drawing on some of the research outlined above, they argue that the effects of developing standards and algorithms on the representation of data, the forms of teaching and learning that are possible, and the notion of the student assumed and enacted, are part of a 'secret code' of the hidden curriculum. They provide examples of how the visualisation of data in digital resources selects what is and is not made visible in ways in which only those who have written or understand the underlying code may be able to understand. The information visualised therefore provides only a partial picture based upon the assumptions in the software, algorithms and ontologies.

When utilising digital visualisations of data in higher education contexts, consideration is needed therefore for questions about the quality and reliability of what is drawn upon and what is coded out as well as what is coded in to make certain data visible. A further question is the semiotic power of the visualisation over the raw data. To have an interactive visualisation of the mapping of, for instance, volcanic eruptions over time is very different from a simple list of places and dates where these events have taken place. At one level, such a visualisation might be more engaging – the knowledge infrastructure being supportive of pedagogy. However, any such visualisation tends to hide the data upon which it draws and the work done to represent it in that particular form. Viewers are not necessarily aware that a small change in these algorithms can produce a completely different picture of the 'reality' that visualisations seem to portend (Wilson 2015). This issue arguably may intensify as educational environments continue to evolve in directions more digitally immersive and interactive.

There are many challenges to exploring the hidden curriculum of digital knowledge infrastructures for pedagogy and research. For example, Kitchin (2014) argues that the source code is often hidden and black-boxed; algorithms are woven into technical systems that are heterogeneous and embedded; they are not fixed and performative; and they are out of control. Kitchin (2013) argues also that the quantitative methods currently taught to undergraduates are hopelessly out of date in this new era of big data. Not only are the methods unsuited for enormous, unstructured datasets with unknown properties, but students also do not develop critical awareness of emerging forms and structures of data, and of how algorithms work in and on data. In other words, higher education is not keeping up with the work and potential of the knowledge infrastructures within which they are entangled.

These are important issues for students and teachers who increasingly rely on digitalised data and interactions in their pedagogic practices and researchers of higher education. In this 'modern techno-social universe', as Manovich (2013, p. 338) terms it, knowledge and the processes of it development are being redefined. Given the invisibility of these dynamics, Berry (2011, p. 4) called for research to make them visible 'so that we can pay attention to both what it is (ontology), where it has come from (through media archaeology and genealogy), but also what it is doing (through a form of mechanology)'. Since his writings, there has been an outpouring of critical research in digital media and software studies, and in general science and technology studies. However, outside of work on learning analytics, there is yet little attention in higher education research to making the hidden curriculum of ontology-building, software and its algorithms more visible. There is a clear need to examine the ways in which software is entangled in pedagogic practices in relation to the forms of representation and the nature of knowledge, and the ways of interacting and knowing that are becoming possible. The hidden curriculum of algorithms and ontologies within the knowledge infrastructures of higher education and those that it draws upon may well be reproducing or reconfiguring inequalities even as the ideology of digital higher education is increasingly emphasising inclusion, participation and openness.

Berry's (2011, p. 5) cautions about making software visible are still worthy of attention: 'looking at computer code is difficult due to its ephemeral nature, the high technical skills required of the researcher and the lack of analytical or methodological tools available'. He proposes that a phenomenology of computation might enable researchers to explore 'the ways in which code is able to structure experience in concrete ways' (Berry 2011, p. 39). This presumably would entail bringing the skills of the ethnographer together with those of the computer scientist, although even that is an over-simplification, as different manifestations of software and data require specific ethnographic and computer science methodologies.

Implications for higher education pedagogy

Given what we would argue to be the sociomaterial enactments of the emerging knowledge infrastructures of higher education, we now want to consider some pedagogical responses to the challenges outlined. Simply reframing academic practices as sociomaterial knowledge infrastructures, engaging with the emerging research in these areas and developing more practice-focused pedagogical practices would be a start when considering what worthwhile teaching entails. The object here is to enable all those participating in these infrastructures to develop a critical attunement to and engagement with, that can see past the persuasive apparent precision of the emergent knowledge and accessibility to new ways of working, learning, intervening and interacting, and to question their limitations as well as identify their possibilities. More broadly perhaps, the aim is to prompt engagement with the digital technologies as part of the assemblages of practice, and not just to accept them as black-boxes that only computer specialists can understand.

How might this be done? Specific suggestions are discussed below. One response is for students and lecturers to be encouraged to learn more about coding processes, ontology-building and the work of knowledge infrastructures and how to engage in such practices themselves. However, in much education, this may be neither feasible nor desirable given existing crowded curricula and a focus on and valuing of propositional knowledge rather than know-how. In these circumstances, it could make more sense for students and lecturers to learn to collaborate more effectively with digital designers and analysts than to try to become computer scientists themselves. Most disciplines still remain separate from engaging with computational experts, for all sorts of understandable reasons, including the vast differences in language, purposes and approaches, even as their practices are increasingly digital. However, to begin with, a key pedagogic strategy will be to have lecturers and students examine their digital activity more critically, and even think about ways to disrupt taken for granted practices, such as developing alternative ontologies for digital data.

Students in all areas can be encouraged to find out more about and how to engage in coding processes and ontology-building that produce certain forms of knowledge and logic that structure thinking. 'Learning to code' has become a polarised debate in education broadly. The argument is that it is possible and even urgent to make visible the hidden work of software code by developing enhanced computer skills in all students. In much higher education however, learning to code is neither feasible nor desirable. However, students can discuss the functions of code as a relatively hidden language. Who gets to see this code? Who should be able to understand code, and at what level? Students also can look more closely at how algorithms built into common software such as Facebook shape the way that they express and represent themselves, interact with others, form preferences, make decisions, and become drawn into particular social groups and patterns. As students move into work, they can become more attuned to making the hidden work of code decipherable and more visible in relation to their practices.

One place for students to begin disrupting their relations with digital media is by critically examining their everyday uses of social media. Facebook algorithms and routines, for instance, shape the content and style of exchange, and the nature of what is taken for knowledge. Patterns of 'friending', favouriting, following, trending – the 'I like' modes of interaction – have become normalised (Van Dijk 2013). More broadly, the fundamental imperatives promoted by digital social media, in particular those of 'openness' and connectivity, deserve disruption. Keen (2012), among others, suggests a return to basic questions: Is openness and sharing necessarily a good thing? If we live online and everything is social, what is outside it? Where is privacy or, what is it that 'privacy' is transmogrifying to become? Such disruptive questions can encourage more systemic thinking among both students and academics. Rather than simply learning ways to protect themselves against the hazards posed by 'openness', or how to avoid 'friending' the wrong thing, students might critically examine their own patterns of social media participation as part of larger cultural trends. Students can, for instance, trawl back through selected traces of their activity, perhaps relating to a particular theme of interest. They can analyse their tweets/retweets over a period, the photos they have posted or favourited, the friends they have accumulated and analyse the identities, values or ways of relating that they are performing online. They might consider more critically how, in sociomaterial terms, software code is inscribing them, and their peers and stakeholders, including those pressuring them to develop 'e-skills', into particular ways of relating, representing themselves, and acting.

Ross (2012) suggests helping students to understand their participation in virtual activities in terms of spectacle, which focuses their attention on the performativity of themselves and others through these engagements. She shows how students can become appreciatively aware of the different ways they become present online and what different identities are performed through the ways their posted content mingles with others' uses. Drawing upon posthuman theory, Bayne (2010) works with students to help them capture, analyse and remix their many 'ghostly' traces in virtual environments, photos and posts and webpages, to both recall and reinvent their past engagements and identities. She engages students in examining those 'uncanny' elisions between presence/absence and here/there that they experience through the multiple synchronicities of virtual engagement. This approach is termed 'productive disruption' (Bayne 2010), and aims to encourage students to reconfigure their sense of the strange and their participation in distributed agency. Students learn not only to disrupt and actively resist the perpetuation of material inequities through human-non-human intra-actions, but also to attune to those surprising possibilities that emerge for alternative ways of being from their digital performances and interventions.

As we have indicated, students as well as lecturers also can learn to collaborate with computer scientists rather than to try to become computer scientists. For Halford et al. (2013), this is the most important area for educational attention. Until students and lecturers learn to collaborate more effectively with computer scientists and vice versa, digital analytics and knowledge infrastructures may well be designed within the vacuums of technological innovation for its own sake rather than for the complex contexts of disciplinary and social worlds. It is argued that a focus on the technological alone can sometimes result in unfortunate and unintended consequences, as, because it can be technologically achieved does not guarantee that something is worthwhile. This is particularly the case when those technologies are being aggressively marketed by commercial concerns as 'solutions' to pedagogical challenges without the underpinning research to support such claims. Collaboration therefore can help students and staff understand the possibilities as well as limitations of software, algorithms, ontology-building, analytics and visualisation and perhaps even to grasp more clearly how they might work most effectively as part of the digitised higher education. It is the capability of the team harnessing different expertise that is central to ensuring knowledge infrastructures are not taken for granted 'matters of fact' but remain open as 'matters of concern' (Latour 2004). However, such team-based approaches often challenge the conventions of assessment of capacity and the assignment of qualifications to individuals in higher education.

In preparing for employment, students can be encouraged also to critically examine new digital technologies being introduced in particular fields in terms of how they influence knowledge and practice. Students can interview experienced practitioners and examine promotional material for these products. How are practices of decision-making represented? What is obscured or over-simplified, or overly emphasised? What happens in practice? What is the nature and extent to which algorithmic structures are actually foreclosing nuances and complexity that are important to professional diagnostics, analysis and problem-solving?

Similarly, students can become critically aware of the methodological problems of working with big data and learn to ask questions of new smart software that appears in their work. What data sets are being merged, how are they captured, what are the inherent linkage problems, and what are the key ethical issues? To what extent are patterns generated from and applicable to large populations being applied inappropriately to individuals? The answers to such questions, as the use of predictive analytics and automated decision-making in different areas become more prevalent, raise important questions about professional and legal responsibility for any failures in practice. Higher education pedagogy will need to help students anticipate the challenges they will face in such digitalised workspaces.

Students transitioning to employment increasingly may need to understand methods and issues of integrating data flow across occupational groups and work systems. As Jaradat et al. (2013) have suggested, these new forms of data often require new systems for transferring data between clients, owners and operators. Workers need to understand the potential points for error or misinterpretation at various interfaces in this data integration, as different forms of data, and different purposes for interpreting it, must be reconciled. Workers also need to assume accountability themselves for examining these points in order to better manage data flows and critically examine the issues in meanings, metrics and ethics that arise. In order to do this, employees who may not ordinarily work directly with data systems need to understand more about data itself and how these systems work, and how to link with other individuals and institutions to integrate practices using this data across work roles.

These questions about the potential expansion of students' and educators' responsibility to critically intervene and more actively engage with big data and coded applications raise the broader issue of professionalism and accountability in this realm. Many students in higher education are studying towards becoming part of a particular profession. All professions, ranging from public services, such as health and social care, to the finance and legal professions, are being profoundly affected by these digital analytics and big data. How should practitioners think about their professional responsibility when algorithms make decisions? How do we understand the professional as a responsible agent when capability is distributed? What does it mean for professionals to work responsibly with 'dirty' big data sets and reductionist algorithms? These sorts of questions can be an explicit part of professional education in higher education. Professionalism is an important aspect of professional education and we could rethink how it is enacted in particular digital environments working through particular digitised problems. This also entails encouraging new professionals to re-imagine principles of responsibility, to develop purposes and learn strategies for using code and big data thoughtfully and responsibly. However, how well versed are existing and new teachers in higher education themselves in relation to these sorts of questions and the challenges posed by digital technologies?

All of the above point to the increasing importance of the work of digital technologies in knowledge infrastructures within higher education, the tracing of which is and is likely to become ever more complex. As Edwards et al. (2013, p. 15) suggest, in articulating what is known, we also need to engage with the 'accidental and systematic means by which non-knowledge is produced and maintained'. Computer code, algorithms and data ontologies are integral to the production and non-production of knowledge and without engaging with the materiality of representation within knowledge infrastructures, there is the potential to lose the development of criticality which is often held to be a key quality that higher education develops. Without the critical attunement of lecturers and students, rather than extending opportunities for openness and inclusion, different exclusions will be inscribed through the hidden curriculum of the emerging digital academic practices. Learning to teach well has always entailed ongoing learning by teachers themselves. The learning associated with engaging digital technologies in worthwhile ways raises challenges far beyond what is often discussed when trying to enable teachers to draw upon such resources. The suggestions we have provided here for higher education pedagogy are intended only to provide a starting point for rethinking education that is digitally mediated – not only for teachers and learners but also for academic developers.

Acknowledgement

This chapter is developed from work within the ESRC funded seminar series Code Acts in Education, http://codeactsineducation.wordpress.com/about/ (grant reference: ES/L001160/1). It draws from previous publications Edwards and Fenwick (2015), Fenwick (2015, 2016) and Fenwick and Edwards (2016).

References

Anderson, T. (2001), 'The hidden curriculum in distance education: an updated view', *Change*, Nov/Dec, pp. 29–35.

Apple, M. & King, N. (1983), 'What do schools teach?', in H. Giroux & D. Purpel (eds), *The hidden curriculum and moral education*, McCutchan Publishing Corporation, Berkeley, CA.

Bayne, S. (2010), 'Academetron, automaton, phantom: Uncanny digital pedagogies', *London Review of Education*, vol. 8, no. 1, pp. 5–13.

Berry, D. (2011), *The philosophy of software: Code and mediation in the digital age*, Palgrave Macmillan, Basingstoke.

Buckingham Shum, S. (2014), 'How do learning analytics "act" in education?', presentation to the Code Acts in Education Seminar, University of Edinburgh, accessed 9 May, http://simon.buckinghamshum.net/2014/05/ how-do-learning-analytics-act-in-education/

Buckingham Shum, S. (2015), 'Learning analytics: On silver bullets and white rabbits', *Medium*, accessed 9 February 2015, https://medium.com/@sbskmi/learning-analytics-on-silver-bullets-and-white-rabbits-a92d202dc7e3

Edwards, P. (2010), *A vast machine: Computer models, climate data, and the politics of global warming*, MIT Press, Cambridge, MA.

Edwards, P., Jackson, S., Chalmers, M., Bowker, G., Borgman, C., Ribes, D., Burton M. & Calvert, S. (2013), *Knowledge infrastructures: Intellectual frameworks and research challenges*, Deep Blue, Ann Arbor.

Edwards, R. (2015a), 'Software and the hidden curriculum in digital education', *Pedagogy, Culture & Society*, vol. 23, no. 2, pp. 265–79.

Edwards, R. (2015b), 'Knowledge infrastructures and the inscrutability of openness in education', *Learning, Media and Technology*, vol. 40, no. 3, pp. 251–64.

Edwards, R. & Carmichael, P. (2012), 'Secret codes: The hidden curriculum of the semantic web', *Discourse*, vol. 33, no. 4, pp. 575–90.

Edwards, R. & Fenwick, T. (2015), 'Digital analytics in professional work and learning', *Studies in Continuing Education*, DOI: 10.1080/0158037X.2015.1074894.

Fenwick, T. (2015), 'What *matters* in sociomateriality: Towards a critical posthuman pedagogy in management education', in T. Beyes, M. Parker & C. Steyaert (eds), *The Routledge companion to the humanities and social sciences in management education*, Routledge, London.

Fenwick, T. (2016), *Professional responsibility and professionalism: A sociomaterial examination*, Routledge, London.

Fenwick, T. & Edwards, R. (2016), 'Exploring the impact of digital technologies on professional responsibilities and education', *European Education Research Journal*, vol. 15, no. 1, pp. 117–31.

Gasevic, D., Dawson, S. & Siemens, G. (2015), 'Let's not forget: Learning analytics are about learning', *TechTrends*, vol. 58, no. 1, pp. 64–71.

Halford, S., Pope, C. & Weal, M. (2013), 'Digital futures? Sociological challenges and opportunities in the emergent semantic web', *Sociology*, vol. 47, no. 1, pp. 173–89.

Harris, C. (2014), 'Big data means big results in higher education', *Tech Page One*, accessed 13 May 2014, http://techpageone.co.uk/en/technology/big-data-means-big-results-in-higher-education/

Jaradat S., Whyte, J. & Luck, R. (2013), 'Professionalism in digitally mediated project work', *Building Research and Information*, vol. 41, no. 1, pp. 51–59.

Kallinikos, J. (2010), *Governing through technology: Information artefacts and social practice*, Palgrave, London.

Keen, A. J. (2012), *Digital vertigo: How today's online social revolution is dividing, diminishing and disorientating us*, St Martin's Press, London.

Kitchin, R. (2013), 'Big data and human geography', *Dialogues in Human Geography*, vol. 3, no. 3, pp. 262–67.

Kitchin, R. (2014), 'Thinking critically about research algorithms', The Programmable City Working Paper 5, www.nuim.ie/progcity, 28 October.

Kitchin, R. & Dodge, M. (2011), *Code/space: Software and everyday life*, MIT Press, Cambridge, MA.

Knight, S., Buckingham Shum, S. & Littleton, K. (2014), 'Epistemology, assessment, pedagogy: Where learning meets analytics in the middle space', *Journal of Learning Analytics*, vol. 1, no. 2, pp. 23–47.

Lampland, M. & Star, S. (eds) (2009), *Standards and their stories: How quantifying, classifying, and formalizing practices shape everyday life*, Cornell University Press, Ithaca.

Latour, B. (2004), 'Why has critique run out of steam? From matters of fact to matters of concern', *Critical Inquiry*, vol. 30, pp. 225–48.

Laurillard, D. (2012), *Teaching as a design science: Building pedagogical patterns for learning and technology*, Routledge, London.

Manovich, L. (2013), *Software takes command: Extending the language of new media*, Bloomsbury Academic, London.

Margolis, E. (ed.) (2001), *The hidden curriculum in higher education*, Routledge, London.

Neyland, D. (2015), 'On organizing algorithms', *Theory, Culture & Society*, vol. 32, no. 1, pp. 119–32.

Pariser, E. (2011), *The filter bubble: What the internet is hiding from you*, Penguin Books, London.

Prinsloo, P. & Slade, S. (2015), 'Student privacy self-management: Implications for learning analytics', in Proceedings of the Fifth International Conference on Learning Analytics and Knowledge (LAK15), pp. 83–92. ACM Press, New York, http://doi.acm.org/10.1145/2723576.2723585

Randall, D., Proctor, R., Lin, Y., Poschen, M., Sharrock, W. & Stevens R. (2011), 'Distributed ontology building as a practical work', *International Journal of Human-Computer Studies*, vol. 69, pp. 220–33.

Ribes, D. & Bowker, G. (2009), 'Between meaning and machine: Learning to represent the knowledge of communities', *Information and Organization*, vol. 19, pp. 199–217.

Ross, J. (2012), 'The spectacle and the placeholder: Digital futures for reflective practices in higher education', Proceedings of the Networked Learning Conference, Maastricht, NL, available online, www.lancaster.ac.uk/fss/organisations/netlc/past/nlc2012/abstracts/pdf/ross.pdf

Snyder, B. (1971), *The hidden curriculum*, Knopf, New York.

Totaro, P. & Ninno, D. (2016), 'Algorithms and the practical world', *Theory, Culture & Society*, vol. 33, no. 1, pp. 139–52.

Van Dijk, J. (2013), *The culture of connectivity: A critical history of social media*, Oxford University Press, Oxford.

Williamson, B. (2014), 'Governing software: Networks, databases and algorithmic power in the digital governance of education', *Learning, Media & Technology*, http://dx.doi.org/10.1080/17439884.2014.924527

Williamson, B. (ed.) (2015), *Coding/learning: Software and digital data in education*, University of Stirling, Stirling.

Wilson, A. (2015), 'Visualizing digital relationships', paper presented to the Stirling Graduate Student Conference, University of Stirling, May 30.

Part II
Practice theories

Chapter 5

Learning to teach as the development of practice

David Boud and Angela Brew

The assumption in most professions is that initial pre-service courses are a necessary preparation for practice. These courses are typically knowledge- and theory-rich and involve some elements of application through supervised placements. The front-end loading of coursework remains the dominant model worldwide and higher education institutions are organised around the provision of such programmes for pre-service and early career professionals in many disciplines.

With regard to the teaching profession, such as for school education, vocational education and training, adult education, or, more recently, higher education, the same assumptions often apply. A basic knowledge of teaching and learning is assumed to be required by all practitioners, and it is assumed that this knowledge can be effectively acquired through the provision of coursework. However, in higher education, there has been considerable resistance to formal teacher training, both in extent and type.

Although there is commonly an assumption that some course-like provision through workshops and structured activities away from the immediate settings of teaching is needed, this front-end loaded model has been challenged for what might be regarded as legitimate and illegitimate reasons. Illegitimate reasons include the assumption that knowledge and systematic development of skill in teaching is not needed; that the PhD and research training is all that is needed for a university teacher and more emphasis on the teaching role distracts from new entrants to the profession getting on to establish their research. Legitimate reasons are those concerned with the effectiveness of such provision.

Becoming a teacher is typically thought to involve acquiring a set of appropriate knowledge, skills and attitudes that can then be deployed, or 'transferred' in whatever setting is required. Courses then tend to employ an acquisition metaphor and to frame learning as if it were an attribute of individuals. Different knowledge and skills may be needed for different sectors of education or for the teaching of different disciplines but it is at this point that adaptation to context ends. In many sectors of education, these features are often translated into competencies and enshrined as such by registration bodies or professional institutes. Ironically, such frameworks typically underpin almost all courses in higher education that permit direct entry into a profession, but not necessarily the profession of teaching in higher education itself.

The limitations of using an acquisition metaphor have been known for some time (Sfard 1998). Hager and Hodkinson (2009) have drawn attention to our dependency on simple assumptions about the transfer of learning that are not borne out by much of the [recent] research and theorising about learning (p. 619). Boud and Hager (2012) point to the problem that the acquisition and transfer metaphors suggest pre-specification and standardisation of the content that is learnt. Indeed, the nature of professional practice is greatly over-simplified by acceptance of the acquisition and transfer metaphors, and professional development viewed as the acquisition and subsequent transfer of content pre-specified by 'experts' ensures that continuing professional development is routinely divorced from actual practice. Boud and Hager (2012) suggest that more helpful metaphors for professional development are those such as participation, construction and becoming. They propose that a more fruitful lens for understanding professional learning is through practice.

Starting from this brief examination of assumptions about what it means to learn to teach, this chapter argues that learning to teach is learning to engage in a particular kind of social practice. It suggests that learning to teach can therefore be fruitfully viewed through the lens of practice theory, as the authors similarly argued in an earlier paper focusing on academic development (Boud & Brew 2013). This practice focus is in contrast to a view that sees learning to teach as the development of personal skills and competencies to perform the task of teaching or seeing it as an entry into a particular disciplinary culture. Learning to teach according to the practice view needs to take place in the environment in which teaching occurs with the practitioners that do it within the micro-contexts of academic institutions (departments, schools and disciplinary groupings). Teaching is seen as an activity that connects the individual with the social. Ways of conceptualising its development need to accommodate that.

Taking a practice approach

What people tend to do when learning to teach is to draw on their own experience. Part of this comes from their own experience of being taught, but there are also strong influences from the social and cultural context in which they operate. That is, in understanding and exemplifying 'what we do around here'. Learning to teach becomes learning to do what those who teach do, in the contexts in which they do it. It is also judged as worthwhile within those contexts, not by educational experts, but by students initially and then by academic peers. If these peers do not value teaching highly, then teaching is influenced accordingly.

In other words, learning to teach is a practice. That is:

> a form of socially established cooperative human activity in which characteristic arrangements of actions and activities (doings) are comprehensible in terms

of arrangements of relevant ideas in characteristic discourses (sayings), and when the people and objects involved are distributed in characteristic arrangements of relationships (relatings), and when this complex of sayings, doings and relatings 'hangs together' in a distinctive project.

A practice approach positions teachers, the social context of teaching and the organisation in which teaching takes place as mutually produced, and where knowing and doing cannot be separated (Gherardi 2000). Teaching is then framed as 'bundles of practices and material arrangements' (Schatzki 2006, p. 1863) or 'systems of practices' (Gherardi 2000, p. 215). Rather than focusing on individuals and their attributes, a practice approach positions practice, what Schatzki (2001, p. 12) calls 'embodied, materially mediated arrays of human activity centrally organised around shared practical understandings' as the central unit of analysis.

This 'practice turn' has been used to describe a set of shifts in theorising about many kinds of social phenomena (Schatzki et al. 2001). It conceptualises all human activity including 'knowledge, meaning, science, power, language and social institutions' (Schatzki 2001, p. 11) as part of the field of practices and does so by eschewing dualities such as individual/social or structure/agency. It grounds thinking in the idea of practices as the primary building block of social life and meaning. The emphasis is on how activities come together through the sayings and doings of the various players involved in them, the artefacts or materials which form part of what happens and the context in which this occurs (Hager, Lee & Reich 2012).

While there is no single unified practice theory, and while Green (2009, p. 2) regards the term as 'inescapably contested, if not essentially contestable' there are common features shared by those theorists who adopt this point of view. Nicolini (2012) has identified a common set of assumptions and principles that have come from several distinct scholarly traditions to create a series of family resemblances (p. 9). His view is that a practice-based view of social and human phenomena is distinctive in that it:

- emphasises that behind all the apparent durable features of our world … there is some type of productive and reproductive work. In so doing it transforms how we conceive of social order and conceptualise the apparent stability of the social world;
- forces us to rethink the role of agents and individuals, e.g. managers, the managed, etc.;
- foregrounds the importance of the body and objects in social affairs;
- sheds light on the nature of knowledge and discourse;
- reaffirms the centrality of interests and power in everything we do.

When looking at learning to teach from a practice perspective we need to consider what acts of teaching involve, who are involved, through what means they are mediated and what the shared understandings are of what is occurring. Teaching, according to this view, is not an act of individual teachers engaging with students in a classroom or the context of a course. It is a socially located set of practices that are framed by structures and expectations of multiple parties.

What then are the sayings, doings and relatings of the practice of teaching and how are they located? Six partly overlapping features of practice are apparent in various practice theories and these can be usefully considered in explicating learning to teach in higher education: embodiment, material mediation, situatedness, emergence, relationality and co-construction.

Embodiment

Practice necessarily implies embodiment: embodied people practice with volition as well as with what they bring to the activity. For Kemmis (2009, p. 23), practice is embodied in that it encompasses what people do, when and where. Further, practice contributes to developing people's identities and their sense of agency. Practices inevitably involve bodies and material conditions. Chapter 6 provides an example of embodiment when a critical friend comments on the way the lecturer uses her body in the practice of her teaching. As Nicolini (2012, p. 3) says:

> The contribution of a practice approach is to uncover that behind all the apparently durable features of our world there is always the work and effort of someone … Practices with no things and no bodies involved are thus simply inconceivable.

People bring their desires, emotions and values to be part of the practice.

Material mediation

Practice involves materials and material arrangements of many kinds. These may include resources, artefacts and tools, physical connections, communication tools and material circumstances (Kemmis 2009). These materials can both limit and enable particular practices. In teaching there are, for example, texts and papers, learning management systems, physical objects and ways in which they are used.

Situatedness

Practice is located in many ways. It is situated in particular ways, in time, in language and in the dynamics of interactions (Gherardi 2008, p. 521). For Kemmis (2009, p. 22), practice 'has aspects that are "extra-individual" in the sense that the actions and interactions that make up the practice are always shaped by mediating conditions that structure how it unfolds'. These may include cultures, discourses, social and political structures, and material conditions in which a practice is situated. Nicolini (2012) draws attention to power, conflict and politics as constitutive elements of social reality and how as such they serve particular interests at the expense of those of other people.

Emergence

Practices change and evolve over time and over contexts. New challenges require new ways of practising; new practitioners introduce new understandings. Practices tend to emerge in unanticipated and unpredictable ways: for example, when people work with others various understandings and interactions emerge (Johnsson & Boud 2010, p. 360).

Practice theories according to Reckwitz (2002, p. 256) (quoted in Nicolini 2012, p. 4) accommodate individual agency since agents embody and carry particular practices in their bodies and minds as they enact particular practices. There is always room for creativity, initiative and individuality as people adapt to the practices in which they find themselves.

Relationality

All people, artefacts, social groups and networks connect and develop in relation to other subjects, social groups or networks, such that they are formed and structured socially (Kemmis 2009). Practice takes place in relation both to others and to the unique features a particular practitioner brings to a situation. Practice is thus embedded in sets of dynamic social interactions, connections, arrangements and relationships. Communities of practice (Lave & Wenger 1993), for example, provide a relational network of interactions to sustain and foster particular practices. In teaching, what is learned is in relation with what has been learned before and what is regarded as acceptable in the context in which one operates.

Co-construction

In addition to its relational nature, practice is also co-constructed with others. The meaning of the practice and the characteristics of practising are the meanings that those involved give to it. These others may be co-workers, but also include in teaching, students, managers, members of the profession or others. Many practices only become legitimate or worthwhile when they are co-constructed with beneficiaries. Teaching is a typical example of this as without student learning, the act of teaching is not meaningful.

Knowledge is co-constructed with others. Only part of what is meant may be articulated, because to become part of a practice is to learn what to say, how to act and what to think. So there are shared implicit understandings (Nicolini 2012, p. 5).

These six features of practice mean that practice cannot be discussed independently of the settings in which it occurs or the embodiment of those undertaking it. Discussion of practice in isolation from practitioners or sites of practice is to misunderstand the nature of practice. It is always constructed with others (in various ways) and in the light of their volition. A practice orientation goes beyond acknowledging the importance of activities, or context, or the agency of people who perform them. It focuses attention on the nature of the interlinked connections between people and with people and artefacts.

To be clear: drawing on practice theory is not about being more practical or more pragmatic or less theoretical. Quite the opposite: it involves actively conceptualising practice and using practice as the lens through which to judge teaching and learning to teach. Practice theory has nothing to do with discredited theory/practice divisions or other binaries, nor does it devalue knowledge and skills.

How do practices persist and change?

Drawing on Schatzki (2006), we can consider teaching as 'bundles of practices and material arrangements' (p. 1863) that persist and frame past, present and future possibilities. They consist of elements of both structure and action. Structure encompasses understandings of the 'how to' of practice, rules, possible ends and goals as well as other appreciations. The existing practice structures sustain a practice by impacting on the material arrangements of that practice within its context. Practices are carried forward through the practice memory of an organisation, such as a department or teaching group, and by all those who enact these practices (Schatzki 2005, 2006). Practices are not set in stone, but change over time and in response to influences on them and the actions of the various players (Kemmis 2007). Some of these influences are contextual, some material, some generated by those who practise. Practices, though, transcend any one person or occasion of practice.

The practice memory of an organisation exists even when practices are not being carried out. It includes the understandings, rules, expectations and types of activity captured in documents, history and infrastructure, e.g. 'we know what a physics degree should look like and how it should be taught'. It persists beyond the individual memories of practitioners. In the enactment of practices teachers and others carry practices forward and simultaneously vary them in the light of their understandings of similar practices from other related contexts – their prior experience as teacher or student, other positions they have held and knowledge they have about what is acceptable. In enacting these practices, teachers' understandings of them become enmeshed with previous understandings of similar practices from other contexts and so practices are both perpetuated and varied (Schatzki 2006).

Kemmis and colleagues (2014) add to this by introducing the notion of practice architecture, which they argue prefigures the practice, shaping it and influencing how it is undertaken. They identifying three dimensions of it: the cultural-discursive, the material-economic, and the social political (Kemmis & Grootenboer 2008, p. 37). The cultural-discursive arrangements of a practice influence what is said and thought in and about the practice (the sayings), the material-economic arrangements influence what is done in the practice (the doings), and the social-political arrangements influence relationships that occur in, and in association with, the practice (the relatings). These dimensions are not distinct, but are interwoven and work together to enable and constrain the conduct of any particular practice.

As practices persist and impact upon past, present and future enactments and possibilities, they influence what is learned, how it is learned and by whom. Through 'teaching and transmitting' (Schatzki 2006, p. 1868) and by individuals describing, examining and questioning, the contextual characteristics and interrelationships among practices embedded in an organisation's practice memory, are learned. This transmitted practice knowledge is not simply replicated. Rather, different people attain different understandings about these practices owing to their previous training and experiences (Schatzki 2005, p. 480). It is these different understandings that contribute to the simultaneous perpetuation and variation of practices.

What then does teaching look like through the lens of practice theory? As we have seen, a practice frame moves teaching from a focus on individuals – whether they are teachers or learners – to the specific practices of teaching and learning and the nature of those practices. It also moves considerations of learning to teach from decontextualised locations separated from the workplace, to locate learning in settings of application (e.g. classrooms and laboratories), to building from practice, that is, the embodied, contextualised activities academics engage in with others including their peers, their managers and students. It does not deny knowledge and skills, but neither does it privilege them in the ways that a conventional training perspective does. It focuses more on what is done and what needs to be done, and less on the attributes of the individuals enacting the doing.

What follows from adopting a practice frame?

How does a practice view start to change the ways we look at the challenges of learning how to teach? The first implication is that it must shift focus away from what the individual teacher knows towards the practice of teaching. What then does actual teaching in higher education involve? From a practice view there is no essential answer to this question. Teaching is what it is. We have to examine what the various practices are that together make up this collection of practices. This takes us immediately to the sites of teaching and what teachers with others necessarily do.

What are the practices of teaching in higher education? Any building of a programme of learning to teach must be based on an analysis of the practices of teaching. Such an analysis must attend to actual practices *in situ* rather than idealised or assumed practices. In a recent study of continuing professional learning among civil engineers, one of the authors undertook a study of the practices through which such engineers learn. The resulting description bore little relationship to the kinds of features inscribed in accounts of competences for professional engineers by their professional body that informs their continuing professional education requirements (Rooney et al. 2013). It was concluded that the ways that sets of competences get generated were conceptually quite different from the approaches needed to discern practices (Reich, Rooney & Boud 2015). The former focused on remembered activities from representatives from an industry who were not necessarily immediate practitioners, the latter from documented current activities of those practising.

There are many ways of looking for and discerning practices in the sphere of teaching, but an important step in doing so is to be able to bracket out some of our conventional educational thinking. Attention needs to turn to the features of the practice, not the characteristics of the practitioner: How does the practice operate? Who is involved? What are the primary sayings and doings of the practice? What artefacts are involved and how do they operate? What conditions are necessary for the practice to occur effectively? A practice has been successfully identified when those who practise can readily agree that it is one of their necessary practices. For example, in a recent as yet unpublished study of assessment practices in which one of us was involved, one of the key practices that was identified was 'bringing a new assessment task into operation' (Boud et al., submitted for publication). This practice is one that all academics easily recognise and see the multifaceted nature of what is involved: it is localised in an institution and course, it involves multiple parties with different responsibilities and it has many variations within it. The materials of assessment policy and procedures for course changes are mobilised. The outcomes have a significant influence on other parties, i.e. students.

While practices can be identified and described by interrogating what we do, it can be particularly helpful to utilise those not directly involved in the process to overcome the problem of only seeing what is already described in the conventional language of teaching and learning. This is a particular trap when looking at the practices of teachers: they are so taken-for-granted that their practice-like character can be rendered invisible. In considering teaching, it can be helpful to continually reiterate the questions: what is the practice seeking to do, what is it for and how does it operate? Thus, lecturing may not be rendered as an act of presenting information to students in a compelling way, but as one of a number of related practices to mobilise and engage students to undertake their own studies. Accounts of the practice vary and the features that are taken into account vary according to the way it is framed.

Is a practice perspective inherently conservative? A naïve understanding of it might lead one to think so. If it merely looks to current practices and prepares novices to reproduce them, it does. However, it also encourages us to look further at what the practices seek to do and how they achieve these ends. In doing this we can look beyond the conventional: preparing someone to lecture, to examine what this practice is for and how it works. Importantly, how does it connect with other practices: such as those involved in student study, to achieve this end?

What are some implications for learning to teach?

A practice perspective leads to a different set of priorities for organising the learning of academics for teaching through:

1   emphasising the development of practices, focusing on the practices in which academics engage and how they might be extended;
2   fostering learning-conducive work;
3   deliberately locating activity within practice, through an emphasis on changing the nature and variety of local.

Emphasising practice development

If practices are central to teaching, then the focus of learning needs to be on how they are enacted and how they develop. This involves an understanding of practices and how they come together to operate in particular ways. Thus, what are key practices in any specific aspect of teaching? What are their characteristic sayings and doings? What are the assumptions that underpin these? What constrains or limits the practice? What is there scope to alter and what is there not? How does the practice purport to do what it seeks to do? As a practitioner positioned in a particular way, and as one perhaps less adept at transacting some aspects of the practice, how can one enter effectively into it? Who else locally might need to be involved? In what ways may they need to be involved?

Practices might be developed through critical examination of current practices and whether they achieve what they claim to do. For example, do comments on student work lead to improved performance in the areas on which comments are made, or do classes stimulate students to spend time on study compared with the setting of particular kinds of task for them?

Fostering learning-conducive work

Some forms of work arrangement are more conducive to learning than others. Considerable potential for development occurs through organising work in ways that support learning (e.g. Felstead et al. 2009).

What forms might learning-conducive work take? This question has been addressed more widely for workplaces beyond education. A study of Norwegian organisations (Skule & Reichborn 2002, Skule 2004) asked the question, what made some workplaces more conducive to the learning of their employees than others? The authors identified that it was the various properties of work that were most important in explaining the differences in the opportunity to learn through work (Skule & Reichborn 2002, p. 10).

The learning conditions that they distinguished as relevant here were: a high degree of exposure to demands from customers, management, colleagues and owners, and to changes in technology, organisation and work methods; managerial responsibility; considerable external professional contact; good opportunities for feedback from work; support and encouragement for learning from management; and a high probability that skills would be rewarded through interesting tasks, better career possibilities or better pay.

Similar factors appear in Ellström's studies of Swedish workplaces. He identified the learning potential of the task in terms of task complexity, variety and control; opportunities for feedback, evaluation and reflection on the outcomes of work actions; the type and degree of formalisation of work processes; organisational arrangements for employee participation in handling problems and developing work processes; and learning resources in terms of, e.g., time for analysis, interaction and reflection (Ellström 2001).

In the UK, Fuller and Unwin (2004) identified features of what they termed expansive and restrictive participation in work. Expansive features of environments that foster learning include: recognition and support for workers as learners, managers giving time to support workforce development and workplace learning, wide distribution of skills through the workforce, workers having discretion to make judgements and contribute to decision-making, opportunities to expand learning through participation in different communities and planned time off-the-job for reflection and learning beyond immediate job requirements (Fuller & Unwin 2010). Many of these expansive features are common in the academic workplace.

While these structural features of the workplace may contribute to conditions conducive for learning, in themselves they do not ensure effective learning will occur. They need to be taken up and realised in local contexts (in the department or work group) as well as the institution more generally. They need to be perceived by participants and utilised as enablers, and managerial practices need to sustain them. The interactive effects of managerial and teaching practices are generally little considered, but teaching can be severely inhibited in unfavourable circumstances for staff. At the most basic level, if teachers are not given opportunities to flourish, how can it reasonably be expected for them to create circumstances in which their students are able to do so? The irony of looking to workplace learning research to inform higher education institutions is that it should be easier to change when the rationale for learning is so much part of the mission and culture of the institution than in conventional industrial environments. That it might not be so in many situations is an important impetus for further investigation.

Learning to teach within a practice view is not limited temporally or spatially. There are always new contexts to respond to, new students with quite different preparations and characteristics and new programmes or types of programme in which teaching occurs. There are also quite radical challenges such as being required to teach online or in another country. Learning to teach is a continuing activity and not limited to those new to the profession. Hutchings and Shulman (1999) highlighted the importance of teachers learning within work contexts in establishing the idea of the scholarship of teaching and learning. They suggested that academics do not sufficiently develop their practice in teaching in the normal process of doing it. Turning the practice of teaching into a scholarly endeavour that goes beyond the particular classroom and engages teachers in scholarly discussions about teaching with colleagues turns teaching into work facilitative of learning.

For academics, practice development involves confronting the competing and sometimes contradictory demands on them, and marrying these disparate requirements. For example, does a peer review system of lectures lead to changes in practices, or to less substantial change, and what effects does it produce? Do work allocations change practices that involve academics spending time on activities that lead to improved student outcomes? It is not usual for academics' research skills to be utilised to solve problems in the academic workplace in the normal course of academic work, but this is implied in the idea of learning-conducive work. It is also the idea behind the notion of the scholarship of academic practice (Brew 2010). As Brew (2010, p. 112) has argued, 'The challenges of academic practice need to become questions for investigation'. Teaching may thus be viewed in the context of academic practice more widely.

It must be acknowledged that teaching involves interactions with a variety of others in a range of contexts that go beyond the immediate work group or department. Much of the learning involved is likely to arise when the exigencies of work are questioned. Some of this learning falls within the conventional boundaries of that work, such as when members of research teams have different interpretations of data, but other learning arises outside and needs to be addressed from beyond the knowledge and skills of the practitioner. One example is when teachers used to taking individual responsibility for a module are grouped to take responsibility for a number of modules. Other learning takes place only when the conduct of work requires it. For example, the introduction of a new virtual learning environment (VLE) that teachers are required to utilise. This means coming to understand how the VLE is going to be used by the group of academics in a specific context and working to ensure that the changed practices have the desired effects on students. The most powerful influence is not the provision of learning opportunities but changing work demands to drive teachers' learning.

Deliberately locating activity within practice

A third focus is to start with an emphasis on changing situations, not changing people. Fundamental to a practice focus, as we have seen, is the notion of locatedness. Practice always takes place in and is positioned with respect to particular contexts and, as Schatzki (2005, 2006) says, contexts contain traces of past practices. Location, however, is not just about physical proximity. Again, as we have seen, what is said and thought about the practice is influenced by its cultural-discursive arrangements; what is done in the practice is influenced by the material economic arrangements; and the relationships that occur in and with the practice are influenced by the social political arrangements (Kemmis & Grootenboer 2008). So deliberately locating activity within practice has a number of elements, any one of which may need to be considered on any occasion of development. These include the spatial, the temporal, the personal, the social and the professional.

Spatial location (where?)

Learning to practice cannot take place independently of sites of practice. A close alignment of activities with sites of practice is needed. So, many aspects of learning to teach need to take place in local sites, and facilitation may need to occur as coaching within practice rather than about practice. The material-economic arrangements are expressed in the spatial location and influence teaching in a variety of ways. For example, teaching sites might include things like: the use of equipment; the arrangement and layout of rooms; the deployment of a learning management system; choosing and using texts; employing casual staff for tutoring or marking.

Temporal location (when?)

Different practices occur at particular times. The practice of course preparation occurs mainly before the start of a semester, the practice of marking occurs within it. There are times when teachers are open to learning, times when they are closed to it. If a major course revision has recently taken place, it may not be appropriate to work on the practice of course design. Alignment of development opportunities may need to take place within normal activities: the common practice of peer observation of a lecture and subsequent feedback conversations is an example of this. The timeliness of development interventions is crucial: a worthwhile conversation in one week of the semester may be irrelevant in another.

Personal location (with which practices?)

Practices are imbued with different personal meanings. The discourse teachers use about teaching, the language they use to communicate with students; the kind of texts involved; curriculum documents which guide the course unit; and many other arrangements are all constitutive of the cultural-discursive arrangements which form part of the practice. At different stages of development of an academic career individuals may be more available to consider some of their practices rather than others. When deadlines are due for a major grant round, then a given person may not be ready to consider aspects of teaching. When workload is being negotiated, some practices are more to the fore than others and priorities may be able to be set.

Social location (with which others?)

As practices always occur in association with other people, social location is an important consideration. The socio-political arrangements of a practice influence relationships between people and between people and objects that are involved in the practice. What learning should occur at an individual level, or with the group who teaches together or with students? Any one person has a limited effect on changing practice, so the community setting of practice is a topic for consideration and a place for learning to take place. What needs to take place with the course team, with tutors, with practitioners, etc.? Another dimension to social location is students and how they might be involved. Practices that work with some students do not work well with others. Students with language difficulties, or who have not been well prepared by previous study, for example, may provide different kinds of challenges and sometimes lead to entirely different practices.

In higher education, social-political arrangements include the relationships that are associated with the everyday practice of teaching. This includes: how students engage with teachers, expectations and practices of work groups, the importance of teaching vis-à-vis research, how policies are used or ignored, relationships which are and are not possible, positioning of teachers in relation to others in departments or programmes, and the hierarchy of the institution. The notion of stewardship in academic development practice discussed in Chapter 7 provides a further example of the socio-political dimension.

Professional location (within which disciplinary contexts?)

The context of practice is much wider than the immediate teaching group. Practices are framed by disciplinary or professional contexts. These act as part of the practice architecture to influence what is accepted as legitimate to be done or to be changed. Learning involves not only exploring what might be possible, but also what is acceptable 'around here'. It also requires consideration of how to operate within particular kinds of working arrangements. How can new ideas be introduced in particular contexts? What makes them more or less likely to be taken up? Some of these considerations are for the immediate working group, but others are constrained or enabled by the disciplinary location. Particular innovations that are commonplace in some disciplines would be difficult for a novice to introduce in others.

Which features of locatedness are pertinent vary in any given instance. What a practice perspective does is to remind us that each needs to be considered, as it is rarely obvious to the individual practitioner nor to those assisting them, which elements may be relevant at any moment.

Conclusion

While teaching in higher education has conventionally been regarded as highly individualistic and perhaps idiosyncratic, this belies the consistency of practices within a given discipline or department. These commonalities suggest that there is shared understanding of what occurs and what is appropriate to occur in teaching in a particular context. Contemporary processes of course development, quality assurance and revision all depend on much higher levels of cooperation and joint planning than have traditionally been the case and this in turn creates circumstances in which greater levels of interaction are regarded as legitimate and worthwhile. In considering practice development, it is increasingly necessary to consider that academic work is becoming more collective rather than individual in nature, involving co-producing practice with others, particularly students and other teachers in a programme.

In this chapter we have argued that professionals engage in practices, they extend these practices and they take up new practices. Learning may be driven by, for example, encountering new groups of students with different needs and expectations, or by working with a new issue not previously identified. Success in learning is judged by how successfully the practice with the new group or new issue is undertaken, not by how much is learned by the individuals involved. Practice drives learning, not only to solve immediate problems, but also to address wider concerns.

A focus on practice development is not only more consistent with the day-to-day experiences of academic work, it also avoids models which imply a deficit on the part of individuals which can only be filled by their own endeavours. If practices, while retaining their practice architecture, are normally evolving and changing, then the insertion of a new player is just part of normal academic practice which can be accommodated along with any other impetus. As the practice is a shared enterprise, then responsibility for learning to teach is similarly shared. Aspects of it, for example, introduction to the language and wider context of higher education teaching, may require the intervention of those beyond the immediate setting. However, learning to teach remains a local responsibility and ways of recognising this and providing suitable conditions for new teachers is a core responsibility of the group (school, department, teaching team) involved. For the most compelling learning occurs when practitioners see it as needed in order to do their work. That is when learning is an imperative, not an option.

References

Boud, D., Dawson, P., Bearman, M., Bennett, S., Joughin, G. & Molloy, E. (submitted for publication), 'Reframing assessment research: Through a practice perspective'.

Boud, D. & Brew, A. (2013), 'Reconceptualising academic work as professional practice: Implications for academic development', *International Journal for Academic Development*, vol. 18, no. 3, pp. 208–21.

Boud, D. & Hager, P. (2012), 'Re-thinking continuing professional development through changing metaphors and location in professional practices', *Studies in Continuing Education*, vol. 34, no. 1, pp. 17–30.

Brew, A. (2010), 'Transforming academic practice through scholarship', *International Journal for Academic Development*, vol. 15, no. 2, pp. 105–16.

Ellström, P. E. (2001), 'Integrating learning and work: Problems and prospects', *Human Resource Development Quarterly*, vol. 12, no. 4, pp. 421–35.

Felstead, A., Fuller, A., Jewson, N. & Unwin, L. (2009), 'Mapping the working as learning framework', *Improving working as learning*, Routledge, London.

Fuller, A., & Unwin, L. (2004), 'Expansive learning environments: Integrating organizational and personal development', in H. Rainbird, A. Fuller & A. Munro (eds), *Workplace learning in context*, Routledge, London.

Fuller, A. & Unwin, L. (2010), '"Knowledge workers" as the new apprentices: The influence of organisational autonomy, goals and values on the nurturing of expertise', *Vocations and Learning*, vol. 3, no. 3, pp. 203–22.

Gherardi, S. (2000), 'Practice-based theorizing on learning and knowing in organizations', *Organization*, vol. 7, no. 2, pp. 211–23.

Gherardi, S. (2008), 'Situated knowledge and situated action: What do practice-based studies promise?', in D. Barry & H. Hansen (eds), *The Sage handbook of new approaches in management and organization*, Sage, London.

Green, B. (2009), 'Introduction: Understanding and researching professional practice', in B. Green (ed.), *Understanding and researching professional practice*, Sense, Rotterdam.

Hager, P. & Hodkinson, P. (2009), 'Moving beyond the metaphor of transfer of learning', *British Educational Research Journal*, vol. 35, no. 4, pp. 619–38.

Hager, P., Lee, A. & Reich, A. (2012), 'Problematising practice, reconceptualising learning and imagining change', in P. Hager, A. Lee & A. Reich (eds), *Practice, learning and change: Practice-theory perspectives on professional learning*, Springer, Dordrecht.

Hutchings, P. & Shulman, L. (1999), 'The scholarship of teaching: New elaborations, new developments', *Change*, vol. 31, no. 5, pp. 10–15.

Johnsson, M. & Boud, D. (2010), 'Towards an emergent view of learning work', *International Journal of Lifelong Education*, vol. 29, no. 3, pp. 355–68.

Kemmis, S. (2007), 'Critical theory and participatory action research', in P. Reasons & E. Bradbury (eds.), *Handbook of action research: Participative enquiry and practice*, Sage, London.

Kemmis, S. (2009), 'Understanding professional practice: A synoptic framework', in B. Green (ed.), *Understanding and researching professional practice*, Sense, Rotterdam.

Kemmis, S., Wilkinson, J., Edwards-Groves, C., Hardy, I., Grootenboer, P. & Bristol, L. (2014), *Changing practices, changing education*, Springer, Dordrecht.

Kemmis, S. & Grootenboer, P. (2008), 'Situating practice', in S. Kemmis & T. J. Smith (eds), *Enabling praxis: Challenges for education*, Sense, Amsterdam.

Lave, J. & Wenger E. (1993), *Situated learning: Legitimate peripheral participation*, Cambridge University Press, Cambridge.

Nicolini, D. (2012), *Practice theory, work and organization: An introduction*, Oxford University Press, Oxford.

Reckwitz, A. (2002), 'Toward a theory of social practices: A development in culturalist theorizing', *European Journal of Social Theory*, vol. 5, no. 2, pp. 243–63.

Reich, A., Rooney, D. & Boud, D. (2015), 'Dilemmas in continuing professional learning: Learning inscribed in frameworks or elicited from practice?', *Studies in Continuing Education*, vol. 37, no. 2, pp. 131–41.

Rooney, D., Willey, K., Gardner, A., Boud, D., Reich, A. & Fitzgerald, T. (2013), 'Engineers' professional learning: Through the lens of practice', in W. Williams, J. D. Figueiredo & J. Trevelyan (eds), *Engineering practice in a global context: Understanding the technical and social to inform educators*, CRC Press/Balkema Leiden.

Schatzki, T. (2001), 'Practice theory', in T. Schatzki, K. Knorr-Cetina & E. von Savigny (eds), *The practice turn in contemporary theory*, Routledge, New York.

Schatzki, T. R. (2005), 'Peripheral vision: The sites of organizations', *Organization Studies*, vol. 26, no. 3, pp. 465–84.

Schatzki, T. R. (2006), 'On organizations as they happen', *Organization Studies*, vol. 27, no. 12, pp. 1863–74.

Schatzki, T. R., Knorr Cetina, K. & von Savigny, E. (eds), (2001), *The practice turn in contemporary theory*, Routledge, London.

Sfard, A. (1998), 'On two metaphors for learning and the dangers of choosing just one', *Educational Researcher*, vol. 27, no. 2, pp. 4–13.

Skule, S. (2004), 'Learning conditions at work: A framework to understand and assess informal learning in the workplace', *International Journal of Training and Development*, vol. 8, no. 1, pp. 8–20.

Skule, S. & Reichborn, A. (2002), *Learning-conducive work: A survey of learning conditions in Norwegian workplaces*, CEDEFOP, Luxembourg.

Chapter 6

Developing professionally
A practice-based perspective

Marie Manidis and Keiko Yasukawa

Introduction

Australian higher education institutions have been undergoing a gradual shift to increasing auditing and accountability at a federal level. New quality standards have been introduced and there is a growing focus on corporate governance and academics' 'professional competence and knowledge in [relevant professional] domains' Tertiary Education Quality Standards Agency, ((TEQSA) 2015, p. 8). Professional development, while not an overt element of these new quality standards, is present nonetheless, subsumed within statements on graduate outcomes, disciplinary content and professional standards. On the websites of many Australian universities graduate attributes are published alongside statements about the institution's commitment to quality teaching and learning.

Another significant trend has been the increased focus on research outputs and research impact in universities in Australia as well as internationally. Doctoral education in particular is seen as having a dual purpose: the production of new knowledge and the development of a researcher. In progressively aligning with the Bologna Process Reform initiatives, Australia seeks to recognise the dual purpose of doctoral education, ensuring research contributes to the advancement of knowledge and develops 'a researcher' – a particular, research-skilled individual (DIISRTE 2012).

There has not been a parallel aim in terms of teaching and learning attributes of the modern-day academic, even though the Bologna Process has put the quality of teaching under scrutiny (Ashwin 2015). Measures of quality that are in place are however unrelated to real classroom learning experiences, resulting in league table comparisons between institutions (Ashwin 2015). Instead of learners having access to powerful forms of knowledge, these measures favour the more prestigious and elite academies (Ashwin 2015). Theorisation and scholarly inquiry about pedagogical practices – for example, questioning an institution-wide model of pedagogy as a framework to guide local teaching practices – have not been part of the quality teaching agenda.

While quality in teaching and learning is desired by university administrators, national governments and European Higher Education initiatives, professional development in teaching and learning at the chalk face is sorely neglected and left to the individual rather than the collective to undertake, as pointed out in Chapter 5 by Boud and Brew. We explore this paradox through the case study of Keiko, an education lecturer, who pursues a solitary quest in learning how to teach and how to become an educator who could enable her students to build scholarly and informed connections between theory and their practice. At this interface of individual-collective practices, Keiko's professional development pursuit embeds one of the key paradoxes of tertiary life: an academic is a solitary figure responsible for, and measured by, their own output, yet at the same time subject to the collective (and desired) discourses and practices of higher education.

Theoretical and methodological approach

Our analysis is undertaken from a practice-based perspective (Gherardi 2008, Schatzki 2006) drawing on theorisations of the learning of social practice(s) and professional learning (Boud & Brew (Chapter 5, this volume), Green 2009a, 2009b, Kemmis et al. 2014, Maton 2013).

Practice-based studies recognise work settings as 'sites' consisting of people, material arrangements and 'practices' which are bound together in time and space. In this paradigm, Keiko, the focus of our case study, as a lecturer/teacher, enacts practices responding to and reflecting the sociomaterial and spatiotemporal features of this university 'timespace' (Schatzki 2010). What she does and how she 'knows in practice' (Gherardi 2006) simultaneously reflect and draw on the complex web of material objects, people, relationships and activities as she initiates her learners into the practices of teaching vocational and workplace numeracy and literacy. Keiko's discourses and activities are 'practices' – arrays of activities – including doings, sayings, seeings and relatings (Kemmis et al. 2014) recognisable to others as tertiary 'lecturing/teaching'. The ways in which learning and knowing in this higher education context unfold as 'the [institution] happens' (Schatzki 2006) are situated phenomena, but ones connecting to, and interrelating with broader nexuses, or 'ecologies' of practices. In our study, these include how the desires of the Australian Vocational Education and Training (VET) system are incorporated into Keiko's learners' metapractices of teaching and learning and professional development (National Skills Standards Council (NSSC) 2013, Productivity Commission 2011). The ecology of practices surrounding the lecturer/teacher is evidenced in Figure 6.1 below.

Kemmis et al. (2014) propose education is a complex interrelated 'ecology of practices', practices into which lecturers/teachers are initiated. Schatzki conceptualises these practices in terms of 'bundles' (2006) as they overlap, intersect, and work with each other, and include in our case study, student learning, teaching/lecturing, professional learning (of the lecturer/teacher), leading and researching – faculty-based, as well as practices at national and international levels.

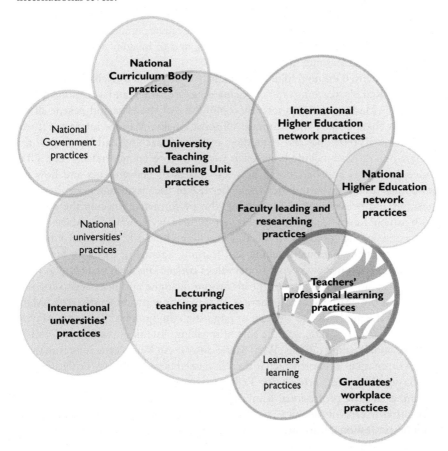

Figure 6.1 The ecology of practices

Developing a collegial partnership

Keiko, a lecturer in the Faculty of Education, initiates an evaluation of her teaching in a discussion with Marie, a lecturer in the same faculty. Keiko approaches Marie (who has a background in VET and teacher education) to be a critical friend to help her interpret and navigate tensions she foresees in her upcoming teaching programme. These are tensions between practices shaped by and perhaps shaping the dynamic relationship of higher education and those in the field to which graduates take their qualifications. This field is the Australian VET system with its own metapractices of teaching and learning and professional development.

Keiko's project is a new programme, the content of which has to tread a fine line between instrumental goals that would enable her learners to work competently within the current requirements of the VET sector, and educational goals that would demand of the learners to critically examine the way the sector positions them as teachers and their students, and to imagine alternative futures for teaching and learning in VET.

In two focused ethnographic (Kornblauch 2005) visits to Keiko's class, Marie observes Keiko's teaching and participates as a learner and occasionally as a colleague. Marie is enrolled into the online site of the class and is sent all the materials (handbooks) and readings. Observationally, Marie is interested in the sociomaterial, relational and embodied aspects of teaching and learning in this programme. These include how Keiko works with teaching artefacts (e.g. CDs, videos, readings and handouts), how she relates to her students and how she embodies teaching through her voice, her use of the classroom space, her hand gestures and her eyes. Marie documents this performativity noting the dexterity with which Keiko leads the learners. At a meta level however, Marie is also interested in the 'politics' of Keiko's teaching: how she 'works around' the exigencies of the national teaching and learning agenda (a focus on regulatory compliance) and her own professional values concerning what pedagogy is *for*.

Marie audio-records parts of the classroom dialogue and interviews several of the classroom learners[1]. In gathering and analysing the linguistic data, Marie draws on the methods and analyses of linguistic ethnography (Rampton, Maybin & Roberts 2014), examining the role of speaking, listening, reading and writing as classroom learning unfolds. What Marie observes in Keiko's teaching is analysed and written up in a report which is then discussed between the two colleagues – a professional learning process for Keiko as she is guided in a reflection of her teaching and the professional learning that has led her, through experience, to her current teaching practice (see Boud & Brew, Chapter 5). Researching and 'doing' professional learning in this way is explained by Kemmis (2012, p. 896):

> in the light of individual and collective self-reflection, to re-orient oneself in the practice of the practice, to re-orient one's understandings of the practice, and to re-orient the conditions under which one practises.

Following an invitation to contribute to this book, Marie and Keiko agree to co-write the narrative and theoretical parts of the chapter, their 'writing' practices intersecting with their 'observer/lecturer' and 'reflective' practices (Kemmis 2012). Seeking to focus on aspects of pedagogy and professional development from a practice-based perspective as a 'reflective' practice itself (ibid.) rather than as a recount, for the dialogue, Marie composes a series of questions which are responded to by Keiko in writing on her own, in her own time. These questions arise from Marie's original report. As neither author edits the other's dialogue these exchanges remain as considered observations and reflections forming the basis of the chapter. The dialogic format provides an opportunity for Keiko to reflect on her practice, while incidentally highlighting many aspects of good practice. Despite Keiko's detailed reflections, we recognise that 'the expert knows more than s/he is able to explicate' (Gherardi 2006, p. 131).

Findings and analysis

An interconnected practice

The preparation for the subject (*Literacy and numeracy in and for work*) includes a range of communications and artefacts to orient and scaffold the learners' engagement with the subject.

Keiko is aware she is a lynchpin in a larger 'ecology of practices'. She knows she must weave the larger policy context and 'official' resources for teaching which conceptualise literacy and numeracy as a set of skills for the practical work of her learners as Language, Literacy and Numeracy (LLN) teachers[2], into a broader pedagogy, one in which literacy and numeracy are conceptualised as socio-cultural practices – a set of life skills for her learners and in turn their VET students.

We begin by focusing on the political aspects of Keiko's teaching:

Marie: You set up three questions at the beginning of the two-day programme. These questions are: 'What do you believe?'; 'Who are you accountable to?'; 'Whose interests are at stake?' In my view, these are big questions about knowledge, about access to socio-cultural discourses of power, about what education is for. Can you say why you used these as a framework for the programme?

Keiko: Yes, these are big questions, but I wanted the group – the learners and I – to acknowledge teaching is a highly political practice, and the subject we were studying is – at that time – a 'hot' policy topic in VET.

With these three questions Keiko not only gives her learners access to the ways in which they should approach the teaching of literacy and numeracy, but she has them entertain reflective questions about *their purpose* as educators, initiating them into reflective practice.

Marie: Keiko, in observing you teaching and tracing the language you use, you constantly weave together and mix up (in a positive sense) theory, practical examples and learner perspectives. This seems to me to provide security and connection for learners. Would you agree?

The intent of my question is to understand how Keiko manages to position herself (or imagine herself) as the learner all the time.

Keiko: I hadn't thought about the notion of providing 'security' until you mentioned it, Marie, but connection, certainly. To be able to 'mix things up' as you say has, for me, been a major achievement. My whole career has been in higher education. I'm not someone who had started her career in the fields that my learners are in, and later on in my career made a shift to higher education. So I've made a very conscious effort to be professionally involved in the sector that my learners work in or hope to work in, so I could feel more credible about my role as a teacher educator. This gives me the real insight I need to know what to teach, where the tensions in teachers' working lives are, what and where the illustrative examples of what I'm teaching are, and so on.

Marie: You inject your talking/lecturing with PowerPoint© slides, videos, group work and open group discussions. How does this help your students' learning?

Keiko: In the subject it was really important to be constantly making theory/practice connections – and at times, interrogating how the policy environment created barriers for certain connections to be made in practice. One of the messages that was central in the subject was the enormous pedagogical benefit of vocational specialists and literacy and numeracy specialists 'working together' in the planning and delivery of vocational courses. But in many of my learners' work environments, this way of working was becoming increasingly difficult due to cuts in funding. And so, some of the practices we discuss in class are not immediately realisable – we need to talk about both: the here and now, and what could be. This is why I show videos illustrating different ways of working. Also, often the first reaction of student teachers to the study of 'policy' is less than enthusiastic. It's when they see how policies can afford or deny ways of working that they value that they become interested.

Marie: In relation to what you have asked me to evaluate as part of your professional development, I would like to focus on the way you provide the learners with two readings which you use to *frame* the contrasting perspectives of the two approaches to literacy teaching you are struggling with. The one reading is instrumental, focusing on literacy for work, and the other takes a more critical perspective on students learning to read and write as social practice. Could you explain your reasons for doing this?

Keiko: Yes, I first get students to read a chapter, 'A Vocabulary of Carpentry' from Mike Rose's book, *The Mind at Work* (2004) – detailing Rose's ethnographic study of carpentry apprentices. We all have our heroes and Mike Rose is my hero because of the way he describes the skilfulness of apprentices and tradespeople who are often dismissed in popular discourses as unskilled, non-academic. His writing challenges these deficit views in a powerful way and dignifies workers and their work. He is able to do this because he knows how to look and see, hear and sense the ways people interact with other workers and with their tools and environment at work. I want my learners to learn to 'notice' their learners/apprentices in the way Rose does, and to see how complex work is, that it is a rich, social, cultural, relational and political practice. This is my first reason for getting my students to read Mike Rose.

The second is to see that literacy and numeracy in the workplace is not just a set of cognitive skills. Literacy and numeracy are part of this sociomaterial practice that can't be understood or isolated from the totality of the practice. We can't come into the work of literacy and numeracy teaching in VET without having a deep sense of what literacy and numeracy looks like as part of the workplace practices. But teachers in Australian VET work with standardised curriculum instruments that abstract and atomise these complex practices into a list of behavioural competencies. After reading Rose's chapter, I hand out one of the units of competency from a curriculum module for carpentry to get students to contrast the ways in which work practices are described by Rose and in the standardised instrument. It's a way of orienting the students to the socio-cultural, practices perspective on literacy and numeracy in this subject.

Marie: You preface each session and then frame how the learners should look at and listen to, a DVD clip. But what I also notice is you select two readings that position 'literacy and numeracy' as either skill sets or ways of participating in social practices. Can you explain how this binary gives learners a clear choice for themselves?

Keiko: Choice is an interesting notion. I would like to think learners make choices at various levels. In their immediate practice, they may have very little 'choice' about what approach to take. Many teachers in the field lament the deprofessionalisation of their work – that they are dictated in their pedagogical approaches by standardised curriculum instruments and tools, especially assessment tools. But policies come and go, and I want students to think and imagine beyond the here and now. They know what the skills-based/human capital approach to literacy and numeracy looks like and feels like because of what we currently have; I want them to know about alternatives. And I want them to think about 'choices' not in terms of what they might or might not do tomorrow in the classroom, but in terms of who they are and who they aspire to be as educators – hence the 'big questions': 'What do you believe?'; 'Who are you accountable to?'; 'Whose interests are at stake?'. I'm sure my learners would see that I have a particular interest in understanding literacy and numeracy as practices. I don't try to hide this, but I think I give my learners space to see for themselves what the practices perspective offers that the skills-based perspective does not. I think after the pilot of this subject, I have been able to do this better. I think initially learners may have felt that they needed to 'choose' a skills-based or a social practices perspective, whereas now, I think learners are able to see what each perspective offers, rather than these being mutually exclusive and incompatible in practice.

Keiko reiterates key points, e.g. 'We have different ways of making meaning with "maths"'. In doing this, Keiko gives students informed, thoughtful and critical options for going forward. By initiating learners into the practices of reflection, Keiko gives them options for their own conclusions: a belief summed up in her words to them – 'That's why you're here – to explore alternate futures'.

A sociomaterial practice

Participants in the programme include 24 adult learners in the class: two males and 22 females. In terms of their backgrounds, most have some connection to (or prior qualifications in) vocational (or literacy) teaching and learning, a pre-requisite for admission into the programme. The classroom is fairly standard: there are desks, chairs (arranged), a whiteboard, a computer, a lectern, student and lecturer name tags, a PowerPoint© screen, light(ing), pens, video resources, CD resources, websites and an online subject page. In her teaching Keiko has expert control of all the materials and equipment and technologies, using this range of diverse learning methods that cater to the variety of learners and learning styles in the room. This is a multimodal and a multi-vocal learning experience.

Teaching (and learning?) is a textured practice (Gherardi 2006). In our view this involves pedagogical and sociomaterial entanglements as it is the warps and the wefts of learning (see Figure 6.2 below), that require constant weaving together by Keiko. Keiko embeds the learning of research skills for her learners in her teaching. She instructs the learners on ways to read the articles she hands out; she scaffolds what they need to do. Keiko articulates what learners should look for in their learning.

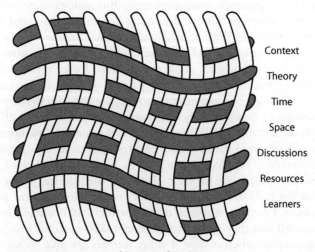

Context
Theory
Time
Space
Discussions
Resources
Learners

Figure 6.2 Interweaving as aspects of lecturing/teaching

Marie: Keiko, you weave context, theory, discussions, resources, learners, language into time and space. How did you learn to do this?

Keiko: In some ways, I think 'theory' is probably the easiest dimension to teach if one is satisfied with a purely academic presentation of theory. I think useful and substantial discussions are generated when learners are able to make connections with the theory and other 'content'. It's taken me over two decades to feel I can talk and 'weave in' content about what is happening and what might be the implications for vocational and adult literacy teaching practices – that is presenting content and in a way that makes connections with my learners. I have spent many years building my connections, confidence and credibility in the field of practice. I've done this through collaborative projects in the field, and engagement with professional organisations, and doing lots and lots of practicum supervision visits. So I have the opportunity to see glimpses of who the students in the field are, what teachers are teaching, how teaching and learning are organised, and so forth. In this way, I have been able to build a deeper understanding of what matters to the field and to the practitioners, as well as what's currently not being imagined that could be considered.

Marie: Keiko, you relate the video content to the reading learners have just talked about. This reading then transforms into group feedback, which is then interspersed with a CD or DVD on the same topic as the reading. In doing this, Keiko, you are stretching and overlaying content, time, space, learning and learners in a going back and going forward zigzag of pedagogy. The weaving involves linear shifts – going forwards and backwards across the content of the subject, across what has been said before and across what is to come. Linking content on Day 2 to content on Day 1 and vice versa, I'd like to ask you how doing this has this been learned in your professional development trajectory?

Keiko: In many ways, my 'career' (life?) has been a serious of accidents that somehow find connections with each other at different times. I came to UTS after completing a PhD in pure maths. I was employed as an educational developer in a community outreach programme to encourage more girls and women to study and work in engineering. Shortly afterwards, I started doing some casual teaching in teacher training of adult literacy and numeracy teachers in the Faculty of Education, and in this way, got more exposed to literacy and language education as well as adult education as a field. After a year in the outreach programme, I was tasked to coordinate a major restructure of the undergraduate engineering courses. Here, I was able to bring some of what I was learning in my work in the Faculty of Education about literacy as a key dimension in any subject pedagogy and about adult education approaches. So I started working with colleagues in the academic literacy centre of the university, and they helped me 'build in' literacy development in the new engineering course. Together – and with some of my engineering colleagues – we designed a subject called 'Engineering for Sustainability' that engineering staff team-taught with the academic literacy colleagues. Many of the engineering colleagues who participated in the teaching of this subject commented on what a significant professional development experience this was to learn to be 'in practice': being learner-focused, attending to literacy development in an engineering subject, to be reflective about their teaching, and to encourage students to reflect. Then when I started to be more involved in the vocational teacher education programmes, I wondered if in our teacher education programme we shouldn't be giving the vocational student (and literacy) teachers opportunities to learn about the practice of 'working together'. That is what this current subject is about, but only after I had completed a national research project on how 'working together' was being carried out in the field, and also another research project about workplace literacy. So, is that zigzagging?

During the programme, Keiko summarises her learning about this for the class: 'We need to be clear of the *purpose* [her emphasis] of this kind of training'.

An embodied practice

Marie: Keiko, I observe you use your body, e.g. your hands, to emphasise meaning. You move around the room when learners are talking; you check how they are going with time; you ask if another 10 minutes is needed. Quiet descends on the room when you appear in the front of the class. Can you talk a little about how you do this? How do you project your presence as commanding?

Keiko: I certainly don't think about how I could have a commanding presence. I think by walking around during group work and checking to see how they are going, chatting to students informally before class and during breaks, I have a sense of the learners' readiness for input from the 'front' of the room.

Marie: In a related question, you very subtly get people to 'listen' to you after there has been an activity or noise. Are you aware of how you do this?

Keiko: It's challenging sometimes to bring the students back together after they have been discussing ideas in groups. But as I said earlier, I do make sure I have a sense of how they are going in the group discussions, and I often ask them something like 'Do you think you can wrap up your discussions in two minutes' so it doesn't come as a total surprise when I try to bring them back together. I often say 'Thank you' as a starting point to the whole group, acknowledging the work they have been doing, and for giving me space to talk. I think students realise that I see the space and time as shared. Sometimes I am at the centre and lead, and at other times I am on the periphery.

A relational practice

Marie: Keiko, could you explain why you use students' names in your teaching? How do you think this shows your recognition and respect for them as people?

Keiko: I think it's essential that each learner is acknowledged and respected, and using their names is a public way of doing so. Teaching is a relational practice (Noddings 2003). We have to establish and sustain the relationship we have individually with learners, and with the whole class.

Professionally, Keiko's response above reflects what we would define as pedagogical 'caring'. This 'caring' is rendered more powerful given the increasing impact of compliance and the corporatisation of tertiary education which is placing a strain on the relational aspect of teaching and learning (Ashwin 2015). We focus on Keiko's caring as a situated activity (Gherardi & Rodeschini 2015) and reflect on how her actions are in a sense an aesthetic component of teaching – an educator's concern for his or her learners. While the rhetoric of higher education is replete with words on 'duty of care' to learners outlined in bureaucratic edicts, few professional development activities address how care might be enacted in the classroom.

Pedagogically, the focus on classroom expertise and professional development pertains predominantly to methodology, subject matter, delivery style and classroom management strategies. However, 'care' remains a strong ethical value of 'professional' practice and actions of care are noticed by learners. One of Keiko's students identifies the fact that Keiko 'gets there [to class] early, is organised with pre-cut name plates and pens'. This care is extended through Keiko's use of pictorial slides – e.g. a building bridges slide, which Keiko goes on to explain via a personal anecdote in relation to the bridges. In this way Keiko weaves together materials with content, with understandings, and with a personal story, which makes the abstract concept practical and personal. In Gherardi and Rodeschini's terms this illustrates how 'care' by one lecturer/teacher might be 'framed as a collective knowledgeable "doing" [of all teaching professionals]. It is not an object or a quality that is added to work; rather, it is "caring", an ongoing sociomaterial accomplishment' (Gherardi & Rodeschini 2015, p. 1).

When the groups are presenting, Keiko is seated at the front of the class. She also constantly looks at and engages with students. She goes beyond the requirements of the programme and offers a session in mid-January (the programme runs late in November just before the December holiday break) so that participants can have additional assistance.

Keiko uses humour a lot. She makes cakes and provides tea for her learners – an additional effort they all recognise and respect in their turn. One student remarks on Keiko's 'homemade morning tea/coffee' and articulates Keiko's teaching as 'implement[ing] TLC' – tender loving care.

Relationally and pedagogically – using language as an interpersonal and a pedagogical resource – spoken and written language is a key part of Keiko's teaching, as with all HE classroom learning. But it can be and is used in very different ways.

Marie: Keiko, you frequently say things in threes: 'a picture, a feel, a sense'; 'we just have to read "stuff", write "stuff", talk "stuff"'; or 'Do I also have a role, an option, a mandate, or a responsibility'? Or 'What would you be looking for? or how would you go about it? or how would you do it?' For me these triple (or more) statements emphasise meaning or emphasise a point. Could you explain why you do this?

Keiko: I think repetition, recasting and emphasis help students to make connections with the points I'm trying to get across, or the question I am asking. Sometimes what they have written down is too abstract or general, and I try to unpack it using language they can use to think about the ideas and the questions more readily, strengthening or weakening the context-dependence and condensation of meanings, what Maton terms the 'semantic wave' (2013). It also, I hope, enables students to feel more comfortable to ask 'Oh, do you mean …' or 'What about …' It gives them different options on how they tackle abstract ideas and concepts. But if I didn't have the kind of engagement with their field, I would probably accept a general, abstract response to questions because I wouldn't have the resources to probe the learners further!

Marie: You telescope for learners what is important to learn and contrast concepts and ideas using language for emphasis and clarity. So for example, you might say 'independence' vs 'dependence' or 'individual' vs 'collective'; or 'human capital', 'resource, skills, exchange potential' or 'numeracy for numeracy's sake or numeracy for tiling's sake'. Or you say 'a case study is studying a case'. Do you do this consciously?

Keiko: Yes, I do, because I think we take so much for granted about shared meanings which aren't actually shared until we unpack them.

Marie: Your gestures also underpin your meanings, so, for example, when you say 'the line of sight …' you use your hands to draw an arc. Are you aware of this?

Keiko: I guess so – I'm increasingly aware of expressions and metaphors that may be idiosyncratic, technical or culturally contingent, so if I can convey meaning through other means I will.

Marie: You use intonation very deliberately. You often leave a gap after saying something important, almost as though for impact. Are you aware of how your voice supplements – or complements – your teaching, and in particular, meaning, in your teaching?

Keiko: I have been told this by colleagues. And I have to be careful too because sometimes when I am reading a quote I really disagree with, say from a politician making sweeping claims about education, my intonation and facial expression give too much away!

Keiko's instructions on group work, arrival times and preparations are clear, repeated and unambiguous. The group feedback is also highly scaffolded; yet she allows the groups to self-organise.

In building knowledge, Keiko always responds to suggestions and input from the learners, i.e. she creates a discussion board space for the learning assessment, which occurs overnight. Spoken and written interactions thus take place in real time.

Keiko gives a lot of space to the learners even when they go on talking at length and once or twice has to move subtly on to another learner's contribution. Keiko always responds to her learners' questions, which she often prefaces with 'and' and not 'but'. In a deliberate linguistic practice, she often repeats what learners have said. So a learner says 'so important' and Keiko says 'which is so important'; or one person says 'Why is it?' and Keiko responds 'I think it's "it" because ...'. This is an effective mirroring strategy recognising and valuing what people have just said.

Discussion

A practice-based approach allows us to focus on Keiko's practices and how these practices are shaped by, and perhaps shape, the dynamic relationship between discourses of higher education metapractices and discourses of the fields to which graduates take their qualifications. Keiko's lecturing and teaching practices are intrinsically a part of the 'ecology of practices' and as such are connected to those of the VET sector, the university, the federal funding bodies, the students' learning practices and the faculty's researching and professional development practices. Keiko's actions and activities in the classroom are instantiations amid a constellation of professional practices. Her actions and activities are 'nested' (Green 2009b, p. 47) in the *practices* of tertiary pedagogy with concomitant dispositions, values and ethics, beyond the immediate here and now of her classroom.

Keiko's teaching, as instantiations of practice, reveals for us the entanglement of pedagogy at the chalk face with its wider ideological connections. Keiko has the learners reflect on what the content of an article is being compared to – or contrasted with. She also reminds her learners that 'teaching is a social practice'. In so doing, Keiko links a critical part of the theoretical component of the subject she is teaching to the broader practice of her *learners'* teaching. Thus, content is linked from the classroom to the wider world, to the broader 'nexus of practices'.

Even though the site we have explored is an Australian university educating vocational teachers with *its* own metapractices of teaching and learning and professional development, there are lessons to be learned which might be applied more systemically and systematically in the university itself. While Keiko selected to inform herself of the relevant professional domain of her teaching and self-initiated this professional development undertaking, we propose such a professional development initiative might fit more systematically within the university's teaching and learning practices. For example, a faculty's practices might shift to adopt a more critical approach to the aims and objectives of the national agenda – whose VET teachers are required to comply with policy frameworks. Or a faculty might work with teachers to include a component of critical reflection in its professional development practices, so that teachers can reflect on – and assist their learners to reflect on – different purposes of education: 'numeracy for numeracy's sake or numeracy for tiling's sake'. Although Keiko has accomplished this, she has done this because as a professional lecturer/teacher, she embodies and enacts the underpinning teleologies (motivations and goals) of her craft.

At the level of practice, Keiko's thoughtfulness and effort on behalf of her students embody broader values of HE: the teleoaffective underpinning (Schatzki 2006) of the professional practice of teaching (Green 2009b). These enactments in her classroom however are not itemised in quality and compliance documents at the federal level of university management domains (TEQSA 2015). Keiko has enacted caring and professionalism because 'she respects her teaching craft' (as stated by one student) and also because of her deep understanding of, and concern about, the shifting metapractices of the vocational sector and what these might mean for the teachers – and *their* learners. Our practice-based perspective has highlighted the interconnected, sociomaterial, embodied and relational dimensions of the practices of tertiary pedagogy. Our empirical data has illustrated how Keiko's *in situ* teaching is inherently tied and responsive to the temporal, spatial, social and material dimensions and discursive and epistemic teleologies of the higher education classroom, but equally connected to the broader 'ecology of practices' of this sector that extends beyond the sector itself.

Finally, our practice-based perspective has illustrated how Keiko has linked not only practices to other practices, but also the subject matter within the classroom, across time and space. She has done this by linking students' comments (discussions in an earlier time) to her subsequent teaching (discussions in the here and now). She remembers what students have seen or said previously and reminds them of this. This has created a continuity of knowing, which recognises the emergent and situated way learning takes places through repetition, reinforcement and recognition. Subject matter is therefore not treated as being in a vacuum – it is intimately connected in her doings (and subsequently in students' learning) to what they might have heard before in other domains of learning and to what they will do in their own practice.

Concluding comments

Marie: But what does all of this tell us about professional development for higher education teachers? What does it mean to you, Keiko?

Keiko: I think it is a rare opportunity to have a colleague to do what you have done for me – to take an interest in my subject, to observe my classroom teaching, to guide my reflection of my teaching! Teaching is such a private activity. We're lucky if anyone even reads and comments on our subject outline and reading list.

The three 'big' questions I ask my students – what they believe in, who they are accountable to, and whose interests are at stake – are questions I ask myself about my own teaching. And having a colleague who has been part of my pilot programme, who knows the context of my learners (VET) as well as our higher education context, and who shares the disciplinary knowledge in adult literacy and numeracy has meant that I could reflect on these questions in dialogue and in writing this chapter.

While this case study is highly contextualised in the teaching practices of a particular subject, and is based on observation-reflection as professional development, it is precisely the particularity and the locally contingent, *in-situ* basis of the case study that has surfaced pedagogical aspects of professional development. When teaching is understood as an interconnected, sociomaterial, embodied and relational practice, then developing one's teaching practice has to attend to the specific time, space, people and materiality of the lecturer's context and beyond. Through these the actions, activities and practices more broadly in the profession, are recognisable.

In summary, developing professionally has been a considered and intentional focus of Keiko's over her life as a tertiary lecturer. This endeavour has provided an opportunity for us to connect Keiko's desire for pedagogical and professional development to the rhetoric of Australia's Tertiary Education Quality Standards Agency. In seeking feedback from a colleague (Marie) on her teaching, Keiko's self-initiated professional development initiative has allowed us to explore the 'practice' of teaching, the practice of professional development and their connections to other practices in the university and beyond. In particular, the (re) articulated links between a 'professionally-attuned' academy with its growing focus on corporate governance and academics' 'professional competence and knowledge in [relevant professional] domains' (TEQSA 2015, p. 8) have been highlighted in instantiations of Keiko's interconnected, sociomaterial, embodied and relational pedagogy. Keiko herself, her methodologies, her identity, her organising, are shown to be 'professionally-attuned'.

Keiko's 'professional competence and knowledge in [her] domains' (ibid.) have been opened up to scrutiny through her own professional development initiative. But other practices in this 'ecology' of practices remain under-critiqued. The instrumentality of the national agenda has forsaken other outcomes of education – in particular those seeking to develop critical views on pedagogy and the development of learners into 'moral beings' (Kemmis et al. 2014) – for outcomes primarily oriented towards workforce development and league table aggregates (Ashwin 2015).

The chapter's practice-based perspective has gone beyond merely describing what lecturers do. This is because a practice-based perspective goes beyond mere descriptions of actions – an approach which practice-based approaches share with behaviourist and positivist paradigms – and describes instead 'the creation of meaning, identity formation, and ordering of activities produced' (de Souza Bispo 2015, p. 314) *in and beyond* the classroom. Thus despite the question-answer exchange between lecturer/teacher and professional developer, our focus has been not only on the teaching actions and activities – what lecturers actually *do* (see Chapter 5) – but on the practices that have been animated by these interactions, which have provoked critical reflections. We recognise these as pedagogical practices within HE, enacted in the classroom, but ones also linked to the 'ecology of practices' beyond, such as the practices of professional development. The latter we identify as primarily centred on regulatory compliance rather than on how these practices might shape (or be shaped by) the meaning, identity and the ordering of tertiary pedagogy for Keiko and for her learners' teaching.

Notes

1   The study was supported by funding from the University of Technology Sydney. The researchers followed ethical guidelines for the evaluation study which included briefing about the aim of the study and obtaining verbal consent of all programme participants. All learner comments have been de-identified and are reported as such.
2   Hereafter referred to as literacy teachers.

References

Ashwin, P. (2015), 'Five ways universities have already changed in the 21st century', *The Conversation* (www.theconversation.com).

de Souza Bispo, M. (2015), 'Methodological reflections on practice-based research in organization studies', *Brazilian Administration Review*, vol. 12, no. 3, Art. 5, pp. 309–23.

DIISRTE (2012), *Australian Innovation System Report*, Department of Industry, Innovation, Science, Research and Tertiary Education, Canberra.

Gherardi, S. (2006), *Organizational knowledge: the texture of workplace learning*, 2nd edn, Blackwell, London.

Gherardi, S. (2008), 'Situated knowledge and situated action: What do practice-based studies promise?', in D. Barry & H. Hansen (eds), *The SAGE handbook of new approaches in management and organization*, Sage, Los Angeles.

Gherardi, S. & Rodeschini, G. (2015), 'Caring as a collective knowledgeable doing: About concern and being concerned', *Management Learning*, DOI: 1350507615610030.

Green, B. (2009a), 'Introduction: Understanding and researching professional practice', in B. Green (ed.), *Understanding and researching professional practice*, Sense Publishers, Amsterdam.

Green, B. (2009b), 'The primacy of practice and the problem of representation', in B. Green (ed.), *Understanding and researching professional practice*, Sense Publishers, Amsterdam.

Kemmis, S. (2012), 'Researching educational praxis: Spectator and participant perspectives', *British Educational Research Journal*, vol. 38, no. 6, pp. 885–905.

Kemmis, S., Wilkinson, J., Edwards-Groves, C., Hardy, I., Grootenboer, P. & Bristol, L. (2014), *Changing practices, changing education*, Springer, Singapore.

Kornblauch, H. (2005), 'Focused ethnography', *Qualitative Sozialforschung/Forum: Qualitative Social Research*, no. 10, September 2012.

Maton, K. (2013), 'Making semantic waves: A key to cumulative knowledge-building', *Linguistics and Education*, vol. 24, pp. 8–22.

National Skills Standards Council (NSSC) (2013), *Improving vocational education and training: The case for a new system*, National Skills Standards Council, Melbourne.

Noddings, N. (2003), 'Is teaching a practice?', *Journal of Philosophy of Education*, vol. 37, no. 2, pp. 245–51.

Productivity Commission (2011), *Vocational education and training workforce*, Commonwealth of Australia, Melbourne.

Rampton, B. Maybin, J. & Roberts, C. (2014), 'Methodological foundations in linguistic ethnography', in J. Snell, S. Shaw & F. Copland (eds), *Linguistic ethnography: Interdisciplinary explorations*, Palgrave Macmillan, Basingstoke.

Rose, M. (2004), *The mind at work: Valuing the intelligence of the American worker*, Penguin Books, New York.

Schatzki, T. R. (2006), 'On organizations as they happen', *Organization Studies*, vol. 27, no. 12, pp. 1863–73.

Schatzki, T. R. (2010), *The timespace of human activity: On performance, society, and history as indeterminate teleological events*, Lexington Books, Plymouth, UK.

TEQSA (2015), *A risk and standards based approach to quality assurance in Australia's diverse higher education sector*, Commonwealth of Australia, Canberra.

Chapter 7

Stewardship as *practice*
'Learning on-the-job' for the academic development newcomer

Tai Peseta and Simon Barrie

While a good deal of this volume revisits the teaching and learning endeavour as the object or phenomenon in focus, in this chapter we use practice-theory as a route into theorising stewardship for the field of academic development. In our experience of the Australian academic development scene, there is a tendency to conflate the practices involved in learning to teach in university settings with those related to the practices of academic development. Indeed, this distinction – between the scholarship of teaching and the scholarship of academic development – is not a new one. If Boyer's (1990) text marked a watershed moment on the international scholarship of teaching landscape, it was only some six years later that a good deal of the research about academic development published in the *International Journal for Academic Development* started to become disseminated more widely, and the texts used to stimulate debate and curiosity about the field.

Our ambition in this chapter is three-fold. We wish to advance a case for how the notion of stewardship (Golde & Walker 2006) offers a fresh view on, and a helpful intentionality to, the learning practices that comprise the field and scholarship of academic development. In particular, our focus is on the newcomer. To this end, we bring together two sets of conceptual resources. The first we take from the cluster of insights attached to the practice-turn in theorising professional work and learning (Gherardi 2000, Reich & Hager 2014). As Boud & Brew have noted in this volume (Chapter 5), this turn has been away from the behaviourist and cognitive traditions where knowledge is acquired by individuals, transferred and applied to new learning situations. Rather, the practice-turn emphasises a concern with the interconnections between bodies, materials and objects, meanings, sayings and doings, and notions of becoming and emergence. Essentially, practices mark collective happenings, and are depicted as emergent effects (and therefore changeable) of relations and collisions between things across bodies, time, space and materials (Hopwood 2014). We draw specifically on the six threads of practice advanced by Reich & Hager (2014): knowing-in-practice, the sociomateriality of practices, practices as embodied, practice as relational, practice as existing and evolving in historical and social contexts, and finally, practices as emergent to tease out the implications of 'learning-on-the-job' as the dominant strategy for inducting newcomers to the work of academic development.

Second, we draw on the concept of stewardship from the US-based Carnegie Foundation project on the future of doctoral education (Golde & Walker 2006). While it is unlikely that they had academic development in mind when they argued that the practice of stewardship ought to be central to the formation of scholars, there is something compelling in how the acts of *generation*, *conservation* and *transformation* – the three domains of stewardship – entail a responsibility to shape the future endeavours of the field. Implied in the notion of stewardship is that there are 'things' that require attending to: a set of practices, ideas, relations, dispositions, and modes of inquiry in need of both nurturing and challenge. We expand on the domains of stewardship later in the chapter.

Finally, we also wish to signal that those already in the field have an ethical commitment (Peseta 2011, Quinn & Vorster 2014) to induct newcomers to the field much more effectively by discussing, researching and theorising its practices in more explicit and sophisticated ways at the points where activity emerges. Without a commitment to stewardship, it is likely that the fast pace, desire for responsiveness, and 'meet your needs' imperatives that currently organise academic development practices will keep it hostage to the diminished discourses of compliance and resistance (Di Napoli 2014).

The field of academic development: contexts for learning

Anyone working in academic, educational or faculty development in universities today will be well aware that there is no one established pathway to the field, to learning about its practices, or going about the work. Unlike education in many professional fields, there is no undergraduate degree and typically no postgraduate degree that offers a steady and transparent route into the field. As a consequence, there is no curriculum that describes the combination of knowledge, knowing, and know-how that constitute the field's practices, and no accrediting body that establishes, regulates and monitors its entry, standards or continuing professional learning. Most academic developers come to the work with some sort of experience of, or care for, university life – as a student, teacher, researcher, scholar or administrator – and they learn what the job is and how to do it, 'on-the-job'. Although it might be said that the arrival of formal award-bearing postgraduate certificate courses in university teaching, learning and academic practice onto the scenes of higher education in New Zealand (NZ), Australia, the UK and South Africa represent the closest effort at instantiating something resembling a curriculum (Kandlbinder & Peseta 2009, Quinn & Vorster 2015), these award courses attend to the practices of university teaching and their relation to student learning rather than the broad scope of academic development practices. To be clear, while there are some similarities, the work does not map neatly across the two domains. And there is of course an ongoing dilemma – generated at least from a practice-theory view – about the degree of alignment between the real and actual practices that constitute a field, and a curriculum designed to prepare people for learning about and negotiating the variety of meanings, contexts and politics which comprise the practices of that same field.

For someone new, academic development is not easy to pin down – in part due to its shifty nomenclature and its movements across complex organisational layers. In some contexts, the preferred term is 'academic' development; in others, the focus is on 'education' development; and yet in others, 'faculty' development or 'instructional' design are used with equal force and favour to mark the terrain. Previously, these markers may have been attributable to national differences (e.g., UK educational development, and in the US instructional or faculty development) although nowadays, these terms can be found across layers of the same institution. More recently, the rise of the learning sciences has challenged the field to respond to questions of scale, especially where enterprise technologies and analytics are providing masses of information about what students do online (how they do them) to feed professional learning opportunities for university teachers (Gasevic et al. 2015). For a new academic developer, Fraser's (2001, p. 5) sense of the role can be helpful here as one attempt at a collective definition (although by no means complete):

> an academic developer is any person who has a role in which they are explicitly expected to work with academics to assist them to reflect upon their academic role in relation to teaching, research, scholarship, leadership, funding applications and supervision of students. An academic developer may also work at a departmental/institutional level in a developmental role.

Even Fraser's succinct definition demonstrates the sheer breadth of the field and its practices.

In the same university, these several versions of academic development can be in play, reflecting different understandings of the nature of professional learning. Its multifaceted nature also implies that choices need making. Is the focus to be directed solely to learning and teaching, to research and research education and development, or activities, systems and policies designed to address the integration of academic work? Who should be involved in the work: students, individual teachers and researchers, subjects/units, teaching workgroups and research teams, academic leaders? How should a unit go about the work: via individual consultations, through offering generic and specific workshops, formal award courses, just-in-time support, developing stand-alone resources, communities of practice, or informal conversation? Where should a unit locate the development activity: online, blended, separate from the routine work practices, or *in-situ* among, and with, colleagues? What theories should inform the unit's practices and what kind of evidence, data and research would best demonstrate its impact and success? These are not insubstantial issues and questions. Despite this variation, in truth many academic development units/groups engage in activities across all five domains. If there is a consistent rationale that helps the field 'hang together', it is perhaps the pressing need to systematically study student learning in order to improve universities' education practices across both teaching and research. More often than not, it is academic development's fidelity to student learning (Peseta 2012) that epitomises its distinctiveness rather than any particular practice, activity, theory or methodology. That broad church approach is often assumed to be one of the field's key strengths.

Navigating the academic development landscape I: processes for 'learning on-the-job'

We know already that transitioning to the work of academic development is not straightforward. We know people arrive at it purposefully at different points in their career (Hicks 1997). We know that people shift to it after long lives – sometimes troublesome and sometimes successful – as disciplinary teachers, scholars and researchers seeking new opportunities to refresh their academic practice. We know that some people get a taste for the work as fellows and adjunct appointments to an academic development unit while they continue to teach in their discipline (McDonald & Stockley 2008). We know it can be a first and sometimes accidental appointment (Peseta 2005). And, we know that it can act as a resting place for academics hoping for respite from histories of itinerant and casual university employment (Manathunga 2006). Because the routes to, and through, the work is rarely uniform, and people bring their own disciplinary histories and professional attachments, it is worth revisiting the following questions. How (and where) do newcomers to the field of academic development learn about its practices? What kind of practice is it, and how are those practices rendered visible and learnable? What are the implications for a field in which 'learning-on-the-job' has become its main mode of induction? Since academic development's practices and modes of inquiry are largely oriented towards tactics designed to support the learning of others (Gibbs 2013), there is merit in exploring the effects, and affects, of 'learning-on-the-job' as the principle method for learning (in) the field of academic development at the point of entry. For one thing, the success of learning-on-the-job for any newcomer is dependent on the fact that the contexts and practices they labour in are set up so that purposeful learning takes place.

Learning-on-the-job about the variety of influences on student learning and how to best develop it, taking into account of disciplinary, institutional and political agendas, warrants significant time and energy in academic development. A newcomer is likely to enact a commitment to student learning by drawing on their nous borne from previous pleasurable and troublesome experiences as a student, teacher, researcher, scholar or administrator. Yet operating as an academic developer solely on the basis of one's own experience, either by commending the replication of personal successful practice to others or by reacting against one's own experiences, presents a set of challenges for the novice.

There is no guarantee that successful previous experience in one context translates effortlessly to the next. It also becomes apparent that operating effectively in any new field not only involves new knowledge, knowing and know-how (Quinn & Vorster 2015), it suggests an additional encounter with existing histories, narratives, memories, and rhythms that circulate within the new local context. This demands developing a feel for the structures, operational logics, and modes of its inquiry practices – akin to Perkins' (1997, p. 49) description of 'epistemic games' as 'patterns of characterization, explanation and justification expressed as "forms, moves, goals and rules"'. Further, Perkins (1997) writes, '[t]hey (epistemic games) are not claims about the world but rather regularities in how we progress toward knowledge and understanding' (p. 52). Indeed, for the new academic developer, their previous experiences, successes, identities, desires and attachments, which are often forged through tough disciplinary and departmental climates, are likely to intersect with the epistemic games in academic development in both predictable and unexpected ways. Without some guiding framework that is in addition to their own experience, there are bound to be unwieldy clashes that require attention. And on occasion, a mechanism for coping with that dissonance may manifest in a longing that the practices of academic development need shifting to become more in line with, and more like, the contexts familiar to them. A significant learning task in academic development is coming to grips with the multiplicity of meanings attached to the project of supporting teachers and institutions to improve student learning in a system rife with contradictory logics (Shore 2010).

Another substantial consideration in learning-on-the-job is whether sufficient attention is given to the actual working contexts in which academic development practices emerge. While institutional strategy always looms large for those in academic development, we draw in particular on the 'micro-cultures' heuristic developed by Roxå & Mårtensson (2015). Their curiosity has been in tracing the effects of micro-cultures – 'traditions, norms and habits in the respective local context' (p. 194) – on informal university teaching development. For us, there is a parallel question about how academic development cultures themselves might also be subject to interpretation via a micro-culture lens. For Roxå & Mårtensson (2015, p. 198), the dynamics of informal learning in micro-cultures rely on the three basic components:

> first, levels of trust (a high or low signal dependant on significance to each other, ties, and belonging); second, the existence of a sense of shared responsibility (accomplishing things together or in parallel, and degrees of negotiation); and third, a developmental agenda (whether the tendency is towards development or preservation).

These three overarching components are then combined in various ways to articulate the characteristics of four micro-cultures: The Commons ('we're in this together'); The Market ('I look after myself'); The Club ('we'll always support each other'); and The Square ('who are these people?').

These are clearly recognisable portraits of academic micro-cultures, offering a piercing analytical device for wrestling with how 'learning-on-the-job' for an academic development newcomer plays out within the local cultures they labour in, and are attached to. Indeed, it begs several questions. Is there a collective vision of academic development that is future oriented? Are there relations of trust between colleagues, and in what ways do they matter to each other? How does negotiation, challenge and experimentation materialise in the practices they develop together? So, not only does a new academic developer need to be able to read the micro-cultures that others in the university occupy (their teaching practices, arrangements, and forms of assemblage), they should also aim to tune in to how the micro-cultures they themselves inhabit within academic development (e.g., in the unit, the project, the workgroup, the teaching team, the research collaboration, etc.) play out, shape up and lead to the emergence of certain kinds of practices and subjectivities over others. It seems to us that learning-on-the-job relies on workgroups and micro-cultures (and those who inhabit them) being able to articulate the features of their practice and forms of organisation to newcomers as an explicit strategy. By keeping these qualities tacit or hidden, a newcomer to academic development – left to their own devices – may find it difficult to determine how best to operate across the institution to influence the teaching, learning and curriculum practices around them.

Navigating the academic development landscape II: 'learning on-the-job' through inquiry practices

In addition to a new academic developer paying close attention to the processes in their own working context, those already in the field have made substantial scholarly efforts to address, theorise, and make more transparent the underlying epistemic games of academic development as an act of professional scholarship and renewal. There is now a prodigious corpus of work available to the novice. Some of it exists in the form of survival guide type advice (e.g. Baume & Popovic 2016) and others, as scholarly research. For us, one approach at organising this effort could be as follows:

1   historical accounts of academic development's emergence within universities, and across national contexts (Sorcinelli et al. 2006, Boughey 2007, Lee et al. 2008, Barrow et al. 2010);
2   ways of thinking about, and strategies for, organising academic development within and across complex and multiple organisational layers (Land 2001, Fraser et al. 2010, Boud & Brew 2013, Gibbs 2013);
3   accounts of academic development activity developed and enacted with, and for others designed to 'address a need' (Bell 2001, Schreurs et al. 1999, Reagan & Bessemer 2009);

4   evidence of the impact and quality of academic development initiatives, tactics and strategies on a range of audiences (Kreber & Brooke 2001, Sword 2008);

5   theories, methods and suggestions for researching and strengthening the research base of academic development (Brew 2002, Boughey & Niven 2012, Sutherland & Grant 2016); and

6   concerns, claims and questions about the identity of academic development, and the epistemological and ontological foundations for its authority (e.g. Grant 2007, Clegg 2009a, 2009b, Peseta 2014, Manathunga 2011, Shay 2012, Quinn & Vorster 2015).

While neither our categorisation nor the references we have included are exhaustive, there is plainly an energetic and active community keen to engage in different (and conceptually difficult) kinds of debate about its work and practices. Our categories might also exemplify narratives or lines of inquiry that researchers in the field are in conversation about. One interesting observation about this list is the absence of scholarship about the field's key people. Although Kandlbinder (2013, 2014) has begun to redress the biographical absence in research about teaching and learning in higher education, the ongoing separation of the concepts from the contexts and events of their development (and the people who helped bring them into being) still plagues professional learning in academic development. For the novice academic developer, one danger is that concepts are put to use with little knowledge of their proper historical antecedents (Kandlbinder & Peseta 2011). Another is that a field ambivalent about telling the stories of its people gives an impression that its concepts and concerns are given, rather than forged through a clash of ideology and material circumstance. For us, the particularities of learning informally 'on-the-job' in academic development are ripe for granular, empirically based investigations. In part, the absence of formal learning through a curriculum formulated by experts (as is the case with other disciplines and professions) together with the variety of pathways to the work means that 'learning-on-the-job' has become the principal mode of professional learning for newcomers in academic development. And this is perhaps no bad thing. As a pedagogical strategy for professional learning, it carries aspects of the six threads articulated Reich & Hager (2014). In our view, *knowing-in-practice* brings to mind that academic developers make decisions and shape practices drawing on a variety of knowledge sources as well as their own embodied knowing. The *socio-materiality of practices* reminds us – as does Fenwick & Edwards' chapter (Chapter 1) earlier in this volume – that non-human objects (and their emergence in contexts) contain real and significant effects on the potential to do and imagine the possibilities for academic development work (e.g. different kinds of technologies – pen, book, classroom, tablet, web-based technologies – permit certain kinds of practices). The *embodied-ness of practices* alerts us to the fact that academic development practices have organisational rhythms and routines in which clusters of bodies move in particular ways at specific times to get things done. Additionally, *practice as relational* foregrounds concepts such as 'ecology, network, choreography and orchestration' (Reich & Hager 2014, p. 425). For a novice academic developer, these terms intimate practices in which people, things, ideas are interdependent – floating together, coming apart, and then re-establishing in new and different ways – as ongoing co-production. As in other fields, practices in academic development are instantiations of regimes and systems of power *evolving in historical and social contexts*. They can be understood as effects of specific arrangements of rules and resources that may *emerge as new practices*. For these reasons, learning-on-the-job is a crucial dimension of how academic developers go about and understand their work and workplaces.

Key for us is the availability of a local academic development micro-culture that engages with understandings of practice in these complex ways. A helpful start would be an examination of the local emergence of the field of academic development both within the university, and nationally. In the Australian context, Percy (2014) reminds us that similar to the field of academic language and learning, academic development is also a higher education sector-wide invention; that is, an institutional project demanding a response focused on student learning, *and* a field of practice implicated in scholarly inquiry. Inasmuch as these sites carry different logics for practice, they can (and do) present as tensions for the new academic developer. And depending on the orientation of the local workgroup/micro-culture, the temptation is often to seek resolution to these tensions when in fact this is the very game academic developers are in, and must learn to live with (Lee & McWilliam 2008).

Stewardship as an intentional practice for learning on-the-job?

> I guess we've got a fairly standard process of induction to the role so we'd have an outline, we'd work through all the elements in their new [academic developer] position description and set out a plan for them to work with someone or get that knowledge or learning from some area of resource within the University or from elsewhere. So we'd set up an induction plan from the induction checklist, they would attend orientation so that they came up to speed very quickly with how this place works and the philosophy of learning and teaching and knowing who is who around here. We'd probably, as we have done in the past, set them alongside someone who's very experienced in our unit so they'd be shadowing that person for some time until they felt you know that wanted to move out on their own.

This extract is from a study carried out by Kensington-Miller et al. (2012, p. 126) in which the authors – new to the New Zealand academic development scene themselves and seeking guidance – interviewed a handful of directors of academic development units prompting them to reflect on their approach to inducting someone new to the role in their own institution. In our view, the response of this director is somewhat familiar and typical of the ways learning-on-the-job manifests for a new academic developer. The institution features heavily, as does the importance of getting a feel for its processes, ways of operating, and the machinery of its bureaucracy. There is an intention that the novice will work to the position description, and that although the job is intended to unfold in an orderly manner, the focus on 'speed' hints at urgency. The job is about 'teaching and learning' rather than broader aspects of the academic role. And while there is a sense of an underpinning philosophy designed to guide the approach of the new academic developer, there is not much assistance about where to find it, how to work with it, or its relation to the university strategy or the scholarly conversations in academic development. Colleagues feature too in this director's approach to induction although no insight is provided about the local practices, or how the work is to be accomplished. And while there is appreciation that a new academic developer needs dedicated attention from someone already schooled in the work – it is unclear what 'experienced' signals. The term 'shadow' gives the appearance of following around a more experienced colleague's daily work life and rhythms, and it assumes that the experienced colleague not only has time to give the novice but also the wisdom to interpret and make judgements that advance the novice's professional learning about the field. Overall, the focus is on the process and structures for professional learning rather than what a novice academic developer should aim to learn from engaging in those practices. What is missing in the account of a practice intended to induct a newcomer is a sense of care for the field. On the one hand, the inculcation of 'care' for, and of, academic development depends on the local micro-culture a newcomer joins and participates in. On the other, a commitment to care might be worked with as a professional value or virtue that animates a field's practices. While there is a literature on the ethics of care in university teaching and learning (Bozalek et al. 2014) motivated in part from the intersections between feminism, politics and social justice agendas, we draw in particular on the notion of care as *stewardship* best fleshed out by the Carnegie Foundation project on doctoral education (Golde & Walker 2006). The obligations of a steward, Golde (2006, p. 9) points out, is not only to the roles and skills designed to develop competence, but to matters of principle intended to provide both integrity and a 'moral compass' when navigating and contributing to the field. More precisely,

> [s]tewards think into the future and act on behalf of those yet to come. A steward of the discipline, then, thinks about the continuing health of the discipline and how to preserve the best of the past for those who will follow. Stewards are concerned with how to foster renewal and creativity. Perhaps most important, a steward considers how to prepare and initiate the next generation of stewards.

Golde's (2006) concern was that the intense effort on the development of research and researchers was narrowing the broad education of students. Her proposal to attend to the education of *disciplinary* stewards suggests that: '[some] one has been entrusted with the care of something valuable on behalf of others' (p. 12). Stewards express care for their practice by demonstrating accomplishment in three domains. The first focuses on *generation*: 'the ability to conduct research and scholarship that make a unique contribution and meet the standards of credible work' (p. 10). The second domain, *conservation*, involves 'under-stand[ing] the historical context of the field – how and when important ideas, questions, perspectives, and controversies arose or fell (or were overturned) [in order to] grasp the span and sweep of the field and locate themselves and their work in the disciplinary landscape' (p. 10). Third is *transformation*, where the emphasis is on communicating the field to a range of audiences.

Of stewardship's three domains – generation, conservation and transformation – it may already be the case that the field of academic development is alert on each of these fronts, but these are worth revisiting, considering the challenges in being a newcomer. In relation to *generation* (domain one), academic developers have been producing quality and useful research for some time, and similar to many professional fields, are active in arguing for an evidence-based approach to educational decision-making in universities. What is perhaps harder to grasp given the diversity of pathways to the work and the variation within and across institutional contexts, are the practices and mechanisms academic developers employ to explicitly teach its newcomers about the assortment of research conversations in the field. Across national contexts, the strategies are likely to be uneven. For instance, in South Africa there is a noticeably strong commitment to growing doctoral study in the field of academic development, which is not really replicated elsewhere as an overt strategy.

In the second domain of *conservation*, it is clearly the case that the field of academic development has seen quite specific theoretical frameworks about teaching and learning rise, flourish and fall over its short history. In this volume, Ashwin points to the utility of 'student approaches to learning' for informing approaches to academic development as well as the critiques levelled at it from various scholars (Haggis 2003). Yet it is important for a novice to appreciate not only that the ideas which underpin academic development are iterative and expand conceptually (e.g., witness the shifts in focus from teaching tips, to teaching conceptions, to teaching design, to socio-cultural understandings of learning and teaching), they should aim to do so with the knowledge and humility that they enter an existing scholarly conversation about academic development at a particular point in its history. For us, a curiosity that asks 'why does academic development look like this *now*?' is one that ought to be cultivated. While new paradigms and institutional concerns will inevitably emerge to supplant previous hegemonies (e.g., the rise of big data, analytics and the learning sciences is the current preoccupation), each development builds on what has gone before. Accounts of those specific intellectual and oral histories are starting to litter the field in a range of national locations, and it is this kind of attitude to conservation that the focus on stewardship is seeking to encourage. In any other discipline or professional field, a critical disposition to the narratives of the field is likely to be par for the course.

Finally, the third domain of stewardship focuses on *transformation*. The field of academic development has been active too in translation and communication advocating on behalf of students, and making both conceptual and evidence-based arguments to communities of university teachers, university leaders, and sector policy makers. And across the globe scene via national and international professional development networks such as the Staff and Education Development Association (SEDA) in the UK, Chinese Higher Education Development network (CHED), Higher Education Learning and Teaching Association in South Africa (HELTASA), the Professional and Organisational Development (POD) network in the US, the Higher Education and Research Development Society Australasia (HERDSA), and the Society for Teaching and Learning in Higher Education (STLHE) in Canada (to name only a handful), the field of academic development can lay claim to *transformational* commitment that focuses on the systematic study of student learning as its raison d'etre. The peak international body for the field is the International Consortium of Educational Development (ICED) and its formation and mission is in large part consistent with the notion of stewardship – enacting a moral duty to care for the professional community. Yet despite being able to show that there are already aspects of stewardship apparent in the field of academic development, our experience teaches us that practices of stewardship are difficult to discern at the micro-culture level – within the actual spaces and locations where newcomers toil and get their first taste of the work.

Stewardship offers a narrative of intention or a philosophy that guides the practices of induction for new academic developers. In helping newcomers come to grips with the work, there may well be a temptation to foreground tasks or what it is institutions want. And while these are laudable aims, on their own they are unlikely to lead to an understanding of the field informed by stewardship. At the micro-culture level, there is a case for encouraging slow, careful, and more deliberative academic development practices designed to induct newcomers to the field. And there is potential for these to be guided by the intention of stewardship. Many practices are deceptively simple: purposeful reading together where the commitment is to understand the field, collective conversations designed to unpack dominant ideas, or developing a shared programme of scholarship designed to break the routines of ordinary habit. Under the conditions of fast capitalism, being in academic development can generate all sorts of anxiety about not doing enough and never being responsive enough. Our view is that practices designed to cultivate stewardship achieve three aims: they help a newcomer navigate the field, they support a micro-culture to hold a mirror up to its practices, and they demand the field take seriously its moral obligation to speak truth to power.

References

Barrow, M., Grant, B. & Brailsford, I. (2010), 'Heroic aspirations: The emergence of academic development in a New Zealand university', *New Zealand Journal of Educational Studies*, vol. 45, no. 1, pp. 33–47.

Baume, D. & Popovic, C. (eds) (2016), *Advancing practice in academic development*, Routledge, London & NY.

Bell, M. (2001), 'Supported reflective practice: A programme of peer observation and feedback for academic teaching development', *International Journal for Academic Development*, vol. 6, no. 1, pp. 29–39.

Boud, D. & Brew, A. (2013), 'Reconceptualising academic work as professional practice: Implications for academic development', *International Journal for Academic Development*, vol. 18, no. 3, pp. 208–21.

Boughey, C. (2007), 'Educational development in South Africa: From social reproduction to capitalist expansion', *Higher Education Policy*, vol. 20, no. 5, pp. 5–18.

Boughey, C. & Niven, P. (2012), 'The importance of research in the South African academic development movement', *Higher Education Research and Development*, vol. 31, no. 5, pp. 641–53.

Boyer, E. (1990), *Scholarship reconsidered: Priorities of the professoriate*, Carnegie Foundation for the Advancement of Teaching, Princeton, NJ.

Bozalek, V. G., McMillan, W., Marshall, D. E., Melvyn, N., Daniels, A. & Sylvester, T. (2014), 'Analysing the professional development of teaching and learning from a political ethics of care perspective', *Teaching in Higher Education*, Vol. 19, no. 5, pp. 447–58.

Brew, A. (2002), 'Research and the academic developer: A new agenda', *International Journal for Academic Development*, vol. 7, no. 2, pp. 112–22.

Clegg, S. (2009a), 'Forms of knowing and academic development practice', *Studies in Higher Education*, vol. 34, no. 4, pp. 403–16.

Clegg, S. (2009b), 'Histories and institutional change: Understanding academic development practices in the global "north" and "south"', *International Studies in Sociology of Education*, vol. 19, no. 1, pp. 53–65.

Di Napoli, R. (2014), 'Value gaming and political ontology: Between resistance and compliance in academic development', *International Journal for Academic Development*, vol. 19, no. 1, pp. 4–11.

Fraser, K. (2001), 'Australasian academic developers' conceptions of the profession', *International Journal for Academic Development*, vol. 6, no. 1, pp. 54–64.

Fraser, K., Gosling, D. & Sorcinelli, M. D. (2010), 'Conceptualizing evolving models of educational development', *New Directions in Teaching and Learning*, vol. 122, pp. 49–58.

Gasevic, D., Dawson, S., Mirriahi, N. & Long P. D. (2015), 'Learning analytics – a growing field and community engagement', *Journal of Learning Analytics*, vol. 2, no. 1, pp. 1–6.

Gherardi, S. (2000), 'Practice-based theorizing on learning and knowing in organisations', *Organization*, vol. 7, no. 2, pp. 211–23.

Gibbs, G . (2013), 'Reflections on the changing nature of educational development', *International Journal for Academic Development*, vol. 18, no. 1, pp. 4–14.

Golde, C. M. (2006), 'Preparing stewards of the discipline', in C. M. Golde & G. Walker (eds), *Envisioning the future of doctoral education: Preparing stewards of the discipline – Carnegie essays in the doctorate*, Jossey Bass, San Francisco.

Golde, C. M. & Walker, G. (eds) (2006), *Envisioning the future of doctoral education: Preparing stewards of the discipline – Carnegie essays in the doctorate*, Jossey Bass, San Francisco.

Grant, B. M. (2007), 'The mourning after: Academic development in a time of doubt', *International Journal for Academic Development*, vol. 12, no. 1, pp. 35–43.

Haggis, T. (2003), 'Constructing images of ourselves? A critical investigation into "approaches to learning" research in higher education', *British Education Research Journal*, vol. 29, no. 1, pp. 89–104.

Hicks, O. (1997), 'Career paths of directors of academic staff development units in Australian universities: The emergence of a species?', *International Journal for Academic Development*, vol. 2, no. 2, pp. 56–63.

Hopwood, N. (2014), 'Four essential dimensions of workplace learning', *Journal of Workplace Learning*, vol. 26, no. 6/7, pp. 349–63.

Kandlbinder, P. (2013), 'Signature concepts of key researchers in higher education teaching and learning', *Teaching in Higher Education*, vol. 18, no. 1, pp. 1–12.

Kandlbinder, P. (2014), 'Signature concepts of women researchers in higher education teaching and learning', *Studies in Higher Education*, vol. 39, no. 9, pp. 1562–72.

Kandlbinder, P. & Peseta, T. (2009), 'Key concepts in postgraduate certificates in higher education in Australasia and the United Kingdom', *International Journal for Academic Development*, vol. 14, no. 1, pp. 19–31.

Kandlbinder, P. & Peseta, T. (2011), *Higher education research & development anthology*, HERDSA, Milperra, NSW.

Kensington-Miller, B., Brailsford, I. & Gossman, P. (2012), 'Developing new academic developers: Doing before being?', *International Journal for Academic Development*, vol. 17, no. 2, pp. 121–33.

Kreber, C. & Brook, P. (2001), 'Impact evaluation of educational development programmes', *International Journal for Academic Development*, vol. 6, no. 2, pp. 96–108.

Land, R. (2001), 'Agency, context and change in academic development', *International Journal for Academic Development*, vol. 6, no. 1, pp. 4–20.

Lee, A., Manathunga, C. & Kandlbinder, P. (2008), *Making a place: An oral history of academic development in Australia*, HERDSA, Milperra, NSW.

Lee, A. & McWilliam, E. (2008), 'What game are we living in? Living with academic development', *International Journal for Academic Development*, vol. 13, no. 1, pp. 67–77.

McDonald, J. & Stockley, D. (2008), 'Pathways to the profession of educational development: An international perspective', *International Journal for Academic Development*, vol. 13, no. 3, pp. 213–18.

Manathunga, C. (2006), 'Doing educational development ambivalently: Applying postcolonial metaphors to educational development?', *International Journal for Academic Development*, vol. 11, no. 1, pp. 19–29.

Manathunga, C. (2011), 'The field of educational development: Histories and critical questions', *Studies in Continuing Education*, vol. 33, no. 3, pp. 347–62.

Percy, A. (2014), 'Reintegrating academic development and academic language and learning: A call to reason', *Higher Education Research and Development*, vol. 33, no. 6, pp. 1194–207.

Perkins, D. (1997), 'Epistemic games', *International Journal of Educational Research*, vol. 27, no. 1, pp. 49–61.

Peseta, T. L. (2005), *Learning and becoming in academic development: An autoethnographic inquiry*, unpublished PhD thesis, the University of Sydney.

Peseta, T. L. (2011), 'Professing in the field of academic development: Is content a dirty word?', *International Journal for Academic Development*, vol. 16, no. 1, pp. 83–86.

Peseta, T. L. (2012), *Academic development and its fidelity to student learning: Problems and possibilities for renewal*, keynote address at the HELTASA Conference, Stellenbosch University, South Africa, Nov. 28–30.

Peseta, T. L. (2014), 'Agency and stewardship in academic development: The problem of speaking truth to power', *International Journal for Academic Development*, vol. 19, no. 1, pp. 65–69.

Quinn, L. & Vorster, J. (2014), 'Isn't it time to start thinking about "developing" academic developers in a more systematic way?', *International Journal for Academic Development*, vol. 19, no. 3, pp. 255–58.

Quinn, L. & Vorster, J. (2015), 'Towards shaping the field: Theorising the knowledge in a formal course for academic developers', *Higher Education Research and Development*, vol. 34, no. 5, pp. 1031–44.

Reagan, J. A. & Bessemer, K. (2009), 'Using action learning to support doctoral students to develop their teaching practice', *International Journal for Academic Development*, vol. 14, no. 3, pp. 209–20.

Reich, A. & Hager, P. (2014), 'Problematising practice, learning and change: Practice-theory perspectives on professional learning', *Journal of Workplace Learning*, vol. 26, no. 6/7, pp. 418–31.

Roxå, T. & Mårtensson, K. (2015), 'Microcultures and informal learning: A heuristic guiding analysis of conditions for informal learning in local higher education workplaces', *International Journal for Academic Development*, vol. 20, no. 2, pp. 193–205.

Schreurs, M. L., Roebertsen, H. & Bouhuijs, P. A. J. (1999), 'Leading the horse to the water: Teacher training for all teachers in a faculty of health sciences', *International Journal for Academic Development*, vol. 4, no. 22, pp. 115–23.

Shay, S. (2012), 'Educational development as a field: Are we there yet?', *Higher Education Research and Development*, vol. 31, no. 3, pp. 311–23.

Shore, C. (2010), 'Beyond the multiversity: Neoliberalism and the rise of the schizophrenic university', *Social Anthropology*, vol. 18, no. 1, pp. 15–29.

Sorcinelli, M. D., Austin, A., Eddy, P. L. & Beach, A. L. (2006), *Creating the future of faculty development: Learning from the past, understanding the present*, Anker, Bolton, MA.

Sutherland, K. & Grant, B. (2016), 'Researching academic development', in D. Baume & C. Popovic (eds), *Advancing practice in academic development*, Routledge, London & NY.

Sword, H. (2008), 'The longitudinal archive', *International Journal for Academic Development*, vol. 13, no. 2, pp. 87–96.

Chapter 8

Cultural-historical approaches to teaching and learning in higher education

Teaching to support student agency

Anne Edwards

Introduction

Being a university student, at whatever age and whether full or part-time, is very rarely an end in itself. It is a period of transitions, into the degree programme and out from it, usually into a workplace. It is a period of potential formation and transformation: recognising fresh possibilities; adapting identities; testing new ideas; making mistakes; and learning. All of these aspects of student life involve being active, interpreting opportunities and demands and responding to them, so that the person who leaves the programme has developed, to be in some way different from the person who entered it. In this chapter the theoretical resources I draw on are cultural-historical ideas on human learning and development in order to bring together the notion of active and agentic learners, involved in transitions as they make sense of the practices in higher education and prepare themselves for the practices of workplaces, with the implications of these moves for those who teach and guide them as learners. The discussions that follow reflect the approach to practice presented by Boud and Brew (Chapter 5), but their origins in cultural-historical theory mean that they focus particularly on the dynamic of agency and demand, as learners navigate different practices. My starting point, therefore, is that the aim of university teaching is to create agentic and critically self-regulating students who are able to take themselves forward as enquiring learners, both during the programme and after they have graduated. This holds true whether students are preparing themselves directly for professions such as medicine, social work or teaching, or are gearing up for further study. While in university they need to gain expertise in the knowledge practices of the disciplines they encounter, in doing so they learn to grasp and deploy key concepts while using the ways of testing and representing, which are valued in these disciplines and linked professions.

We should not, therefore, underestimate the demands that the aim of supporting informed and agentic lifelong learners makes on university teachers. First, each student is different, so each will create a different learning trajectory and, without expert guidance, some may be unable to overcome hurdles or may get distracted. Second, despite this sense of responsibility to students, nurturing agency in learners involves letting go: losing control while ensuring that the curriculum can be accessed and assessment criteria are met. Letting go, of course, does not mean walking away, but entails the kind of reciprocity that encourages the exercise of student agency as they begin to interpret, navigate and master the knowledge practices, including testing claims to knowledge, which mark the fields they are entering.

I suspect it would be difficult to disagree with most of the truisms outlined so far. But, in order to inform developments in how students are supported as learners, we need to move from these everyday understandings to conceptualise them, so that ideas can be taken away, tested and fashioned to suit local conditions without losing their essence. This is where theory becomes a tool for thinking and planning. The theoretical foundations of this chapter are in the work of Vygotsky and draw on developments of his cultural-historical analyses by those interested in learning, agency, practices, motives, identity and transitions. Because cultural-historical accounts of learning are premised in a dialectic of person and practice, there is a dual focus, on students and the demands their learning makes on teachers, and the demands teachers make on students. Having outlined what a cultural-historical approach to learning means for teaching, the chapter concludes with a practical resource aimed at helping university teachers to develop the reciprocity that encourages student agency and learning.

Cultural-historical approaches to learning

As I have already begun to indicate, Vygotsky's Marxist psychology meant that his approach to learning and development recognised that learning happens through a continuous dynamic between person and practice; we are shaped by the practices we inhabit, but we also shape them as we act in them. This dialectic of person and practice, and its relationship with learning, is described by Vygotsky as a process of both internalisation and externalisation, taking in new ideas and testing and using them in actions in activities (Vygotsky 1998). Consequently, university teaching is not a homogeneous practice, with techniques that apply uniformly across disciplines and professions. Rather it is both a position within a practice of, for example, mathematics or nursing and a specialist practice, for example, university teaching of mathematics or nursing. This nested position of the practice of teaching, within a disciplinary or professional practice, is important because teaching involves helping learners to both act in and act on the practices in which they are developing expertise as mathematicians or nurses.

Another key feature, found in Vygotsky's writing on child development, is that there is a qualitative difference between learning and development. Learning involves grasping and employing new concepts, which add to one's understanding of a phenomenon; while development involves a more profound repositioning within a practice and is the outcome of several, or even many, new understandings. This distinction is relevant when considering how learners move between practices, where new demands are made on them (Hedegaard 2012), requiring them to learn quickly if they are to position themselves comfortably in the new practice; but the distinction also points to how the student-teacher relationship may change, quite profoundly, over time as students' expertise in a practice grows.

These shifts over time were made clear in an Oxford masters' thesis which examined changes in the relationships between students and their supervisors over the course of a DPhil in education (Wagstaff 2009). In her observations of supervision sessions, Wagstaff found that in the first year of a study, supervisors focused on creating common knowledge of the problem to be researched, encouraging students to bring their own knowledge to defining the purpose of the study, while also introducing other ideas from the discipline and explaining the demands of a DPhil. By the final year of study, supervisors and students were relationally engaged in joint problem-solving as they worked on analyses and interpretations of findings, jointly constructing new understandings of phenomena. The positioning of supervisor and student therefore changed as the student became more expert in the practice of research within the discipline and able to act on, as well as in, its knowledge practices.

Unpacking Vygotsky's dialectical approach to learning therefore takes us straight to the agency of the learner, the demands in practices and how students interpret and respond to those demands to propel themselves forward, as they engage in and with the knowledge practices of the field. Let us therefore look at each of these three aspects in turn; while considering the implications for those who are supporting them as learners.

Agency

Vygotsky, writing in Russia in the 1920s and early 30s, did not, to my knowledge, use any equivalent of the term 'agency'. But he paid great attention to building the capacity to work conceptually, using powerful and culturally valued ideas as tools, rather than working with everyday context-bound understandings. Working conceptually particularly involved what he termed 'higher order thinking', a form of self-regulation that enabled people to organise and deploy these conceptual tools to take forward their intentions (Vygotsky 1998). Stetsenko and Arievitch have recently captured the dialectical aspects of this argument in a way that is relevant for recognising higher education as a period of potential self-transformation: '[with these conceptual tools], ... people not only transform and create their environment; they also transform and create their lives, consequently changing themselves in fundamental ways and, in the process, gaining self-knowledge' (Stetsenko & Arievitch 2004, pp. 482–83).

This notion of agentic and self-transforming action on the world also, I suggest, involves the sense of responsibility, which was captured by Taylor in his 1977 definition of an agent: 'We think of the agent as not only partly responsible for what he does, for the degree to which he acts in line with those evaluations, but also as responsible in some sense for those evaluations' (Taylor 1977, p. 118).

Again we return to teaching as enabling learners to take increasing responsibility for their interpretations of demands and responses to them.

These two attempts at describing agency, the first avowedly cultural-historical and the second with similar philosophical roots, bring together agency and intentional action within activities in ways that are crucial to enabling students to create transformational learning trajectories. This view is explained in cultural-historical terms by Roth who has pointed to how agency unfolds in the acts that comprise the actions taken in activities which are themselves located within institutional practices (Roth 2006). This linking of actions, activities and institutional practices is central to how teachers design learning environments, which reflect the demands to be found in the practices of the discipline or area, and how they work pedagogically within them.

Demands in practices

From a cultural-historical perspective, practices are inhabited, consist of activities and constitute institutions such as university departments or workplaces, which are themselves located in wider policy environments with their own practices and cultural values. Practices, such as mechanical engineering or social work, carry histories, values and purposes; are emotionally freighted and therefore contribute to the formation of identity (Edwards 2010). And, as I have already indicated, they are shaped and reshaped by the people who act in them

Practices therefore make demands on those who engage with them, expecting specific ways of thinking and behaving. In universities demands in knowledge practices will include following reporting conventions and using the ways of evaluating and arguing that are valued in a subject discourse such as engineering; alongside behaviours such as honouring project hand-in times and doing the pre-reading for classes, which are part of general student practice. Of course, to be able to respond to the demands, students need first to recognise them and then believe that they can respond. Recognising and responding agentically to these kinds of demands is easier for students who have prior experience of something similar. Very different dialectics, with different learning outcomes, arise when students either do not recognise the demands, or recognise them but find them overwhelming and exercise their agency through working around them and not engaging with them. The implications for teachers are not only that they should make the demands clear to everyone, but they should also be equally clear about the resources available to help meet the demands and ensure equal access to them. Again these implications need to inform the design of learning environments, as well as the interactions within them.

Propelling oneself forward as a learner

The design of learning environments is perhaps most evident when considering the activities that comprise a course of study. Student agency and the demands in knowledge practices are brought together in these activities, and in the pedagogies through which they are implemented. When writing about young children as learners, Vygotsky used the idea of the social situation of development (Vygotsky 1998). By this he did not mean a benign configuration of people from whom one might learn. Instead, he saw it as a dialectical relationship between a person and the social conditions in which they acted and, through their actions, created themselves.

A social situation of development in this sense is always potential; it only arises when a learner is active, recognises and responds to the demands she or he encounters in a practice and is learning. In addressing the demands, she or he learns and moves forward towards being repositioned in a practice, in the way that the DPhil students in Wagstaff's study did in the practice of educational research. This repositioning involves seeing the familiar in fresh ways, informed by newly acquired conceptual insights, making new connections and being able to see new possibilities for action. The crucial point here is that the learner creates the social situation of development. Not recognising or avoiding demands means that the learning expected in a course of study does not occur and there is therefore no development, or self-transformation, in relation to the knowledge practices of the subject or profession.

A cultural-historical reading of practices recognises their nested nature. A practice, such as teaching social work in higher education, is located in and informed by the practice of social work and at the same time is located in university institutional practices, such as quality assurance regimes, which are in turn located in and informed by wider societal practices. Leont'ev, a close colleague of Vygotsky in Moscow in the late 1920s, summarised the iterative relationship of person and societal conditions as follows: '... society produces the activity of the individuals forming it' (Leont'ev 1978, p. 7). Human agency is therefore evidenced in our ability to work on and change the conditions in which we act. Where students and teachers can be agentic, practices are not necessarily static but can be responsive and emergent, as fresh demands are recognised, new knowledge brought into play and values and motives questioned and reconfigured in the person-practice dialectic. We shall return to this point in the final section of this chapter when a resource for reflecting on pedagogy is introduced.

Students' motives

Motive is a concept which has so often been worryingly over-simplified in texts on learning, in particular the intertwining of motive, agency, identity and practice is not always recognised. A cultural-historical account of motive, drawing on ideas developed by Leont'ev in his work on activity theory, offers a way of bringing these four components together. Doing so helps to identify the careful calibrations of support and demand that mark responsive teaching for student agency, as learners navigate the demands of university and shape their identities.

The terminology Leont'ev used when discussing motive, 'object of activity' and 'object motive', were key to his efforts to overcome what he saw as weaknesses in a psychology that separated personal motives and societal conditions. This separation was a problem for him because of his iterative view of person and societal conditions or practices. He argued that that the dialectic of person, in activity, in a practice, in society, gives rise to the object motive, which in turn directs the participation of an actor in an activity. He explained the overlapping and interconnected relationship of the object motive and object of activity, as follows: 'The main thing that distinguishes one activity from another, however, is the difference in their objects. It is exactly the object of activity that gives it a determined direction. According to the terminology I have proposed, the object of activity is its true motive' (Leont'ev 1978, p. 17).

This rather opaque explanation needs unpacking. First, objects of activity, such as a problem to be worked on, cannot be regarded as a given; students, and their teachers, may interpret it in different ways and so respond to different aspects of the problem by drawing on what they recognise and regard as important. Engeström, in his contribution to the development of activity theory, has usefully described the object of activity as the problem space at which the participants in an activity system are directing their energy (see Engeström (2015) for his explanation of activity theory). In higher education, an activity system may be a class or a course. In a university class, the object of activity could be a mathematics problem, or a piece of text, a case study and so on. In this chapter I am not drawing extensively on Engeström's ground-breaking work on collective activity systems, as my focus is on how the learning student is supported rather than how the learning system changes, and I am therefore closer to Leont'ev's concern with the person in practice than Engeström's focus on systemic change.

Nonetheless, Leont'ev's explanation of object motive does take us to the practices that students are entering, by raising the question of how students are helped to recognise the object of activity as it is understood in those practices. For example, how do students learn to interpret a poem in ways that are valued within the knowledge practices of literary criticism, or interpret a case study according the professional expectations of social work?

In crude summary, as learners approach an object of activity, such as a case study, they will project onto it what matters for them, which is what Leont'ev meant by object motive. The object motive, what matters, gives direction to how the task is tackled and therefore what the activity becomes for them. What matters may be completing the task rapidly to free up time for other activities, or accomplishing it quickly to show how clever they are. Or it may be that what matters is connecting one's own experience, for example poverty, with features of the case study. More complex object motives, might involve hiding one's lack of understanding, or avoiding discussion because the case invokes traumatic memories. But each personal object motive will mean that one task may become several very different activities within the one group of students.

This variation is not necessarily problematic; it has already been argued that learners create their own learning trajectories. But it may be detrimental if the variation includes students' object motives which prevent engagement with the knowledge practices represented in the course and presented in the demands of the task. There is now a great deal of research on motivation which shows that learners approach demands if they believe that their actions will be effective (Elliot & Dweck 2005). Again, we return to how learning environments are designed so that the route to accomplishing a task is demystified and that access to useful resources, including digital, is equally distributed.

Students' identities and transitions

Successful task accomplishment and the feedback it receives is where motivation and identity can connect. Holland's anthropological work on agency, identity and practices combines the person-practice dynamic, which is so central to cultural-historical approaches, with the reciprocity and importance of feedback, which marks the approach to identity taken by G. H. Mead. Much of Holland's focus has been on what she terms 'the authoring self' (Holland et al. 1998, p. 169), who creates an identity as she or he interprets, navigates and works in and on practices. The examples the team draw on in their 1998 book include identities shaped by developing expertise in the practice of 'romance' in 'Southern University' in the US, and how members of Alcoholics Anonymous (AA) created a practice of not drinking, in which they became expert.

In these discussions Holland and her colleagues usefully describe social settings, such as AA, as 'figured worlds' of practices, which may be interpreted and acted in with growing expertise to allow particular forms of the authored self to emerge. The influence of Mead is found in the focus on how feedback informs identities; while the dialectic that Vygotsky brings to their work on identity, is seen in their interest in '... co-development – the linked development of people, cultural forms, and social positions in particular historical worlds' (Holland et al. 1998, p. 33).

Holland's work is an important contribution because her anthropological methods allow a detailed tracking of actions in activities in the figured worlds of practices, to reveal how demands in these figured worlds are met or avoided in ways that contribute to self-authoring. Though she does not talk of object motive in Leont'ev's sense, her attention to actors' developing expertise as they take forward what matters for them in the student practices of a southern US university has strong resonance with object motive. We can see in her work how, for example, demands identified by the successful practitioners of romance call forth their responses as flirtatious young women and, over time, help them become more expert and repositioned in the practice of romance.

These ideas are highly relevant for examining the student self-transformations that can happen at university. In one DPhil study, Francis showed how masters degree students used net-based affinity groups to create and test identities, which they then used in face-to-face interactions in the university. He drew on Holland's studies to reveal just how much identity work can occur when students encounter new practices and have the freedom to experiment (Francis 2010, 2013). In another DPhil study, Lundsteen used the ideas as a framework for examining how student interns in an investment bank interpreted and navigated the practices of the trading floor to create identities which meant they would be offered positions on graduation (Lundsteen 2011, Lundsteen & Edwards 2013). In another Oxford DPhil, Banda drew on Holland's work with Lave on 'history in person' (Holland & Lave 2001) to examine the impact of short management courses on participants' identities and to observe how the reciprocal relationships that sustained their former identities in the workplace, remained unchanged after the course ended (Banda 2011). Her conclusions questioned the value of courses which aimed only at empowering individuals. All three of these studies focused, as did Holland's work, on the trajectories of individuals as they made sense of and acted in practices.

Others working with cultural-historical ideas have attended more specifically to transitions, how people move between practices, negotiate and act in them (Dreier 1999, Hedegaard & Edwards 2014) and the identity changes that can arise when entering new practices (Beach 1999). Like Holland, these authors recognised the mutually constitutive nature of the relationship between person and practice. But Beach's work most directly relates to the focus on self-authoring, which is so relevant to the transitions that occur as learners move in and out of university.

Beach's main argument was that transfer is an inadequate metaphor for understanding how people enter new settings and use the knowledge they have brought with them. Instead, he discussed transitions between practices with a particular focus on the identity shifts that occur when people operate in different practices. His key idea was 'consequential transitions', arguing that transitions are of consequence to the actor when there is: 'a developmental change in the relation between an individual and one or more social activities ... Transitions are consequential when they are consciously reflected on, often struggled with, and the eventual outcome changes one's sense of self and social positioning' (Beach 1999, p. 114). His are rich arguments and, although based in transitions between schools and workplaces, his reminder that these developmental changes involve personal struggles is helpful for university teachers too.

A consequential transition may involve repositioning oneself in a practice, such as becoming a competent researcher after previously only reading research studies. But they can also apply to movements between practices, such as entry to university or the workplace. One feature in Beach's analysis is the idea of 'developmental coupling', which 'encompasses aspects of both changing individuals and changing social activity' (Beach 1999, p. 120). Here, Beach drew on Leont'ev to explain how these developmental couplings are also located in the broader themes of cultural conditions. His conclusion was that we should make formal educational settings less boundaried and therefore easier for students to make transitions in and out.

The implications of this suggestion for higher education are perhaps seen most clearly in provision that aims at easing entry into universities for students from backgrounds where experience of higher education is limited; and in courses which involve work placements. Gutierrez's cultural-historical-based work on remediating the university, through student engagement with sociocritical literacies, shows how the practices of higher education can be demystified (Gutierrez et al. 2009). Work in the discursive space that is created prepares students for the practices of higher education and allows them to see themselves as informed participants.

Work placements within courses for professional preparation present different problems. They usually require students to make transitions and negotiate work practices without the direct help of university staff. While few course designers think students will simply transfer and apply ideas encountered in university in the workplace, there is perhaps too little attention to the nature of the transitions that students make as they move to placements and from placement to placement (Edwards in press). In a current DPhil study, Tan has followed four student teachers on a one-year post-graduate training programme as they each were placed in two different schools for practical experience. One striking and unexpected finding is how difficult the transition from the first to the second school placement was for the students. This was true of students who had successfully negotiated identities as beginning teachers in the first school as well as those who had not (Tan in progress). These studies call for attention to the identity aspects of transitions and the work of both Holland and Beach is particularly helpful in clarifying the challenges.

All of the research mentioned so far has focused on cultural-historical analyses of how students act in and on practices. But because of the dialectical nature of learning, it points to what university teachers may need to do to create and sustain conditions which are conducive to the productive self-authoring of students and their repositioning in practices. At the same time these analyses recognise the cultural conditions of university teaching, such as constraints of uniform quality assurance regimes and the different expectations of professional associations and learned societies. So let us turn our attention to how university teachers create the conditions for student transformations within the knowledge practices of a discipline or area.

Enabling student agency while teaching

I have emphasised knowledge practices, the ways of reasoning and representing that are valued in specific domains, but am not suggesting that these practices are static. They are open to scrutiny and to shifts as people act in and on them, bringing different prior experiences and using new technologies. I have therefore argued that university teachers are best seen as located within these knowledge practices, working in and on them, alongside students helping them recognise and respond to objects of activity. Vygotsky consistently suggested that the function of the teacher is to organise and be part of the social environment so that learners might create relationships with the environment, which are conducive to their learning (Vygotsky 1997). This view of teaching is entirely consistent with the idea that the social situation of development is created by learners who recognise and respond to demands; while the role of the teacher is to help learners to interpret and tackle these demands. Vygotsky, in his advice to beginning school-teachers, warned against a view of teacher as direct instructor (Vygotsky 1997). Instead, he suggested that teachers should create learning environments in which they act as resources for learners, increasing the demands on them as they move forward.

Elsewhere I have discussed these ideas in relation to a teaching-learning sequence, which shows a shift in agency from teacher to learner (Edwards 2014). If these shifts are to represent increasing expertise in a domain, whether mathematics or social work, Leont'ev's ideas on object of activity and object motive alert us to (i) how learning environments need to be resourced to enable students' engagement with what matters in the domain; and (ii) feedback needs to focus on the expertise needed to work within its knowledge practices. Consequently, the design of learning environments needs to identify what is being navigated by the students as they enter practices, for example, institutional expectations, resources to support actions and ways of reasoning and representing, and to make these demands and resources explicit for students. In addition, the design needs to be sensitive to how students are navigating these figured worlds, by revealing, for example, students' intentions, the personal resources they bring and their interpretations of the demands.

Derry's analyses of the pedagogic implications of Vygotsky's work help us address these challenges. A philosopher within the cultural-historical field, Derry has reflected on how students' experience is recognised and brought into play in pedagogic interactions, so that their understandings can be worked with and their learning supported. Influenced by the work of Dunne on the 'rough ground' of experience (Dunne 1993), Derry has argued that the conceptual potential of the unarticulated experience that students bring to formal learning situations has often been overlooked in educational policies. 'There may be a domain of knowing which is nuanced and not consciously acted on, but which is nevertheless rich in conceptual content, and is often ignored by policy makers to the detriment of their intended aims and outcomes' (Derry 2000, p. 154).

I would suggest that this underplaying of the knowledge, which is latent in student experience, can also be true of university teaching. The challenge is to connect these domains of everyday knowing with the powerful and publicly validated concepts that make up a discipline or profession, in ways that nurture students' agentic control over their own learning trajectories. Derry's response to the gap she identified was to turn to Sellars (1956), McDowell (1996) and Brandom (2000) (Derry 2000, 2008) to argue for learning environments in which everyday understandings can be referenced to robust concepts in the 'space of reasons'. Talking of learning as building strong systems of interconnected concepts, she suggests that pedagogies, where it is legitimate to ask for and give reasons, allow students to connect their everyday understandings, based in experience, with the powerful concepts that enable expert engagement in a domain. She explains as follows:

> Brandom's careful study of concept use argues that concepts by their nature are not isolated from one another; to have conceptual content is just for it [a concept] to play a role in the inferential game of making claims and giving and asking for reasons. To grasp or understand such a concept is to have practical mastery over the inferences it is involved in – to know, in the practical sense of being able to distinguish, what follows from the applicability of a concept, and what it follows from.
>
> (Derry 2008, p. 17)

The 'space of reasons' in this sense, is premised in the Vygotskian view that teachers work in practices alongside students, monitoring, offering resources and increasing demands. But it also points to the need to elicit and work with students' prior experience and to encourage, and respond to, students' questions, as much as one might expect students to respond to teachers' questions. In summary, to enable students to connect agentically with the knowledge practices embedded in a course, teachers need to position themselves as expert participants in the knowledge practices of the area. Their role there is to assist students in recognising and engaging with these practices.

This is not an argument against presenting key ideas in lectures; Vygotsky was clear that learners need to become familiar with the language that carries concepts before they can manipulate the ideas themselves. But it is an argument for taking seriously what students bring to learning encounters and for demystifying the practices they enter as novices so that they can work with the ideas as they learn to connect their private sense-making with publicly powerful knowledge.

Learning how to work with student agency

The arguments in this chapter are not intended as points for reflection only in induction programmes for teachers who are new to working in higher education. The kinds of demands the arguments make on university teachers call for strong knowledge of the area covered in a course, the capacity to elicit and work with what matters for students, when also helping them to progress within a domain. While many novice teachers can manage to do this, these are also relevant points for reflection for more experienced colleagues. This may be particularly so when working with students who come from backgrounds where higher education is not the norm, or who are studying part-time and dealing with complex sets of transitions and identity shifts.

With the editors of this volume I am involved in a project, funded by the South African National Research Foundation (NRF), aimed at developing participatory parity for students across a wide range of professions and in very different South African universities. For the study I have developed a simple resource to help the kind of reflection called for by a cultural-historical approach to student agency. Ethical approval for the study has been gained from each participating university.

There are two versions of the resource: Table 8.1 is for teachers and Table 8.2 is for students. In the study we have not been prescriptive about how frequently these two reflective templates are used, how they are adapted to specific groups and courses, or about the extent that the reflections in them are shared between teachers and students. The template has a history of adaptation. The 8.1 version was first used with senior leaders in children's services in England, to help them focus on how they worked pedagogically as leaders, and has subsequently been developed to work with other professional groups to take forward their reflective conceptualisations of their own work (Edwards 2015).

Its adaptability arises from the strong theoretical framing that underlies it, as all versions of the template are based on the cultural-historical ideas discussed here. The starting point in Table 8.1 is an activity where a teacher is attempting to help students develop as confident learners. The term 'confident' is used rather than agentic, as confidence is one way of describing informed navigation of the figured world of the course. Once an activity has been selected and outlined briefly, the teacher lists the actions they took in the activity, then reflects on how their actions related to their aims or intentions for the activity. In the present NRF study, teachers' intentions include taking seriously what the students bring to the potential learning encounter. Finally, the teachers' attention is taken to the conditions they have created for student learning and how those might be adjusted to help build a stronger link between their own actions and intentions, and ultimately to identify whether institutional expectations are inhibiting their preferred pedagogy with these students. In this way teachers can gather evidence to inform how they adjust their design of the learning environment. The evidence can also be used to support arguments for institutional changes, such as access to resources, the length of sessions, the types of collaboration with work placements and so on.

In Table 8.2 we see a similar process of questioning for individual students. The intention here is twofold. First, students come to articulate what they are bringing from the rough ground of experience to interactions in formal university settings. Second, if they share these reflections with their teachers, how much or how little they have brought to the activity is likely to provoke further reflections on pedagogy on the part of the teachers.

The overarching aim of both templates is to make explicit both elements in the learning dialectic: (i) teachers' actions in the activities, which constitute the learning environment she or he has designed; and (ii) the possibilities for connecting student experience with course demands to harness their agency as learners and enable them to position themselves as active agents in a knowledge practice such as social work.

Table 8.1 A reflective template for teachers

ACTIVITY: Very briefly describe one everyday activity in the last week where you were working with students to help them develop as confident learners.

ACTIONS: What did you do during the activity (i.e. what actions did you take)? (For example, explained the purpose of the session, listened to how they were interpreting and understanding the task, walked around the pairs as they reflected on their work placements, gave 1:1 feedback on XX, etc.). You can mention as many actions as you like.

AIMS: What are the long-term goals behind how you worked with the students? How do your actions in this activity relate to these goals?

CONTEXT: What, if anything, would help you to take forward your aims with the students? What institutional changes would you like to see?

Table 8.2 A reflective template for students

ACTIVITY: Very briefly describe one activity in the last week where you felt effective as a learner.

ACTIONS: What did you do during the activity i.e. what actions did you take? (e.g. explained how I did xxx to two other students, recognised the connection between x and y, etc.) You can mention as many actions as you like.

ADVANTAGES: What did you bring to the activity? (e.g. I've known about xxx for a long time, I prepared by doing zzz, the topic is important and interests me because … etc.) You can mention as many points as you like.

CONTEXT: What was it about the session that meant you could draw on what you brought to the activity?

Concluding reflections

The view of university teaching presented here pays attention to the knowledge practices of specific domains. It therefore follows the practice turn outlined by Boud and Brew in Chapter 5, but it emphasises, a little more than they have done, that different fields of study will place different demands on students. In pursuing a cultural-historical approach to practice I have particularly argued that the teacher is positioned in the practice alongside students: helping them recognise and approach demands; enabling them to draw on the resources they bring from their own life experiences; and ensuring that they are supported by the resources in the university environment, which will include the teacher.

Where I agree wholeheartedly with Boud and Brew is in their critique of application models of learning, their warning against focusing on the individual, and their recognition of how practice and person are mutually constituting. These implications of the practice turn for university teaching are immense, calling into question homogenising quality assurance systems and demanding indicators, which reflect the reciprocity of pedagogies, which engage directly with different knowledge practices, and which take seriously the nurturing of student agency for critically reflective self-regulating lifelong learning.

References

Banda, B. (2011), 'Connecting management education with the workplace', DPhil thesis, University of Oxford.

Beach, K. (1999), 'Consequential transitions: A sociocultural expedition beyond transfer in education', *Review of Research in Education*, vol. 24, pp. 101–39.

Brandom, R. (2000), *Articulating reasons: An introduction to inferentialism*, Harvard University Press, Cambridge, MA.

Derry, J. (2000), 'Foundationalism and anti-foundationalism: Seeking enchantment in the rough ground', in V. Oittinen (ed.), *Evald Ilyenkov's philosophy revisited*, Kikimora Publications, Helsinki.

Derry, J. (2008), 'Abstract rationality in education: From Vygotsky to Brandom', *Studies in the Philosophy of Education*, vol. 27, pp. 49–62.

Dreier, O. (1999), 'Personal trajectories of participation across contexts of social practice', *Outlines*, vol. 1, no. 1, pp. 5–32.

Dunne, J. (1993), *Back to the rough ground: 'Phronesis' and 'techne' in modern philosophy and in Aristotle*, University of Notre Dame Press, London.

Edwards, A. (2010), *Being an expert professional practitioner: The relational turn in expertise*, Springer, Dordrecht.

Edwards, A. (2014), 'Designing tasks which engage learners with knowledge', in I. Thompson (ed.), *Task design, subject pedagogy and student engagement*, Routledge, London.

Edwards, A. (2015), 'A tool for public services research and development', *International Journal of Public Management*, vol. 11, no. 1, pp. 21–33.

Edwards, A. (in press), 'The dialectic of person and practice: How cultural-historical accounts of agency can inform teacher education', in J. Clandinin & J. Husu (eds), *International handbook of research on teacher education*, Sage, New York.

Engeström, Y. (2015), *Learning by expanding*, 2nd edn, CUP, Cambridge.

Elliot, A. & Dweck, C. (eds) (2005), *Handbook of competence and motivation*, Guilford Press, New York.

Francis, R. (2010), *The decentring of the traditional university: The future of (self) education in virtually figured worlds*, Routledge, London.

Francis, R. (2013), 'The agency of the learner in the networked university: An expansive approach', in G. Wells & A. Edwards (eds), *Pedagogy in higher education: A cultural-historical approach*, Cambridge University Press, Cambridge.

Gutierrez, K., Hunter, J. & Arzubiaga, A. (2009), 'Remediating the university: Learning through sociocultural literacies', *Pedagogies: An International Journal*, vol. 4, no. 1, pp. 1–23.

Hedegaard, M. (2012), 'The dynamic aspects in children's learning and development', in M. Hedegaard, A. Edwards & M. Fleer (eds), *Motives in children's development: Cultural-historical approaches*, Cambridge University Press, Cambridge.

Hedegaard, M. & Edwards, A. (2014), 'Editorial: Transitions and children's learning', *Learning, Culture and Social Interaction*, vol. 3, no. 3, pp. 185–87.

Holland, D., Lachicotte, W., Skinner, D. & Cain, C. (1998), *Identity and agency in cultural worlds*, Harvard University Press, Cambridge, MA.

Holland, D. & Lave, J. (eds) (2001), *History in person: Enduring struggles, contentious practice, intimate identities*, James Currey, Oxford.

Leont'ev, A. N. (1978), 'The problem of activity in psychology', in *Activity, consciousness and personality*, Prentice Hall, Upper Saddle River, NJ, accessed 17 July 2015, http://Marxists.anu.edu.au/archive/leontev/works/1978

Lundsteen, N. (2011), 'Learning between university and the world of work', DPhil thesis, University of Oxford.

Lundsteen, N. & Edwards, A. (2013), 'Internship: Navigating the practices of an investment bank', in G. Wells & A. Edwards (eds), *Pedagogy in higher education: A cultural-historical approach*, Cambridge University Press, Cambridge.

McDowell, J. (1996), *Mind and world*, Harvard University Press, Cambridge, MA.

Roth, M. (2006), 'Agency and passivity: Prolegomenon to scientific literacy as ethico-moral praxis', in A. Rodriguez (ed.), *The multiple faces of agency*, Sense Publishers, Rotterdam, accessed 17th September 2015, http://web.uvic.ca/~stemed/assets/PDF/Roth103.pdf

Sellars, W. (1956), 'Empiricism and the philosophy of mind', in H. Feigl & M. Scriven (eds), *Minnesota studies in the philosophy of science – vol 1. The foundations of science and the concepts of psychology and psychoanalysis*, University of Minnesota Press, Minneapolis, MN.

Stetsenko, A. & Arievitch, I. (2004), 'The self in cultural-historical activity theory', *Theory and Psychology*, vol. 14, no. 4, pp. 475–503.

Tan, D. (in progress) 'Student teachers' learning to teach' (working title), DPhil thesis in progress, University of Oxford Department of Education.

Taylor, C. (1977), 'What is human agency?', in T. Mischel (ed.), *The self*, Blackwell, Oxford.

Vygotsky, L. S. (1997), *Educational psychology*, St Lucie Press, Boca Raton, FL.

Vygotsky L. S. (1998), *The collected works of LS Vygotsky vol. 5, child psychology*, Plenum Press, New York.

Wagstaff, S. (2009), 'Relational agency within dyadic doctoral supervisory relationships', masters thesis, University of Oxford.

Critical and social realism

Critical and social realism as theoretical resources for thinking about professional development and equity

Sue Clegg

Introduction

This chapter sets out some of the key tenets of critical and social realism and indicates why this theoretical framing provides us with resources for thinking about learning to teach and higher education more generally. Most readers will be familiar with simple forms of realism which claim that our ideas about the world refer to a world which exists independently of our constructions of it. For most of the twentieth century the dominant manifestation of this kind of realism was positivism. What distinguishes critical realism is a more sophisticated account about the nature of the social and physical worlds and how we can make knowledge claims about them. Critical realism also stands against forms of irrealism – that is views of the world which deny the possibility of a connection between our thoughts and sense making and the world beyond our constructions of it. Post-structuralism has been the dominant form of irrealism, or idealism, in the second half of the twentieth and into the twenty-first century.

Debates between these traditions matter because they offer different accounts of the status of claims about our objects of enquiry, whether these be teacher learning or the nature and causes of inequality. Different traditions have competing views about whether we can legitimately claim that one account is better than another, the grounds for such judgements, and whether there is something special about scientific (in its broadest sense) knowledge or not. In thinking about the nature of theorising we are making these assumptions explicit and opening them to examination rather than leaving them implicit. As such, all social theory involves some underlying assumptions as well as substantive claims about how things, including people, work or how they are construed. Although we use broad terms like critical realism, poststructuralism, and positivism, different authors within these traditions have varying emphases. As with any other area of social theory, critical realism denotes a theoretical field which operates at different levels of argument and with a number of key theorists, not all of whom agree with one another. There are, however, some core ideas that this chapter will outline in making an argument that critical and social realism offers rich theoretical resources for thinking about professional development and equity which are the core concerns of this book.

Critical realism, or transcendental realism in Roy Bhaskar's (1978, 1979) account, acts as a philosophical under-labourer for substantive social scientific work. It provides a powerful analysis of the inadequacies of both idealism and positivism. In their place it argues for a depth ontology in which the domain of the real encompasses not just experiences (our sensory perceptions of things) and events (actual occurring things) but also underlying mechanisms. These, often non-observable, mechanisms are nonetheless real and Bhaskar argues that it is they that produce the world of events which we come to experience in the here and now. The focus of Bhaskar's work, therefore, is primarily philosophical in clarifying what the world must be like in order for us to make sense of the practice of science. Critical or social realism, however, also offers substantive sociological analyses. Margaret Archer (1995) is the key theorist of a morphogenetic approach to analysing social life. Morphogenetic being literally 'beginning of the shape' from the Greek for shape (morphê) and the genetic referring to how it is formed. This is developed in Archer's work to ground an explanatory methodology:

> The 'morpho' element is an acknowledgement that society has no pre-set form or preferred state: the 'genetic' part is a recognition that it takes its shape from, and is formed by, agents, originating from the intended and unintended consequences of their activities.

In keeping with the rejection of idealism and positivism that underpins all critical realism, Archer develops a critique of their sociological manifestations in the form of downward, upward, and central conflations and argues the need for analytical dualism (Archer 1995).

She argues that structure and agency constitute two linked but irreducible levels of social reality. Such conflations are the result of a failure to understand the dualism that is entailed. Her morphogenetic approach allows for an analysis of structural constraints and enablements and for the emergence of the *sui generis* powers of persons (Archer 2000). The third major theorist I will draw on is Andrew Sayer (2011) who, in keeping with the emancipatory thrust of Bhaskar's early work, makes a powerful case for the normative purposes of theorising. Sayer's (2005, 2011) work combines philosophical elaboration and substantive sociological claims in his defence of a social science that can speak meaningfully to the question of why things matter to people and also, crucially, why things matter to us.

This chapter is structured into main three sections and some concluding remarks. The first section deals with ontological and epistemological questions and indicates some of the methodological implications these have for researching higher education. It also touches on the ways critical realist ideas have been influential in bringing knowledge questions more firmly into focus, especially when combined with the social realist concerns of the sociologist of education

Basil Bernstein (2000). The second section elaborates the substantive sociological work of Margaret Archer (1995, 2000, 2012) and, in particular, pays attention to her work on agency which has proved powerful in thinking about both student and teacher learning and action. Finally, the third section explores the writing of Andrew Sayer (2005, 2011) and considers normativity and the development of legitimate arguments for the recognition of the importance of values in theorising.

The three sections are inter-related and taken together provide an argument for why critical realism is good to think with and, in particular, good for theorising about teaching and the social purposes of higher education. Critical realism does not offer a theory of learning as such, but it does give an account of both what human beings are like and their potentialities. It is these human potentials that underpin learning and, as we can see in the chapters that follow, scholars working within a broadly critical realist paradigm have turned their attention to theorising the specifics of teachers learning to teach and their professional development. Equally significantly, critical and social realism embodies sets of normative concerns that are central to debates about the purposes of higher education. Critical realism connects accounts of the ways things are to claims about why things can and should be different. Critical realism's underlying philosophical claims underpin an emancipatory values-based form of argumentation which is central to equity and social justice arguments.

Ontological, epistemological and methodological considerations

Critical realism in its Bhaskarian form takes as its starting point the intelligibility of science and then proceeds by way of philosophical transcendental enquiry to establish what the world must be like in order for science to be possible. A transcendental argument according to Andrew Collier (1994), one of Bhaskar's more accessible interpreters, turns on the ways philosophy can help clarify a practice:

> One specific way in which philosophy can turn light on a practice is by what have been known, since Kant, as transcendental arguments. In such arguments, we ask 'what must be true in order for x to be possible?', where 'x' usually refers to some feature of human activity.
>
> (Collier 1994, p. 20)

The practice in Bhaskar's case is science. Doing science (including, as I will elaborate later, social science) is a social activity which assumes the transitive dimension of the knower (the scientist and her practice) but also an intransitive dimension of what is being known about. Critical realism's insistence on the 'aboutness' of science is key since it involves an emphasis on ontology, not just epistemology. As such, transcendental realism starts from a rejection of the epistemic fallacy which reduces knowledge to the knower, which is at the core of all idealism, whereby ontology is reduced to epistemology. Critical realism is equally critical of positivism and empiricism in their many forms which reduce what is known to experience, i.e. that which can be observed. Instead, critical realism proposes that for science to be intelligible the real cannot be reduced to either experiences or the world of events. What science is interested in is the elucidation of the real underlying mechanisms and tendencies which produce events and experiences. In this stratified view of reality mechanisms are real and it is their operation which produces the world of events. Another way of putting this is that transcendental realism posits a depth ontology not a flat atemporal world of experiences and events in the here and now. Non-visible trans-factual mechanisms are real and not just useful constructs or models:

> The world consists of things, not events. Most things are complex objects, in virtue of which they possess an ensemble of tendencies, liabilities and powers. It is by reference to the exercise of their tendencies, liabilities and powers that the phenomena of the world are explained.
>
> (Bhaskar 1978, p. 51)

Bhaskar (1978) reaches this conclusion through his analysis of experimental work whereby scientists by dint of their practices seek to produce empirical regularity in highly artificial and controlled environments (the laboratory). This allows them to test out what mechanisms and powers are at work by isolating particular mechanisms and predicting outcomes in controlled experiments. Empirical regularity is rare outside the non-controlled environment of the laboratory because in the open systems in which we live multiple mechanisms are at work. This means that in the real world it is difficult to predict what will happen, which is why complex systems are difficult to understand. Explanations of climate change, for example, are complex precisely because there are multiple mechanisms so predicting what will happen at any one point in time is not possible, but what scientists can do is point to the underlying mechanisms which are producing the tendencies and patterns we can observe. Because we live in open systems and there are multiple mechanisms, not all of which may be operative at the same time, there is an asymmetry between explanation and prediction. Lack of prediction is not a failure of science, rather the purpose of science is explanation. Any view of science that is based on a notion of Humean regularity – causality as B invariably following on from A – fails the test of intelligibility since these sorts of occurrences are rare and do not have explanatory power. The Humean view reduces explanation to prediction, one thing following on from another, but it does not tell us why this is happening. Bhaskar's argument pays attention to the material and social practices of doing science. He does not deny the importance of the epistemological, but his elucidation of the ontological dimension allows for a defence of scientificity and the special status of scientific explanation. Critical realism provides an account of how we can make (always fallible) judgements about the truth claims of explanations of a world which exists independently of our knowledge of it. It, therefore, accepts epistemic relativism, science is an inherently human activity, but rejects the idea that this entails judgemental relativism.

But what of social science – the objects of enquiry we are concerned with in this volume are intensely human and social. The problem of 'naturalism', namely the extent to which society and nature can be studied in the same way, has bedevilled debates about the nature of the social sciences since the nineteenth century. Bhaskar (1986) makes two important points. Firstly, that the objects of social science are only relatively enduring – not only is our knowledge of them fallibly human but also that as human beings we reproduce and transform the very societies and processes we are studying. The distinction between transitive and intransitive remains but the intransitive dimension is always relational. Secondly, that experimental closure is not possible in the social sciences for ethical and practical reasons, and so the strong test of alternative explanations afforded in (some) natural sciences is not available to us. This also means that that prediction is not possible in the social sciences since we cannot replicate the closed conditions which make predication possible. Nonetheless, the principle form of explanation, which is of elucidating the underlying mechanisms which can account for the emergence of patterns of events, remains the same. The purposes of understanding and explanation in scientific work are common to both the natural and social sciences although the methods at our disposal are different. Bhaskar's position is, therefore, one of critical naturalism, rather than crude naturalism, as he recognises the ontological differences that pertain in the social world while at the same time identifying the common elements of the scientific project. This account of the non-possibility of experimentation is controversial as whole areas of social science are based on experimentation, notably in psychology, but replication is low and the explanatory power of its theories are limited as the variables manipulated tend to be trivial when confined to the artificial environment of the psychology lab. The argument, however, has broader resonance in the debates about evidenced-based policy and practice. This movement is premised on assessing the quality of social scientific work based on the closeness of its proxies to the 'gold standard' randomised control trails used in the natural sciences. Critical realists would argue, however, that this version of 'evidence' underlying the evidence-based movement is flawed (Clegg 2005). There are important methodological implications for realist evaluations. Ray Pawson (2006), Pawson & Tilley (1997), a critical realist who does not accept the need for Bhaskarian transcendental arguments to ground his own critical realism, points out that the problem that besets programme evaluation is that interventions work in some situations and not in others, but we are none the wiser as we do not know why. In effect we do not understand the underlying mechanisms that are generating the different outcomes at the level of the actual events we observe. He suggests that realistic evaluations should identify and evaluate the effectiveness of different mechanisms, not particular interventions, thus paying much greater attention to the theoretical work involved. A good example in higher education of the failure of looking at just interventions was demonstrated by the systematic review established to identify the effectiveness of personal development planning (PDP). The review identified unconnected examples of where something had 'worked' (mostly in the US) but yielded no insights into the underlying mechanisms and, therefore, no ideas as to why PDP worked, which could have been useful for learning how to teach (Clegg 2005).

Of course, we cannot derive knowledge of what mechanisms are at work by philosophical reasoning, but we can derive an argument about what is entailed in explanation and we can also offer an account of why it is that we can claim that some explanations are (fallibly) better than other others. This has methodological implications and Andrew Sayer in his book *Method in social science* provides insight and guidance on the process of retroduction: 'a mode of inference in which events are explained by postulating (and identifying) mechanisms which are capable of producing them' (Sayer 1992, p. 107). In particular, he describes the processes whereby we need to abstract from the particularities of the concrete situation and exclude those things which have no significant effects in order to isolate and concentrate on the things that do. Like Pawson (2006), he points to the limitations of much quantitative work in the social sciences which fails to make these distinctions. A further implication of critical realism, highly relevant to education and educational research, is the insistence that our knowledge is about some something and, therefore, not arbitrary. Knowledge claims are central to education and critical realism has been mobilised by some authors (Wheelahan 2010, Maton 2014) in their defence of the significance of esoteric disciplinary knowledge which can be distinguished from everyday common sense knowledge (vitally important though that knowledge may be). This work combines critical realism with another tradition of theorising which draws on the Durkheimian distinction between the sacred (specialised religious knowledge produced by priests and their like) and profane (everyday knowledge). Disciplinary knowledge is a modern form of sacred or specialist knowledge. Basil Bernstein (2000), an influential English sociologist of education, built on Durkheim's (1995) work in analysing the relationship between knowledge, curriculum and pedagogy by showing how disciplinary knowledge is recontextualised into curriculum and pedagogy and the struggles this entails. These arguments have taken on new force with a range of thinkers arguing the need to 'bring knowledge back in' (Young 2008) and in particular to consider the challenges of 'epistemic' access (that is access to specialist knowledge) for students who do not come from elite backgrounds. This is controversial since the thrust of much educational research has been towards social constructivism in recognising the meaning-making process of learners and tending towards a foregrounding of the knowledge of learners, not that of teachers and the structure of disciplinary knowledge. In a recent paper, Zipin, Fataar and Brennan (2015) have challenged the social justice credentials of Bernsteinian approaches. They argue instead for a greater focus on the everyday resources that learners (in their examples mostly in schools) bring to learning. However, Moore and Muller (1999) in their influential paper, 'The discourse of "voice" and the problem of knowledge and identity in the sociology of education' argued that identity politics and a poststructuralist celebration of diversity undermined considerations of epistemic warrant and knowledge. They argued that it is essential to recognise the structure of knowledge in the design of curricula which gives access to powerful knowledge, and that voice epistemologies, which privilege the question of who the knower is, undermine this. Access to the structure of knowledge is vital for the least privileged students as the educational system ensures that the elite always do. The strength of Wheelahan's work is that, in developing her critique of vocational education offered primarily to the underprivileged, she underpins her Bernsteinian social realist argument with a critical realist philosophical stance.

Concerns with social justice constitute a key element of critical realist thinking. An important part of critical realism's Bhaskarian legacy was his insistence on the connection between critical realism and concerns with human emancipation (Bhaskar 1986). If we can identify the underlying mechanisms which are producing injustice or suffering then we can show under what conditions it could be otherwise. In these circumstances the argument becomes that *ceritus paribis* (other things being equal) we should change it. He argues that the denial of a connection between the 'ought' and the 'is' is a product of false philosophical reasoning, engendered by a Humean view of the world. Authors like Leesa Wheelahan (2010) have combined critical realism and Bernstein's (2000) and Young's (2008) social realism to make a passionate case for the least privileged students having access to powerful knowledge. These ideas are an important resource in teachers learning about teaching, and in particular to thinking about developing the curriculum in ways that promote access, as a number of writers working in the South African context have noted (Case 2014, Luckett 2015, Shay 2013, Wolff & Luckett 2013). Jenni Case (2014) for example suggests caution in the introduction of a problem-based curriculum in engineering as the unintended consequence might be that this makes epistemic access for the least privileged students more difficult rather than facilitating it. Suellen Shay has pointed to problematic cases where the recontextualising principles of the curriculum in earlier years of a degree may not provide an adequate basis for conceptual knowledge building at more advanced levels (Shay 2013) and Kathy Luckett (2015) is extending critical and social realists' ideas (Maton 2014) into the extremely challenging area of thinking about de-colonising the curriculum in the humanities. At the centre of all these concerns are social justice issues which increasingly should, and hopefully do, form part of teachers' learning to teach in increasingly diverse higher education systems.

This section has shown the way critical realism operates at a philosophical level as an under-labourer for the substantive work of theorising about the social world. It has also indicated that it provides an important resource for theorists whose central concerns are social and epistemic access. While philosophical reasoning is not conclusive in settling these substantive matters, the Bhaskarian legacy has been productive in thinking about methodology and in underpinning arguments that are vitally important in theorising higher education and teaching.

The next section will turn to the substantive sociological and analytical work of Margaret Archer as an important example of critical realist theorising in action.

Archer, morphogenesis, and on 'being human'

Margaret Archer has built a substantial body of theoretical work which directly confronts the problem of structure and agency that has so troubled sociological work. She is insistent that the structural cannot be reduced to individual actions (upward conflation), but equally individual agency is not a product simply of social structure (downward conflation). She is also critical of what she calls central conflation, whereby structure is always reproduced in the actions of persons, which in effect produces a continuous present and erases historicity. To overcome these weaknesses she proposes an analytical dualism whereby we can analytically separate structure and agency over time. Time becomes the key to understanding how structural conditioning at time 1, socio-cultural interaction at time 2 to 3 results in structural elaboration (morphogenesis) or structural reproduction (morphostasis) at time 4.

Much of Archer's work concentrates on elaborating the emergent properties of people. She points out in her book *Being human* (2000) that dominant accounts, particularly in poststructuralism, have too thin a view of persons to capture the capacities to reflect and act on our commitments which are central to being human. She argues that human beings are fundamentally evaluative in their relations with reality and that the 'inner conversation' is critical in understanding how human beings come to make commitments:

> The 'inner conversation' is how our personal emergent powers are exercised on and in the world – natural, practical and social – which is our triune environment. This 'interior dialogue' is not just a window on the world, rather it is what determines our being in the world, though not in times and circumstances of our choosing. Fundamentally, the 'inner conversation' is constitutive of our concrete singularity. However, it is also and necessarily a conversation *about* reality. This is because the triune world sets us three problems, none of which can be evaded, made as we are. It confronts us with three inescapable concerns: with our physical well-being, our performative competence and our self worth.
>
> (Archer 2000, p. 318)

Human beings in Archer's account are strong evaluators with the full range of personal powers who confront their triune environment in the natural, practical and social orders and who perforce possess embodied knowledge, practical knowledge, and discursive knowledge (see the diagram in Archer 2000, p. 162 for a mapping of the relationship between the nature of the world and our knowledge of it). This view of people has significant implications for how we think about learning and also to how we can think about commitments to social justice and equity.

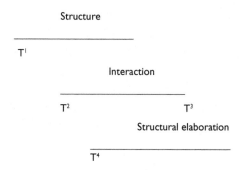

Figure 9.1 The morphogenetic sequence

(Archer 1995, p. 76) Crucially, this analytical separation allows us to distinguish structurally emergent properties (SEPs), culturally emergent properties (CEPs), and the emergent properties of people (PEPs) (Archer 1995).

She also analyses our capacity for what she calls corporate agency (see the detailed discussion in the chapter that follows), which is when people come together to promote or defend collectively identified projects:

> Organised interests groups represent the generation of a new emergent property amongst people (a PEP), whose power is the very special punch they pack as far as systemic stability and change are concerned. Only those who are aware of what they want, can articulate it to themselves and others, and have organised in order to obtain it, can engage in concerted action to reshape or retain the structural and/or cultural features in question.
>
> (Archer 2000, p. 265)

One way of thinking about the emergence of professional development and equity agendas is precisely in terms of the emergence of new corporate agents from the 1960s onwards (Clegg 2009). A new area of professional/academic development was created by a new layer of teaching protagonists to support teacher learning (and also in some national contexts to directly support students) and to urge greater attention to student learning and not simply to the discipline and research. As a particular group of teaching advocates, academic developers have also been important supporters of research into student learning and the knowledge base now available in learning to teach has significantly expanded.

Archer's account of the emergent properties of people also transcends the Cartesian dualism of reason and emotion which have dogged debates about higher education (Clegg 2013). She regards emotions as emergent commentaries relating to physical well-being, performative achievement, and self-worth entailed by our triune environment (natural, practical and discursive). Emotions shift from first order to second order as they become further articulated and elaborated through our internal conversations (Archer 2003). This dialogue, according to Archer (2000), cannot be construed as being driven by either logos (the word) or pathos, but instead both are intertwined. She argues that there are three significant moments: discernment, deliberation and dedication. Emotionality for Archer (2000) plays an important part in the vivid inner life of personhood which comes to define our identities, and emotions are central to her understanding of human beings as strong evaluators. Emotions are:

> socially *constituted* properties which are emergent from the internal relationship between the subjects concerns and society's normativity
>
> (Archer 2000, p. 215)

Normativity and values, which are central to understanding the possibilities of shaping higher education in more socially just ways, are thus not cut off from emotion; rather emotion is central to our commitments and powers to act.

In her more recent work Archer (2007) has empirically explored different forms of reflexivity which she identifies as communicative, autonomous, meta-reflectivity, and fractured. These positions represent different dominant personal orientations to being in the world. She has also suggested that we can distinguish the dominant forms of reflexivity which characterise different historical periods (Archer 2012). The present period is characterised by accelerated morphogenesis both structurally and culturally, which makes it harder to read and predict what is happening. This is a not based on a view that structure is becoming less important as some theorists of 'individualised individualism' (Beck & Beck-Gernsheim 2002) have suggested. Structure still presents actors with potentially devastating consequences and, as she points out, the banking crisis would be a good case in point. Equally we can see the ways in which major structural changes in higher education systems (the move to mass higher education, increasing privatisations, students as paying customers, etc.) are changing the conditions under which teachers come to learn to teach in ways that are not always fully understood as we struggle to make always fallible evaluations of the possibilities in a situation. Archer argues that the intensification of morphogenesis, at both cultural and structural levels, presents actors with 'contextual incongruity'. This renders communicative reflexivity, which relies on confirmation of our views from others and ties people to their natal origin, and the rational calculation of autonomous reflectivity which underpins social mobility more problematic. Communicative reflexivity, which might have once formed a basis for inter-generational learning about teaching, is more problematic as the challenges facing younger academics are more uncertain, as Louise Archer (2008) has pointed out. Similarly, autonomous reflectivity becomes more problematic as it becomes less not more clear what the routes to academic success are. At a system level Margaret Archer argues that meta-reflexivity becomes the dominant orientation (although not necessarily the most common in a numeric sense). Meta-reflexives:

> are 'contextually incongruous' and also contextually unsettled. They are *subversive* towards social constraints and enablements, because of their

willingness to pay the price of the former in the attempt to live out their idea and to forfeit the benefits of the latter.

(Archer 2007, p. 98)

These sorts of ways of committing and making their way through the world renders meta-reflexives less dependent on more linear trajectories of staying put or social mobility. Increased incongruity is also likely to produce greater levels of fractured reflexivity as people cease to be able to make sense of the situations in which they find themselves.

The dominance of meta-reflexivity, however, also suggests that in periods of uncertainty we are likely to see new sorts of corporate agency emerging. This is an especially interesting phenomenon for higher education which has seen the re-emergence of different forms of social activism, e.g. 'Rhodes Must Fall' (2015). The move by students to get the statue of Cecil Rhodes removed from the centre of the campus at University of Cape Town was at one level about the continued symbolism of colonialism, but it was also about the experiences of black students of a largely elite and historically 'white' curriculum and their experiences in an institution still dominated by white staff. The emergence of students as new collective agents, which has intensified in the struggles over fees, is not just an example of new collective agency, but arguably of meta-reflexivity towards the conditions of higher education and one which, moreover, presents teaching staff with contextual incongruity and a requirement for meta-reflexivity with regard to teaching, the curriculum, and indeed their own identities in the situation. These new conditions also make the arguments about powerful knowledge, rehearsed above, even more contentious as these new agents confront the question of 'whose knowledge' in different ways (Clegg 2015, Luckett 2015).

Archer's work has been criticised for paying too little attention to the habitual in social life and for placing too much emphasis on reflexive or deliberative action. It could also be argued that the account she gives in *The reflexive imperative in late modernity* (2012) considerably underestimates the extent to which traditional elites can continue to thrive even in the face of accelerated morphogenesis. Nonetheless, Archer presents us with a large body of theorising about the capabilities and capacities of persons to act. Her morphogenetic analysis offers an approach to understanding emergent powers that does not collapse the structural, cultural and personal and points us to the central importance of temporality and historicity for the work of theorising in and about the social world.

Normativity and 'why things matter to people'

I have already noted that an important part of the Bhaskarian legacy was critical realism's insistence on the connection between ought and is, between an evaluative stance to the world and substantive claims about it. One of the most distinctive theorists following through on these insights is Andrew Sayer. In his book entitled *The moral significance of class*, Sayer (2005) makes a sustained argument that class matters because it 'creates unequal possibilities for flourishing and suffering' (Sayer 2005, p. 218). His position is that flourishing and suffering are both ideational and material and physical and that, therefore, both recognition and egalitarian responses are entailed. What makes this moral, as well as substantive claim about the way things are, is his argument that:

> Newborns are unquestionably of equal moral worth, equally needy, equally deserving of a good life, yet class inequalities quickly ensure that their life chances are decidedly unequal ... We need not only a politics of recognition but a rejuvenated egalitarian politics of distribution that confronts the injustices of class openly ... In fact redistribution in itself would be an advance in terms of the politics of recognition.
>
> (Sayer 2005, p. 232)

His distinctively critical realist stance also involves the claim human well-being can provide a basis of morality sometimes regardless of how this suffering and flourishing are construed. In other words, there is a substantive objective dimension to morality, not only a subjective one. In common with Archer (2000) this view of humans is rooted in an understanding of the primacy of practice and as humans beings as not only social beings. In his analysis of class, however, Sayer draws not only on Archer but also on the French social theorist Pierre Bourdieu to provide a more nuanced analysis of the relationship between habitus (structured dispositions) and reflexivity and conscious deliberation. His analysis of the underlying mechanisms which produce inequality and the mis-recognition involved in attributing life chances to the striving of individuals, as neo-liberalism would have us believe, instantiates the Bhaskarian claim that, however difficult in practice, things could be otherwise. This is particularly significant for arguments about education which produces inequalities (and not just those attributable to class) while at the same time seeming to promise the possibility of unfettered social mobility.

More recently Sayer (2011) has drawn together his thinking about the relationship between social science, values and ethics in his analysis of 'why things matter to people', drawing on insights from both social science and moral philosophy. His insistence on human beings as essentially evaluative beings, and that reason and emotion are entwined not contraries, are profoundly Archerian themes. He argues for a form of moral realism based on the idea that:

> Our moral beliefs are directly or indirectly about matters of fact – the capacities and susceptibilities of our cultivated natures. Those facts about flourishing or suffering are what we seek to establish through moral evaluation ... here it is vital to note that we too are part of the world, not positioned outside as external observers, though our ideas are about things that are independent of them.
>
> (Sayer 2011, p. 259)

Crucially, therefore, he also challenges social scientists not only to consider the normativity of those they study but also our own normativity. This is particularly important where we confront theory–practice contradictions. He argues that we should check that the way we account for others' behaviour (for example, that of teachers) is not at odds with the way we account for our own behaviour (for example, as researchers of teachers and teaching). It is not that these contradictions are necessarily resolvable but they should always give us pause for thought (Clegg, Stevenson & Burke 2016).

One general argument that Sayer makes from his broad involvement with ideas from across the social sciences and moral philosophy, where problems have traditionally been analysed in different ways, is the need for post-disciplinarity. This might seem to be challenging, but it is underpinned by his rejection of forms of irrealism which would risk rendering such post-disciplinary commitments arbitrary. He argues that all forms of irrealism:

> tend to dissociate people from their relationship to the world and reduce them to relationships which are purely horizontal, subjective, discursive or conventional and are not about anything.
>
> (Sayer 2011, p. 247)

His recognition and analysis of normativity is, therefore, underpinned by the fundamentals of critical realism outlined in Part I. Sayer's post-disciplinarity is radically different from the sorts of generic vocational curriculum of the learning-to-learn type criticised by Leesa Wheelahan (2010) as further disadvantaging the most disadvantaged students. It is rather the basis for a more critical exploration of the theoretical tools we have available. As well as reflecting real differences in the natural kinds being studied it is important to recognise the historicity of the emergence of disciplines themselves. Even Bernstein, who dedicated much of his work to analysing the significance of disciplinarity for education, acknowledged that:

> The evolution of a range of singulars, specialised knowledge structures of the division of discursive labour, is very much a phenomenon of the last century. The development of English was linked to the development of nationalism and Britain's international position at the end of the nineteenth century.
>
> (Bernstein 2000, p. 54)

The challenge Sayer is posing is for us to develop ways of doing social science differently. This project is in keeping with the profoundly normative concerns of this book and the range of disciplinary perspectives that contributors have drawn on in their analysing teacher learning.

Critical realism is good to think with

The overall claim of this chapter is that critical realism is a productive framework for theorising. I have written elsewhere about the dangers of thinking of theory with a capital T, as if adding in a theorist or two makes our work theoretically sound (Clegg 2012). My account of critical realism in this chapter suggests that it can under-labour for social science in the sense of making important philosophical arguments about the nature of scientific work. Critical realism offers an alternative to the flat ontologies of both positivism and poststructuralism. It is interesting to note that many of the strengths of critical realism are echoed in the 'affective turn' in social science, particularly within feminism, as well as in the 'practice turn'. The practice turn has sought to recognise the importance of materiality, the body, and emotions (Schatzki et al. 2001), and is specifically addressed in both of the earlier parts of this book.

Critical realist arguments have significant methodological implications. They preclude seeing simple evaluations of the effects of intervention as being decisive and point instead to the importance of being able to gain insight into the underlying mechanisms at work. Empirical work requires under-girding with theoretical work if it is to be productive. Moreover, Archer's work suggests that we need to take account of emergence and historicity and her morphogenetic approach is especially productive in thinking about how we can account for change or stasis. She presents us with both a rich body of methodological insight and substantive social theorising, and her work on the emergent properties of people is especially suggestive in thinking about education and forms of reflexivity. Finally, I have argued that Sayer presents us with a number of challenges about how we theorise about ourselves and others, about how we reach normative conclusions, how we think about the possibilities for change in the world and what the obstacles to those changes are. Emancipatory themes were central to the early work of Bhaskar and have remained a defining feature. Sayer suggests that we need to do critical social science differently in a post-disciplinary mode, but he also builds on the rich resources of feminist and other critical writing. Critical realism does not do the work for us, but, as the chapters that follow show, can provide us rich and multi-layered resources with which to work.

References

Archer, L. (2008), 'The new neoliberal subjects? Young/er academics' constructions of professional identity', *Journal of Educational Policy*, vol. 23, no. 3, pp. 265 –85.

Archer, M.S. 1995, *Realist Social Theory: The Morphogenetic Approach*, Cambridge University Press, Cambridge.

Archer, M. S. (2000), *Being human: The problem of agency*, Cambridge University Press, Cambridge.

Archer, M. S. (2003), *Structure agency and the internal conversation*, Cambridge University Press, Cambridge.

Archer, M. S. (2007), *Making our way through the world*, Cambridge University Press, Cambridge.

Archer, M. S. (2012), *The reflexive imperative in late modernity*, Cambridge University Press, Cambridge.

Beck, U. & Beck-Gernsheim, E. (2002), *Individualization*, Sage, London.

Bernstein, B. (2000), *Pedagogy, symbolic control and identity, theory, research, critique*, Rowan & Littlefield, Oxford.

Bhaskar, R. (1978), *A realist theory of science*, Harvester Press, Brighton.

Bhaskar, R. (1979), *The possibility of naturalism: A philosophical critique of contemporary human sciences*, Harvester Press, Brighton.

Bhaskar, R. (1986), *Scientific realism and human emancipation*, Verso, London.

Case, J. (2014), 'Problematising curriculum: Contemporary debates in engineering education', in M. Young and J. Muller (eds), *Knowledge, expertise and the professions*, Routledge, London, pp. 143–56.

Clegg, S. (2005), 'Evidence-based practice in educational research: A critical realist critique of systematic review', *Sociology of Education*, vol. 26, no. 3, pp. 415–28.

Clegg, S. (2009), 'Histories and institutional change: Understanding academic development practices in the global "north" and "south"', *International Studies in the Sociology of Education*, vol. 19, no. 1, pp. 53–65.

Clegg, S. (2012), 'On the problem of theorising: An insider account of research practice', *Higher Education Research and Development*, vol. 31, no. 3, pp. 407–18.

Clegg, S. (2013), 'The space of academia: Privilege, agency and the erasure of affect', in C. Maxwell & P. Aggleton (eds), *Privilege agency and affect*, Palgrave Macmillan, Basingstoke, pp. 71–87.

Clegg, S. (2015), 'The necessity and possibility of powerful "regional" knowledge: Curriculum change and renewal', *Teaching in Higher Education*, vol. 21, no. 4, pp. 457–70.

Clegg, S., Stevenson, J. & Burke, P. (2016), 'Translating close-up research into action: A critical reflection', *Reflective Practice*, pp. 1–12, http://dx.doi.org/10.1080/146239 43.2016.1145580

Collier, A. (1994), Critical Realism, Verso, London.

Durkheim, E. (1995) (first edition 1912), *Elementary forms of religious life*, The Free Press, New York.

Luckett, K. (2015), *Gazes from the post-colony: An analysis of African epistemologies using legitimation code theory*, paper presented at the LCT Conference, Cape Town 17–19 June.

Maton, K. (2014), *Knowledge and knowers: Towards a realist sociology of education*, Routledge, Abingdon.

Moore, R. & Muller, R. (1999), 'The discourse of "voice" and the problem of knowledge and identity in the sociology of education', *British Journal of Sociology of Education*, vol. 20, no. 2, pp.189–206.

Pawson, R. D. (2006), *Evidence-based policy: A realist perspective*, Sage, London.

Pawson, R. D. & Tilley, N. (1997), *Realistic evaluation*, London: Sage.

Rhodes Must Fall (2015), Cape Town, South Africa, accessed 10 September 2015, http://rhodesmustfall.co.za/

Sayer, A. (1992), *Method in social science*, Routledge, London.

Sayer, A. (2005), *The moral significance of class*, Cambridge University Press, Cambridge.

Sayer, A. (2011), *Why things matter to people: Social science, values and ethical life*, Cambridge University Press, Cambridge.

Schatzki, T. R., Cetina, K. K. & Savigny, E. (2001), *The practice turn in contemporary theory*, Routledge, London.

Shay, S. (2013), 'Conceptualizing curriculum differentiation in higher education: A sociology of knowledge point of view', *British Journal of Sociology of Education*, vol. 34, no. 4, pp. 563–82.

Wheelahan, L. (2010), *Why knowledge matters in curriculum: A social realist argument*, Routledge, Abingdon.

Wolff, K. & Luckett, K. (2013), 'Integrating multidisciplinary engineering knowledge', *Teaching in Higher Education*, vol. 18, no. 1, pp. 78–92.

Young, M. (2008) *Bringing knowledge back in: From social constructivism to social realism in the sociology of education*, Routledge, London.

Zipin, L., Fataar, A. & Brennan, M. (2015), 'Can social realism do social justice? Debating the warrants for curriculum knowledge selection', *Education as Change*, vol. 19, no. 2, pp. 9–36.

Chapter 10

Teaching in higher education as a collective endeavour

Peter Kahn

Introduction

Many of the tasks entailed in university teaching are characteristically performed by an individual, whether giving a lecture or convening a seminar. A lecturer usually stands in front of a class of students on his or her own, or a single technician will explain to a group of students how to operate a piece of equipment. The collective dimension to teaching is muted at best. If teaching is stereotypically seen as involving actions of the individual, then we should not be surprised that the dominant theories used to frame how to teach in higher education are focused on individual competence. Indeed, Boud (1999) suggested that programmes of professional development for teaching in higher education typically focus on training and developing individual members of staff as resource for their institutions, on the lines of human capital theory (Lepak & Snell 1999).

Kandlbinder and Peseta (2009) identified a set of theoretical perspectives that were particularly likely to be adopted on such programmes, including reflective practice (Schön 1983), constructive alignment (Biggs & Tang 1999) and the scholarship of teaching (Boyer 1990). Such perspectives typically promote an individual framing of teaching in higher education. For instance, Kahn, Goodhew, Murphy and Walsh (2013) argued that the original model of the scholarship of teaching offered by Boyer concentrates on the practice of individuals. The influence of such theories is also apparent in the emphasis on individual competence that is evident in professional standards frameworks such as the UK Professional Standards Framework for teaching and supporting learning in higher education (Higher Education Academy 2011). It is to be expected, furthermore, that development programmes will not only promote these theories to participants, but will themselves be influenced by them.

Is this framing of what it means to teach and to learn to teach one that is fully adequate? Are there core aspects of the teaching role that go beyond one's own individual expertise as a practitioner? If so, what would the implications be for the process of learning to teach in higher education? There is significant scope for social theory to underpin investigation of these questions. One of the advantages of a critical realist theorisation is the scope it offers for critique, as Clegg (2014) argued.

Indeed, the early work by Bhaskar (1979) that helped to establish critical realism as a field was itself focused as a critique of the contemporary human sciences. However, the emphasis within critical realism on developing comprehensive and non-reductive explanations for social phenomena also means that the paradigm is well suited to a theorisation that takes in a wider basis than the theoretical perspectives currently in possession within the field of academic development.

Critical realism is also closely associated with the pursuit of social justice, as Clegg observed in the previous chapter. Bhaskar (1986) argued that theories in the social sciences are not neutral, but are both ridden with values and impregnate commitments. He suggested that an understanding of the causal mechanisms in play within social reality should engender a commitment to emancipatory action. If education is understood and unfolds in particular ways then, according to Bhaskar (1986), there will be ethical implications for the way that lecturers both teach and learn to teach. He principally understood emancipation as a form of self-determination, in which the lives of subjects are determined by sources that are desired rather than undesired by them. However, Bhaskar (1986) also recognised a shared dimension in that emancipatory action requires solidarity with others if a transformation of social structures is to occur. If we ignore the collective dimension to university teaching, it is likely that scope for the advancement of social justice will narrow.

Such perspectives inform the analysis in this chapter of what is entailed in learning to teach, although the argument also addresses some limitations in the approach to emancipation advocated by Bhaskar (1986). It is clear that individually focused capacities are still required to teach well. This chapter, though, seeks to employ critical realist perspectives to understand the collective dimension to teaching in higher education, and the means that might be employed to help those who are teaching as they learn to undertake their varied roles.

Teaching as a disciplinary practice

Teaching in higher education is characteristically undertaken within disciplinary settings or in settings with a scholarly focus for cross-disciplinary engagement. Each discipline has its own language, knowledge base and ways of perceiving the world, as Becher and Trowler (2001) argued. Entry into a given academic tribe primarily rests on the acquisition of specialist disciplinary knowledge and expertise, as acquired when securing a doctorate. The command of one's subject matter is central to participation in the tribe, and it is this command that a teacher seeks to help his or her students to acquire. It is intriguing, though, as Shulman (1986) pointed out, that our current processes to examine doctoral students remain closely related to the forms of teaching in evidence within medieval universities: oral exposition (lecture) and defence of a thesis (disputation). The mastery of the lecture and the disputation have historically been acquired on a tacit rather than an explicit basis (Eraut 2000), on the basis of experience rather than formal instruction. Until relatively recently, lecturers typically have been expected to replicate the modes of instruction that they experienced when they themselves studied as students. Knight and Trowler (2000), furthermore, have argued that colleagues in a given department maintain common working practices when teaching. There are advantages in maintaining common teaching practices within a department. Students benefit from receiving a consistent educational experience. The capacity to adopt practices that are acceptable and meaningful to one's colleagues represents an important baseline for learning to teach. Kahn and Walsh (2006), for instance, argued that it is reasonable for lecturers to justify their teaching in part through an appeal to established practice within their immediate setting.

The term 'morphostasis' refers to those processes that tend to preserve the existing structural aspects of a system, with 'morphogenesis' referring to those processes which tend over time to transform the structural aspects of a system (Archer 1995). At least until somewhat recent times, teaching in higher education has been characterised by morphostasis. Clegg explored in the previous chapter how interaction between the agents operating within a system either leads to structural elaboration or reproduction. One might argue for using terms such as 'change' and 'stability' rather than 'morphogenesis' and 'morphostasis' when seeking to make sense of teaching. However, at least for the purposes of theorising in this chapter, the use of these latter terms helps us to draw attention to the processes in play, and assists in connecting our argument to critical realist theorising.

Archer (1995), however, claimed that morphostatic scenarios become increasingly untenable as pressures for change mount. The extent to which the world of higher education is now characterised by change rather than stability is a central issue, one that has a significant influence on what is entailed in learning to teach. Archer (2007) held that social change is now endemic in today's morphogenetic society, while Barnett (1999) suggested that our world is characterised by supercomplexity, in which the means that we use to understand the world and our place within it are themselves contested. One's view of what it means to learn to teach depends in significant part on the extent to which one acknowledges change as an integral feature of higher education today.

Transformation and the capacity to teach

It is important to understand the nature of the pressures for change before considering the implications for the process of learning to teach. If a department perceives that its existence is under threat, then new teaching practices may be required to attract students or to convince managers of the viability of the department. Gibbs, Knapper and Picinnin (2008) identified a set of departments in research-intensive institutions that could objectively be characterised as manifesting excellent teaching. In each case he was able to identify an external threat to the future of the department as a significant factor in realising that excellence. However, the range of pressures for change in teaching that now operate within higher education is genuinely wide. Regulatory changes provide a particularly compelling motive for change – as has occurred in many European countries as a result of the Bologna process to integrate higher education (Keeling 2006). Drives for greater accountability have been particularly powerful in the UK, with the Quality Assurance Agency for Higher Education (2014) requiring institutions to specify the outcomes and methods of teaching, learning and assessment that are employed in programmes. The use of learning technology constitutes a particularly widespread driver for change in teaching (Laurillard 2013). Indeed, technological pedagogical content knowledge (Mishra & Koehler 2006) has been added as a specific sub-domain to pedagogical content knowledge. In addition to these drivers, Altbach, Reisberg and Rumbley (2009) cite global shifts that relate to the massification of higher education, growth in transnational education, moves towards widening access, the advance of private higher education, partnerships with industry, and so on. Other shifts in society at large have also impacted on higher education, whether the growing recognition of the need for sustainable education or the value of addressing historic inequalities in participation in higher education.

Critical realist perspectives would suggest, though, that such pressures do not operate on those teaching in higher education in some automatic fashion; just as social justice is not an inevitable outcome of change. Archer (1995) argued that while pressures may exist for change, individuals and groups need to act together if morphogenesis is to result. Archer (1995) used the term 'corporate agency' to refer to the way that individual agents join together in order to formulate and advance mutual interests. Corporate agency is focused on systemic change, whereby corporate groups change the structure of the system. Archer (1995) contrasted this form of agency with primary agency, whereby agents work within existing systems. Primary agents are those who act within a system that is shaped by others, even in cases where they act together. A department or institution in which no change has occurred in teaching over an extended period can be characterised as a morphostatic scenario. By contrast, the pursuit of changes in teaching necessitates the capacity to act together with others as a corporate agent. If excellent teaching involves responding constructively to pressures for change, then the capacity to teach is closely related to the capacity to act as a corporate agent.

Learning to pursue change with others

It is important to understand how lecturers and others engaged in teaching can respond creatively and wisely to pressures for change. This depends upon an appreciation of the ways in which a group of people collectively act so rather than otherwise in the pursuit of mutual interests. One key lesson from Archer (2003) is that reflexivity plays an important role in mediating the influence of structure on the agency of individuals. Reflexivity as a term refers to the ordinary mental capacity to consider oneself in relation to the social contexts that one encounters. Archer (2003) argued that the agency of individuals becomes increasingly concrete as concerns lead to action, under the influence of reflexivity and within given structural settings that constrain and influence that action. We have already seen in Chapter 9 that Archer (2003) identified a set of characteristic modes of reflexivity. Variation in the way that structure impacts on agency results in part from differences in the way that individuals engage in reflexivity. It is reasonable to consider the possibility that similar principles operate in relation to corporate agency.

Archer (2013) used the term 'collective reflexivity' to denote the reflexivity that subjects employ with regard to their social relationships in particular. Donati (2011a) referred to 'we-reflexivity' as the means by which agents employ (internal) reflexivity in order to guide their (external) relations with others. However, the focus on joint action is not to the fore in this description of we-reflexivity, with Kahn (2014) using the term co-reflexivity to refer to this more specifically. Archer (2013) suggested that social theorists have barely begun to address ways in which collective reflexivity shapes and influences our interpersonal relations.

Teaching as a priority

It is clear, in the first instance, that the exercise of corporate agency needs to be supported by reflexivity. In a morphostatic scenario where corporate agency for the development of teaching is highly restricted, one might possibly expect to see the restricted reflexivity that Donati (2011a) called 'we-reflexivity close to zero' or the near non-reflexivity of Archer (2012). Kahn (2014) argued that extended forms of reflexivity are a central feature of learning, and this would be true as much for the learning of teachers as for students. Where change is involved, it is clear that the interests that are at stake in teaching span efficient processes, social relations, whose interests are served, and other areas. These interests relate to each of the three main characteristics modes of constructive reflexivity identified by Archer (2003), namely autonomous reflexivity, communicative reflexivity and meta-reflexivity. As Clegg noted in the previous chapter, these different forms of reflexivity are shaped in significant part by social influences. The complexity of the interests that are entailed in corporate agency around teaching favour extended expressions of reflexivity.

Possibilities for extended reflexivity, though, depend on the extent to which teaching and the need to adapt teaching to a changing world is considered a priority by lecturers themselves. There is a significantly greater chance of teaching being accorded a priority by a group of members of staff if there is a connection with a genuinely significant issue at stake for the discipline, department or institution, as Kahn et al. (2013) contended. This is evident also in many professional disciplines in which a commitment to the future of the profession underpins the readiness to change. It is, however, relatively difficult for programmes of education focused on personal competence to connect to such compelling reasons for action – such programmes should look to outcomes for the work group as much as to outcomes for the individual. Any outcomes for the work group would need to be negotiated on an ongoing basis, and could not be determined in advance by a programme team. Boud (1999), indeed, argued that there is good reason to situate academic development within sites of academic practice.

There is also an inherent dominance from research that needs to be taken into account. Bernstein (2000) argued that several different fields of activity are in play, in which separate discourses take place with their own rules and patterns of language use. Teaching is constituted as a field of reproduction, with its own discourse and patterns of language use. It depends on an earlier reconstitution of knowledge, which also forms part of a wider pedagogic discourse. Such pedagogic discourse, though, contrasts with the discourse associated with research. Bernstein (2000) referred to research as a field of production, in which new knowledge is created. Bernstein (2000) argued that contestation occurs between these fields for control of educational activity, but that research as a discourse is typically more dominant. It is generally recognised that higher levels of prestige are associated with research as opposed to teaching. Chalmers (2011), indeed, reported widespread agreement in the research literature on the low status which universities give to teaching, even if progress has been made in recent years.

One's configuration of concerns forms an important part of personal identity for Archer (2007). According to this view, learning to teach within a changing environment entails learning to give at least some priority to teaching-related concerns. The readiness to exercise corporate agency represents a key threshold in the process of learning to teach. Otherwise lecturers can remain as primary agents, swept along by an agenda that is set by others. However, Reed (2005) noted that corporate agency does not, of itself, confer strict social identity. He pointed out that the model offered by Archer (1995) is only completed by the articulation of roles that the 'You' can occupy; and through which individuals gain social identity. Morphogenesis is particularly associated by Archer (1995) with the establishment of new roles. The success of corporate agency is manifest when the interests are embodied in the social order through a new configuration of roles, given that roles represent a key means by which the social order is constituted.

Sustaining collective reflexivity

Given the importance of collective reflexivity to responding to change, it is important to consider what sustains such reflexivity. Corporate agency entails a communicative dimension that ensures an awareness of the interests of colleagues. Dialogue is particularly needed when seeking to agree on novel purposes or practices. Roxå and Mårtensson (2008) suggested that most teachers rely on a small number of significant others for conversations that are characterised by their privacy, by mutual trust and by their intellectual intrigue. The data that they presented suggested that university teachers rely on a limited number of individuals to test ideas or solve problems related to teaching and learning. Individual teachers were seen to have small 'significant networks', where private discussions provided a basis for conceptual development and learning in ways that were quite different to 'front stage' public debate about teaching in committees.

Individual teachers seemed to have more significant conversations and larger networks where the local culture was perceived to be supportive of such conversations. Learning to teach in contexts where change is endemic involves learning to value such conversations.

Dialogue can, however, serve as a focus for inaction. Where reflexivity is marked by an absence of agency on the part of individuals, Archer employed the term 'fractured reflexivity'. Kahn (2015) suggested that there is scope for co-reflexivity to fracture in relation to learning. If one experiences frustrations with the collective aspirations that are in possession, then a fractured response could result. It may be the case that reflexivity around teaching degenerates, we can say, into a series of complaints. Dialogue would then simply amplify the overall volume of complaints, directly serving a morphostatic purpose. Dialogue can support the status quo in other ways, whether in talking down prospects for change or in focusing on the most satisfactory aspects of current provision.

Donati and Archer (2015) further highlighted the relational basis for collective reflexivity. Gustavsen (2001) similarly suggested that the capacity for new forms of action is closely affected by the extent to which a rich and diverse network of professional relationships is present. The nature of the social relations that are in place has a significant influence on the capacity of those involved to undertake the collective reflexivity that supports corporate agency. Donati (2011b) specifically highlighted reciprocity in social relations as a central feature of what humanises these relations. Boud (1999) argued that reciprocal peer relations are particularly likely to lead to learning amongst academics. By contrast, relations that are constituted by processes of domination and competition are harder to combine with extended reflexivity that is directed at constructive action. Flann (2010) argued that where an individual is subject to domination by others, then reflexivity can be suppressed. The social relations one maintains closely influence one's capacity to act as a corporate agent. On this count, learning to teach in a changing world involves building reciprocal relations with others.

Teaching as emergent co-action

Learning to teach involves growth in one's capacity to act as a corporate agent in order to meet new aspirations and needs as they arise in a changing world. However, even beyond change in practices and structures, teaching involves a range of further demanding forms of co-action. Walsh and Kahn (2009) argued that teaching is an inherently troublesome activity that involves emergent working. It is not possible to pre-determine from the outset those actions that will be required when teaching. This is especially so given the challenges of working with students, for whom learning incorporates an inherent dimension of uncertainty and struggle. Interaction with students and colleagues places significant demands on one's social relations, reflexivity and capacity to engage in dialogue.

A collective endeavour with students

Teaching involves developing an understanding of one's students, and the challenges that they face as learners. If one does not understand what will inspire or intrigue one's students, then one's teaching will be lacklustre. Palmer (2009) argued that it is essential to develop good rapport with students, both to find inspiration for the dedication that is required as a teacher and to catalyse the interest and engagement of students. Lecturers will always need to come to understand the capacities and experiences that students bring with them to their studies. Constructive forms of collective reflexivity are needed for members of staff to appreciate their students. Clearly it is possible to respond to perceived inadequacies in the student body with a fractured reflexivity that does not manifest itself in constructive action – in time-honoured fashion. Even without change in society, the interests and capacities of students are inherently different from those of their teachers. It is easy, for instance, for lecturers to forget the uncertainties and challenges that mark out learning as a difficult. Work on threshold concepts has been helpful in drawing close attention to these challenges (Meyer & Land 2006). Learning to teach should incorporate an explicit engagement with understanding the challenges that students face in developing mastery within their subjects. Shulman (1986), indeed, highlighted this as a central aspect of pedagogical content knowledge.

Social relations between staff and students are thus an essential consideration in what constitutes excellent teaching. The quality of the social relations that are maintained through different modes of teaching is important to consider – doubling the size of a seminar group or cutting out personal tutorials affect the nature of the social relations in place. Different teaching methods affect the scope for dialogue with students as an integral feature of learning. There may be scope for a shared determination of what is entailed in learning, as is often the case in enquiry-based learning or when students undertake research as a part of their studies (Kahn & O'Rourke 2004). Kahn (2014) suggested that such modes of learning may result in students exercising higher levels of agency in relation to their own learning. Similarly, the organisation of university life beyond the classroom has a significant impact on the extent to which social relations are realistic between staff and students. Tutors historically maintained relatively close personal relations with their students, although clearly there will have been extensive variation. John Henry Newman (2008) observed that he would dispense with examinations rather than with the requirement to live as a resident in a college. A clear rationale exists for the make up of the academic staff to reflect the student body, as Astin (1993) argued. The relational goods that are present within an ethnic community convey a significant advantage in establishing relations between staff and students from that community, providing a basis for communicative reflexivity and for the establishment of trust. New public management has gained extensive ground in universities in recent years (De Boer, Enders, & Schimank 2007), but this approach to management tends to neglect the relevance of social relations in a search for efficiency gains. A focus on social relations between staff and students is similarly absent from the perspectives noted earlier in the chapter that are typically promoted in programmes of professional development on teaching. If education in universities is conceived to be mutually determined, then the possibilities of emancipation for students are significantly enhanced.

Teaching together

Some aspects of teaching are constituted on an overtly collective basis. Team teaching offers particular possibilities for learning to teach. Archer (2000, pp. 182–84) argued that a sharing of practice is essential for new forms of discursive knowledge to impact on practice. There is similarly scope for shared practice to ground the process of learning for inexperienced members of staff. When someone new to teaching is first faced with the uncertainties of their professional environment, there is scope for a collective reflexivity that helps them to chart their own way forward, on a similar basis to communicative reflexivity. Shulman (2005) argued that many settings for professional education incorporate signature pedagogies, characteristic forms of teaching and learning. There is significant overlap between signature pedagogies offered by Shulman (2005) and the presence of distinctive professional environments. Signature pedagogies are closely grounded in particular sociomaterial settings, whether studios, fields, stages, operating theatres, laboratories and so on. Such settings provide extensive opportunities for shared practice and for collective reflexivity, whether resulting from interactions around equipment, common tasks, residency and so on. In order to teach together in these settings one needs to acquire a familiarity and attentiveness that takes in the social and material dimensions. In relation to learning within an operating theatre in medical education, for instance, Lyon and Brew (2003) argued that the most successful students were able to attend to the immediate physical environment and the social relations that were present, and they were able to relate the emotional impact of the surgery to their work and education.

Collective responsibility for higher education

Curricula are established as result of collective endeavour. A curriculum represents a plan for learning (Taba & Spalding 1962). More specifically, we can view a curriculum as an ordered series of foci for learning. It would, in principle, be possible to envisage an apprenticeship model of higher education, in which a master passes on his or her expertise to one or more apprentices (Lane 2005). The master might determine the focus for learning on the basis of his or her own acquired expertise. Higher education, however, almost from its very beginnings developed as a communal form of education in which the foci for learning were established on a collective basis. Ridder-Symoens (2003), indeed, demonstrated that shared responsibility for determining the organisation of the studies to be pursued in universities was established during medieval times. Learning to teach involves learning to act as a member of an institution. If a lecturer or tutor comes to a teaching role with the expectation of being able to frame a course of study as he or she sees fit, then disappointment is likely to abound. An emergent form of co-action is again entailed in this aspect of teaching, one that also depends upon collective reflexivity. If a departmental or faculty committee has a role to approve the specification for a module or programme, then in order to teach well one needs to recognise the legitimacy of this situation. Discussions with committee members prior to the meeting at which a decision is to be made will seem entirely reasonable if the determination of the curriculum is seen as a collective responsibility. In the face of differences with colleagues, it can be only too easy to revert to criticism, complaint and anxiety – to fractured reflexivity.

Collective responsibility for higher education is also in evidence in relation to the quality assurance and enhancement that institutions maintain, whether programme approval, monitoring of programmes or periodic review of programmes. It is important to develop the capacity to offer constructive peer review when learning to teach, as well as the capacity to respond well to the critique of others. Some institutions have begun to exercise more direct forms of control over teaching – but there is clearly a danger that imposing particular modes of teaching or the use of specific resources will undercut scope for corporate agency and other forms of emergent co-action that is more attuned to the needs and aspirations of students.

Beyond one's immediate context for teaching

Different settings for teaching do, indeed, incorporate varying scope to work collectively with others. The systems that are in place or the number of students that one is teaching may make it difficult to develop social relations with colleagues or one's students. Colleagues may be unwilling to engage in curricular change that responds to one's own deeply-held concerns. The increasingly dominant focus on preparing students for the labour market (Bok 2009) may make it difficult to respond to other agendas. It remains the case that the practice of teaching is constrained in a range of ways. The sociomaterial perspectives that have been advanced within this book highlight these constraints in helpful ways. Gourlay and Oliver in Chapter 2, for instance, argued that an emphasis on reflective practice may inculcate in lecturers a positive orientation to active learning, and a readiness to use assessment to ensure students act in desired ways. Edwards and Fenwick in Chapter 4 argued that technology serves to reconfigure practice.

The analysis of this chapter would suggest, however, that a space still remains for the intentional action of individual tutors and groups of tutors to shape practice. Smith (2010), indeed, has argued that systems involving persons are *proactively* emergent, with human intentional action both occurring within the system and influencing the emergence that results. It is clear that the capacity to re-frame existing forms and structure, and to evade constraints, constitutes an integral aspect of what it means to teach well. The capacity to think imaginatively in dialogue with others in relation to the constraints that one faces is a feature of an excellent teacher. This essentially represents a meta-reflexive response to the social contexts within which one finds oneself, enabling a tenacious pursuit of social ideals. For instance, regulations constrain the actions that are possible within universities, but it may be possible to argue for an interpretation of the regulations that fits with one's intended course of action. Barnett (2013) has suggested that there is scope to broaden the ways in which we imagine life within universities. It may be that a work group or institution can be helped to acquire a wider breadth of vision in order to be ready to consider new forms of education. Markus and Nurius (1986) argued that each person has the capacity to represent possible futures for itself, giving expression to their ideals and hopes. The self-knowledge that is developed through formulating such representations has been employed in a range of ways to support individual growth. There is scope for a similar formulation of possible collectives, future collectives, whereby a group engages in dialogue and actions designed to formulate possible futures for itself.

There will be a role for paradigms such as critical realism in helping to establish forms and systems of education that enhance the possibilities for emancipation. The capacity for critique is an essential feature of an excellent teacher. Lacey (1997), however, argued that the move from holding a theory to becoming committed to a value is less straightforward than Bhaskar (1986) suggested. Lacey (1997, p. 236) argued: 'The promise of Bhaskar's argument is that there is a quick rational move from coming to accept theories in the social sciences to adopting value judgements partial to emancipation'. He suggested that further value judgements are entailed in this transition. Lacey (1997) pointed out that a commitment to emancipation requires both appreciating the actual limits of current structures and developing forms of organisation that could provide a basis for new social structures. Only if a theory is developed or understood from within an emancipatory movement did Lacey suggest that Bhaskar's argument is fully applicable. Learning to teach can be regarded as learning to engage in activism, even if this is not taken as far as the approach advocated by critical pedagogy (McLean 2006).

The setting within which one practices education is important. The pursuit of social justice within higher education is the work of a lifetime. One might take up roles and positions partly on the basis of the scope for shared emancipatory commitments, particularly in settings where emancipation is an urgent concern. It is also important to recognise that one's reflexivity is influenced by the context within which one exercises agency, as Kahn (2014) argued in relation to student learning. Learning to teach should involve learning to take care over the choice of context within which one teaches. One might even actively search out an institutional or departmental setting where others manifest compatible commitments to education or where scope for good scope is present for corporate agency. Learning to teach is not simply about learning to perform in a seminar room or to design a course, even if it might be most straightforward for programmes of professional development to concentrate on such issues.

Conclusion

Teaching in higher education *is* a collective endeavour. It requires the commitment and agency of teachers, learners and others in order to be undertaken well. Excellent teaching is determined on a wider basis than simply the individual competence of lecturers. An awareness of these wider underpinnings is important for anyone to learn to teach or to improve their teaching. One does not necessarily need to employ the theoretical viewpoint offered in this chapter in order to teach well, but it remains the case that an appreciation of the generative mechanisms that shape teaching and learning is of value. One of the purposes of this present book is to extend the range of theoretical perspectives that are employed to make sense of both teaching in higher education and the field of academic development. This chapter has been able to provide an explanation for a range of issues that are not normally addressed when considering the process of learning to teach in higher education, taking in the role that both change and uncertainty play in relation to collective activity. On this view, learning to teach in the shared and changing world that is higher education involves acquiring the capacity to undertake corporate agency. It involves learning to engage in constructive and extended forms of collective reflexivity, and to maintain capacity for critique, dialogue, collective practice and social relations.

The account in this chapter is offered as a resource on which to enhance the development of teaching in higher education. Those seeking to develop teaching either as individuals or on behalf of disciplines and institutions should pay explicit attention to the collective dimension to teaching. Consideration of these issues could play an important role in the design of academic development programmes and in the way that faculties seek to develop their own capacities for teaching. It could assist in the design of professional standards frameworks or the development of new signature pedagogies. There is scope to illuminate the pursuit of social justice within higher education as a result of the theoretical perspectives outlined in this chapter.

There is value in acquiring a breadth of vision when teaching in higher education. Learning to teach should involve coming to recognise the full range of influences on one's teaching. There are many advantages from viewing teaching as a collective endeavour. By contrast, a focus on individual competence leaves one ill-equipped to deal with shifts in the higher education sector that work against emancipation. A theoretical lens that is grounded in comprehensive forms of explanation constitutes a valuable asset in coming to understand what is entailed in learning to teach.

References

Altbach, P. G., Reisberg, L. & Rumbley, L. E. (2009), *Trends in global higher education: Tracking an academic revolution*, Sense Publishers, Rotterdam.

Archer, M. S. (1995), *Realist social theory: The morphogenetic approach*, Cambridge University Press, Cambridge.

Archer, M. S. (2000), *Being human: The problem of agency*, Cambridge University Press, Cambridge.

Archer, M. S. (2003), *Structure, agency and the internal conversation*, Cambridge University Press, Cambridge.

Archer, M. S. (2007), *Making our way through the world: Human reflexivity and social mobility*, Cambridge University Press, Cambridge.

Archer, M. S. (2012), *The reflexive imperative in late modernity*, Cambridge University Press, Cambridge.

Archer, M. S. (2013), 'Collective reflexivity: A relational case for it', in C. Powell & F. Dépelteau (eds), *Conceptualizing relational sociology: Ontological and theoretical issues*, Palgrave Macmillan, London, pp. 145–61.

Astin, A. W. (1993), 'Diversity and multiculturalism on the campus: How are students affected?', *Change: The Magazine of Higher Learning*, vol. 25, no. 2, pp. 44–49.

Barnett, R. (1999), *Realizing the university in an age of supercomplexity*, Open University Press, Maidenhead.

Barnett, R. (2013), *Imagining the university*, Routledge, London.

Becher, T. & Trowler, P. (2001), *Academic tribes and territories: Intellectual enquiry and the culture of disciplines*, Open University Press, Maidenhead.

Bernstein, B. B. (2000), *Pedagogy, symbolic control, and identity: Theory, research, critique*, Rowman & Littlefield, Lanham, MD.

Bhaskar, R. (1979), *The possibility of naturalism: A philosophical critique of contemporary human sciences*, Harvester Press, Brighton.

Bhaskar, R. (1986), *Scientific realism and human emancipation*, Verso, London.

Biggs, J. B. & Tang, C. (1999), *Teaching for quality learning at university*, Open University Press, Maidenhead.

Bok, D. (2009), *Universities in the marketplace: The commercialization of higher education*, Princeton University Press, Princeton, NJ.

Boud, D. (1999), 'Situating academic development in professional work: Using peer learning', *International Journal for Academic Development*, vol. 4, no. 1, pp. 3–10.

Boyer, E. L. (1990), *Scholarship reconsidered*, Carnegie Foundation for the Advancement of Teaching, Princeton, NJ.

Chalmers, D. (2011), 'Progress and challenges to the recognition and reward of the scholarship of teaching in higher education', *Higher Education Research & Development*, vol. 30, no. 1, pp. 25–38.

Clegg, S. (2014), *Realism as a theoretical resource*, University of the Western Cape, South Africa, October.

De Boer, H., Enders, J. & Schimank, U. (2007), *On the way towards new public management? The governance of university systems in England, the Netherlands, Austria, and Germany*, Springer, Berlin.

Donati, P. (2011a), 'Cultural change, family transitions and reflexivity in a morphogenetic society', *Memorandum*, vol. 21, pp. 39–55.

Donati, P. (2011b), *Relational sociology: A new paradigm for the social sciences*, Routledge, London.

Donati, P. & Archer, M. S. (2015), *The relational subject*, Cambridge University Press, Cambridge.

Eraut, M. (2000), 'Non-formal learning and tacit knowledge in professional work', *British Journal of Educational Psychology*, vol. 70, no. 1, pp. 113–36.

Flann, H. (2010), 'Emotion, and the silenced and short-circuited self', in M. S. Archer (ed.), *Conversations about reflexivity*, Routledge, London, pp. 187–205.

Gibbs, G., Knapper, C. & Picinnin, S. (2008), *Departmental leadership for quality teaching – an international comparative study of effective practice*, Leadership Foundation for Higher Education, London.

Gustavsen, B. (2001), 'Theory and practice: The mediating discourse', in P. Reason & H. Bradbury (eds), *Handbook of action research: The concise paperback edition*, Sage, Thousand Oaks, CA.

Higher Education Academy (2011), *The UK professional standards framework for teaching and supporting learning in higher education*, Higher Education Academy, York.

Kahn, P. E. (2014), 'Theorising student engagement in higher education', *British Educational Research Journal*, vol. 40, no. 6, pp. 1005–18.

Kahn, P. E. (2015), 'Corporate agency and co-reflexivity in institutional work', European Conference on Educational Research, Budapest, Hungary, September.

Kahn, P. E., Goodhew, P., Murphy, M. & Walsh, L. (2013), 'The scholarship of teaching and learning as collaborative working: A case study in shared practice and collective purpose', *Higher Education Research & Development*, vol. 32, no. 6, pp. 901–14.

Kahn, P. E. & O'Rourke, K. (2004), *Guide to curriculum design: Enquiry-based learning*, Higher Education Academy, York.

Kahn, P. E. & Walsh, L. (2006), *Developing your teaching: Ideas, insight and action*, Routledge, London.

Kandlbinder, P. & Peseta, T. (2009), 'Key concepts in postgraduate certificates in higher education teaching and learning in Australasia and the United Kingdom', *International Journal for Academic Development*, vol. 14, no. 1, pp. 19–31.

Keeling, R. (2006), 'The Bologna process and the Lisbon research agenda: the European Commission's expanding role in higher education discourse', *European Journal of Education*, vol. 41, no. 2, pp. 203–23.

Knight, P. & Trowler, P. (2000), 'Department-level cultures and the improvement of learning and teaching', *Studies in Higher Education*, vol. 25, no. 1, pp. 69–83.

Lacey, H. (1997), 'Neutrality in the social sciences: On Bhaskar's argument for an essential emancipatory impulse in social science', *Journal for the Theory of Social Behaviour*, vol. 27, no. 2-3, pp. 213–41.

Lane, J. (2005), *Apprenticeship in England, 1600–1914*, Routledge, London.

Laurillard, D. (2013), *Rethinking university teaching: A conversational framework for the effective use of learning technologies*, Routledge, London.

Lepak, D. P. and Snell, S. A. (1999), 'The human resource architecture: Toward a theory of human capital allocation and development', *Academy of Management Review*, vol. 24, no. 1, pp. 31–48.

Lyon, P. & Brew, A. (2003), 'Reflection on learning in the operating theatre', *Reflective Practice*, vol. 4, no. 1, pp. 53–66.

McLean, M. (2006), *Pedagogy and the university: Critical theory and practice*, Continuum, London.

Markus, H. & Nurius, P. (1986), 'Possible selves', *American Psychologist*, vol. 41, no. 9, p. 954–69.

Meyer, J. H. F. & Land, R. (2006), *Overcoming barriers to student understanding: Threshold concepts and troublesome knowledge*, Taylor & Francis, London.

Mishra, P. & Koehler, M. (2006), 'Technological pedagogical content knowledge: A framework for teacher knowledge', *The Teachers College Record*, vol. 108, no. 6, pp. 1017–54.

Newman, J. H. (2008) (first published 1873), *The idea of a university*, Yale University Press, New Haven, CT.

Palmer, P. J. (2009), *The courage to teach: Exploring the inner landscape of a teacher's life*, John Wiley & Sons, Hoboken, NJ.

The Quality Assurance Agency for Higher Education (2014), *The UK quality code for higher education: A brief guide*, The Quality Assurance Agency for Higher Education, Gloucester.

Reed, M. (2005), 'Reflections on the "realist turn" in organization and management studies', *Journal of Management Studies*, vol. 42, no. 8, pp. 1621–44.

Ridder-Symoens, H. de (2003), *A history of the university in Europe: Volume 1, universities in the middle ages*, Cambridge University Press, Cambridge.

Roxå, T. & Mårtensson, K. (2008), 'Strategic educational development: A national Swedish initiative to support change in higher education', *Higher Education Research & Development*, vol. 27, no. 2, pp. 155–68.

Schön, D. A. (1983), *The reflective practitioner: How professionals think in action*, Basic Books, New York.

Shulman, L. S. (1986), 'Those who understand: Knowledge growth in teaching', *Educational Researcher*, vol. 15, no. 2, pp. 4–14.

Shulman, L. S. (2005), 'Signature pedagogies in the professions', *Daedalus*, vol. 134, no. 3, pp. 52–59.

Smith, C. (2010), *What is a person? Rethinking humanity, social life, and the moral good from the person up*, University of Chicago Press, Chicago.

Taba, H. & Spalding, W. B. (1962), *Curriculum development: Theory and practice*, Harcourt, Brace & World, New York.

Walsh, L. & Kahn, P. E. (2009), *Collaborative working in higher education: The social academy*, Routledge, London.

Chapter 11

'Extreme teaching'

Exercising agency in difficult contexts

Chris Winberg

South African higher education: a landscape of extremes

Globally, the academic profession faces many challenges, including the pressures of mass higher education, fiscal constraints, rating systems, new technologies and changing attitudes towards accountability and how universities are managed. In the South African context, the post-apartheid expansion of student enrolment and the expectations of a society undergoing significant social change place particular pressures on university teachers and their institutions. There are concerns across the higher education sector in South Africa that 20 years of post-apartheid higher education policy and legislation have not produced sufficient changes in the system. South African higher education is marked by social and material inequalities that continue, through deeply embedded cultures and practices, to reproduce these inequalities (Cooper 2015, Bozalek & Boughey 2012). While there have been funds available to redress historical imbalances, many of the difficulties are systemic and related to broader socio-economic factors. The disparity in staff–student ratios, access to resources and demography of the student population across different universities serve to perpetuate historical inequities (Leibowitz & Bozalek 2014, Badat 2012). A particular concern is the low participation and success rates of black South African students (CHE 2013a). This has led to the proclamation of a crisis in South African higher education, with a particular focus on a need to enhance teaching and learning through quality enhancement mechanisms (CHE 2013b), a summit on 'Higher Education Transformation' (DHET 2015), and growing student activism, calling for the 'de-colonisation' of the higher education system and for the provision of free higher education (Baloyi & Isaacs 2015). These turbulent environments make South African higher education an extreme case, particularly for university teachers seeking to practice socially just pedagogies in support of student learning and development.

The specific background to this study is an institution undergoing complex changes, including the merging of previously advantaged and previously disadvantaged institutions, the attainment of university status, and an institutional drive towards higher degree programmes, research and technology innovation. This has resulted in a multi-site institution with multiple campuses housing different faculties (or sections of faculties), creating divisions, differences and inequalities across sites. The context is thus an extremely challenging one for teachers in professional and vocational fields, whose primary identities are derived from their professions and their passion for teaching and bringing young people into the profession.

The institution in this study, the Cape Peninsula University of Technology, was awarded university status in 2005. South African Universities of Technology were created by decree, that is, they were not expected to meet any particular criteria to be awarded the title 'University of Technology'. The South African higher education system is intended to be hierarchical, with research-intensive universities occupying the highest level, the comprehensive universities focusing on mass higher education, and the universities of technology focusing on technology-based qualifications to 'meet the needs of industry' (Engel-Hills, Winberg & Rip 2016). The Cape Peninsula University of Technology is an undergraduate 'teaching-intensive' university, with the majority of its programmes being industry-accredited three-year diplomas; post-graduate candidates comprise only 5 per cent of its enrolments. Ironically, improving the status of teaching at such a university is difficult because it has to compete with research recognition. While there are strong incentives for staff to achieve research outputs, there are far fewer incentives for staff to achieve teaching excellence. Productive researchers have achieved high levels of status in the institution, while excellent teachers have not.

Additional challenges faced by the institution include new funding mechanisms that require the institution to achieve high pass rates, as failure to meet these targets will incur penalties. Thus meeting the targets is a key concern for managers. The institution is also required to increase its current 32,000 student enrolments to 36,000, but without expanding its current complement of 1,000 permanent and 500 contracted academic staff. Thus university teachers are expected to do more with less. The South African Department of Higher Education and Training provides teaching development grants as a national-level enabling mechanism in support of increased enrolments and ambitious targets, as well as the necessary professional development to accompany this, but for a number of reasons (see e.g., Boughey 2013), these grants have not been effective. Institutional structures, systems and policies have been developed with the intention to meet the targets and support teaching and learning, however enabling systems and structures have been difficult to implement (see e.g., Winberg & Garraway 2016).

The question that this study then seeks to address is: what are the mechanisms by which university teachers are able to commit themselves to the attainment of teaching excellence, and how much are they constrained by the challenges of the context in which they teach?

The interplay of structure, culture and agency

The theoretical resources provided by Archer's (1995, 2000) social realism show how structure and culture, and their generative powers of constraint and enablement, shape the situations in which subjects find themselves, but also show how social practices produced through different modes of reflexivity enable action, even in constraining social environments. These resources are used to explain how personal emergent powers can enable teaching excellence despite extremely difficult contexts.

The study builds on the work of others who have drawn on Archer's social realist framework (e.g., Ashwin 2008, Case 2015, Kahn 2009, Quinn 2012) to explain the ways in which the difficulties of context are negotiated in the development of a teaching agency. Social realism offers a way of understanding the dynamics of context and agency at different levels of the educational system. Social realism acknowledges the power of structure and culture and, equally, affirms the powers of human agency and creativity (Elder-Vass 2010). Structural and cultural contexts can support or constrain the achievement of teaching excellence, but it is how teachers respond to these constraints and enablements that can produce structural, cultural and personal transformation.

The interplay of structure, culture and agency is thus an important concept for understanding university teaching. The structural features associated with policy, funding mechanisms, leadership and resources – as well as the cultures and discourses of different departmental groups and departmental leaders – impact teaching practice. The study reveals the influence of these enablements and constraints on the exercise of teaching agency. At both the structural level (e.g., teaching and learning policies, review processes, teaching and learning committees, reward systems, etc.) and the cultural level (e.g., departmental discourses and practices, concern (or lack thereof) for the educational project and the functionality of the teaching environment) there are enabling and constraining factors. While structural and cultural features can be separated analytically, they are often interlinked and co-determining, creating either a vicious or a virtuous cycle. Archer (2012) argues that the structural and cultural features of systems have causal powers; in the case study we see how the university teachers circumvent, or are thwarted by, contextual and cultural constrains, or are empowered by structural and cultural enablers. A social realist approach is thus appropriate to an exploration of teaching agency within the higher education system, in a way that takes into account the complexity of multi-directional relationships.

Teaching as a critically reflective practice

Central to the idea of teaching excellence in the literature is 'reflective practice'. Dewey (1910) was an early proponent of its importance for rational action. Dewey's principles of reflective practice were taken up by Schön (1983, 1987) who extended these principles to explain skilful practice, including skilful teaching practice. Later scholars argued that Schön's conceptual framework ignored the importance of context in professional education and introduced the concept of *critical* reflection. Freire (1985) understood that both teachers and their students should be liberated from social oppression. He made the point that teachers make conscious political choices, such as to be ethical in thoughts and actions. Excellent teachers, Freire argues, are disposed to change: they acknowledge their personal attitudes and are self-aware of the processes of change. Freire saw critical reflection as the culmination of a movement from social conditioning to critical reflection towards praxis. Mezirow (2000) proposes three types of reflection for transformative action: 'content reflection' in which the subject thinks deeply about the content of what was taught/learned; 'process reflection' in which the subject considers and evaluates the strategies used to teach or to facilitate learning; and 'premise reflection' in which the subject confronts personal assumptions and values. The concept of critical reflection has entered many fields of education. Bryan and Recesso (2006) in computer engineering describe teachers' reflective activities as a deep engagement with values, beliefs and assumptions. Critical reflection is intellectually unsettling; its outcome is changed practice, with a social justice focus across many fields and professions (Benade 2015). Critical reflection 'lays bare the historically and socially sedimented values at work in the construction of knowledge, social relations, and material practices ... it situates critique within a radical notion of interest and social transformation' (Giroux 1983, pp. 154–55). Critically reflective teaching practice challenges both strategies and beliefs about teaching and learning within the wider socio-economic and political fabric of society and is concerned with exposing and challenging discourses, narratives and discursive practices at play within society.

Reflexivity in society

While educational researchers are familiar with the concept of critically reflective teaching practice, sociology uses the term 'reflexivity' to explain critical reflection in broader social contexts. Reflexivity refers to the capacity of subjects to recognise the forces of socialisation and to alter their positions within the social structure. The concept of reflexivity has taken on a new centrality in sociology, particularly with regard to the dynamics of change in the social processes of late modern societies (Caetano 2014). Giddens (1984) suggests that there are degrees of reflexivity, ranging from everyday reflexivity to more intense forms where more is at stake. A low level of reflexivity would result in individuals being largely shaped by social structures while high levels of reflexivity would enable individuals to shape their own norms, tastes, politics, desires, and so on. Archer (2003) emphasises the heterogeneity of reflexivity modes, while her stratified view of the subject attempts to bridge individual and social realms.

A stratified view of the subject

Archer (2000) offers a stratified view of the subject, proposing four strata: 'the self, the person, the agent and the actor' comprising the individual human subject. These layers build on one another as the subject moves from self-awareness to awareness of others, and towards developing unique interests, concerns and ways of interacting with others, and eventually towards more purposeful actions in the world. In elaborating what is meant by 'agency', Archer argues the need to distinguish between collective agents and individual actors:

> The reality experienced by the collectivity is not reducible to the personal reactions of its members; nor is the subjectivity of the latter understandable without reference to the objectivity of the former.
>
> (Archer 1995, p. 120)

Transforming our positions in society is possible but 'their transformation depends partly upon the subjective reflexivity of primary agents in seeking to play an active part in re-shaping society's resource distribution' (Archer 2000, p. 11). Primary agents can respond to social or institutional structures and cultures by forming new collectivities that share a desire for transformative action. As such, they become corporate agents. Corporate agents have 'capacities for articulating shared interests, organising for collective action, generating social movements and exercising corporate influence in decision-making' (Archer 2000, p. 266). The capacity to bring about social transformation is accomplished through particular modes of reflexivity.

Archer describes reflexivity as an 'internal dialogue', a condition of existence in society that 'activates the causal powers of structures and allows individuals to project their actions based on the articulation between personal concerns and the conditions that make it possible to accomplish them' (Caetano 2014):

> The internal dialogue entails disengaging our ultimate concerns from our subordinate ones and then involves elaborating the constellation of commitments with which each one of us feels we can live.
>
> (Archer 2000, p. 11)

The internal dialogue is the practice through which we 'make up our minds ... by questioning ourselves, clarifying our beliefs and inclinations, diagnosing our situations, deliberating about our concerns and defining our own projects' (Archer 2003, p. 103). Reflexivity, exercised by internal dialogues, not only mediates the impact that structures have on agents it also conditions individuals to respond to particular social situations in particular ways. Archer argues that while structural properties shape the situations that agents face, their modes of reflexivity define their concerns, and that social practices are produced from agents' reflexive deliberations.

A typology of reflexivity

Although reflexivity is common to all individuals, it is exercised in diverse ways, depending on the relations that subjects establish within their social contexts, their interests and concerns. 'Communicative reflexivity' arises from internal conversations that require confirmation by others before resulting in specific courses of action. 'Autonomous reflexivity' is achieved through self-contained inner dialogues that lead directly to action without the need for validation by others. 'Meta-reflexivity' is the reflexive critique that subjects direct at their own internal conversations, which often involves problematising social conditions and striving for social justice. 'Fractured reflexivity' is a consequence of inner dialogues that fail to deal critically with social circumstances and can intensify personal stress and social disorientation. Archer's typology does not imply that subjects are limited to a single mode of reflexivity; it suggests that agents are likely to have developed preferred or dominant modes of reflexivity. More recently, Archer (2012) has sought to refine this typology in the light of social change in contemporary societies, geographical mobility, improved educational levels and greater cultural diversity (Caetano 2014).

Researching reflexivity

In line with a realist approach, the study is based on the collection of data at the level of the 'actual' (i.e., events that occurred, such as the conferring of a teaching award) and the 'empirical' (i.e., how recipients experience their worlds and how they describe their practice or concerns) in order to hypothesise the 'real' (or causal mechanisms) (Maxwell 2012). The interview schedules were developed by the larger research group to enable the identification of structure, culture and agency and their interplay, as well as to enable comparison across participants and sites. The data for this study was obtained from interviews with ten academic staff members in professional or vocational fields (e.g., engineering, health sciences), all of whom had been recognised for their teaching excellence.

Table 11.1 The research participants

University teacher	Discipline/field	Position	Teaching excellence award
Interviewee 1	Engineering	Senior Lecturer	International award
Interviewee 2	Business	Lecturer	Departmental award
Interviewee 3	Science	Lecturer	Faculty award
Interviewee 4	Engineering	Head of Department	National award
Interviewee 5	Science	Lecturer	Faculty award
Interviewee 6	Engineering	Lecturer	National award
Interviewee 7	Education	Senior Lecturer	National award
Interviewee 8	Business	Lecturer	Departmental award
Interviewee 9	Health Sciences	Professor	International award
Interviewee 10	Health Sciences	Lecturer	Departmental award

Participants in the study had been recipients of various teaching awards, such as the institution's annual departmental or faculty teaching excellence awards, others had received national recognition (e.g., commendations at national conferences or through professional bodies), and two of the participants had received international recognition: Interviewee 1 had received an international e-learning award, while Interviewee 9 had been a member of a team that jointly received an international professional education award. Some of the research participants had received more than one award; Table 11.1 shows only the most recent award. In the interests of maintaining confidentiality neither the staff member, his/her department, or award is named.

The intention was to identify dominant modes of reflexivity across the ten interviews. Scambler (2012) points out that we are all capable of expressing our internal dialogues to external others, although there are few research methods that offer concrete ways of doing this. He contends that what matters in the data is the nature of the understanding produced by each participant's speech act and how the researcher 'abducts' inference of the real.

This study is part of a larger South African research project funded by the South African National Research Foundation that included eight universities. The project obtained ethical clearance from the lead institution, and subsequently from each participating institution. The interviews were conducted by external researchers and transcribed by a professional transcriber. The interviews were verified by the interviewer and interviewees. The interview transcripts were subjected to close reading and discourse analysis with the purpose of identifying patterns or recurrent modes of reflexivity.

Findings: committed teachers' modes of reflexivity

Participants in the study are academics in a poorly-resourced institution serving mainly poor and working-class students and in a sense can be understood as 'assigned to positions on society's distribution of resources' (Archer 2000, p. 11). However, they exercised modes of reflexivity that enabled them to prioritise the teaching of students, above the status that they might have attained by focusing on research, or the financial benefits that returning to professional practice might have provided.

Their commitment to the education of their students enabled such teachers to engage in practices against the structural and cultural constraints present in difficult contexts. The discourse analysis of the teachers' interviews revealed patterns in the ways in which the participants understood 'good' teaching, collegiality, professionalism, underpinning concerns and motivations, and what might enable or constrain 'good' teaching practice. The findings suggest that internal conversations are central to how teachers engage inwardly to define and clarify their teaching philosophies and evaluate their teaching practices. While the findings are presented in separate analytical categories, following Archer's typology of reflexivity, there is considerable overlap between them.

Communicative reflexivity: multidirectional relationships

Communicative reflexivity links subjects to the aspirations and life worlds of their immediate communities, and while this is often thought of in somewhat negative terms (as the inability to take action without the approval of others), communicative reflexivity can be understood more positivity as a form of collegiality. Teaching expertise is distributed in higher education and collaborative networks play a strong role in its attainment by individual teachers (Knight 2002). The academic staff interviewed did not see themselves in solitary pursuit of teaching excellence against the structural and cultural challenges of the institution. The university teachers interviewed spoke about the communities, colleagues and collaborations that supported or had influenced their practice:

> I must say ... this whole scholarship of teaching ... of reading ... of understanding ... of ... trying to see why are the students doing this ... reading books ... reading articles ... has been a strong influence on me.
>
> (Interviewee 6)

> another great influence is the [Faculty] Teaching and Learning Committee ... that's the great influence on my teaching.
>
> (Interviewee 4)

Consultation and collaboration has been an important part of traditional university collegiality and flattened hierarchies. Such collegial traditions have potential for communicative reflexivity (while stronger, hierarchical management practices do not):

> I had a lot of support from the previous HOD who really was trying to understand teaching and learning and working towards it and ... went with me to conferences and wrote papers together to present ... so that was a tremendous support and it was nice because it's the first time I had experienced that ... but then that HOD left and we got another HOD who knows nothing about teaching and learning and quite honestly is not interested.
>
> (Interviewee 6)

Relationships are at the heart of teaching and learning, including relationships with peers, teaching and learning specialists, managers and, most importantly, the contingent relationship between teacher and student (Ashwin 2008, Case 2015). The participants understood the basis of good teaching as multidimensional – and in a constant state of change and development as they responded to diverse students' needs and the changing environment:

> I ... think that I'm as much a learner as I am a teacher because I learn from the students every day. I learn from them. I see teaching and learning as a communal enterprise between me and the students.
>
> (Interviewee 6)

Archer exemplifies communicative reflexivity with reference to 'people who can understand and enter into the subject's concerns and preoccupations to such an extent that they can complete and confirm their friend's tentative thoughts by their talk together' (Archer 2012, p. 147). While the communicative reflexivity exercised by participants in this study was not this intimate, there were rich descriptions of interdependent relationships with trusted colleagues and a responsiveness to students that opened up possibilities for innovation and change in teaching practice.

Autonomous reflexivity: pride and professionalism

Autonomous reflexivity is an internal dialogue with a clear performative intention. Autonomous reflexives typically develop individual projects that capture their interest or concerns (Archer 2012). In some cases, the autonomous internal conversation can be accommodating of others, or can modify itself to the objectives of collective action, particularly when these align with the purposes of an autonomous reflexive. Archer (2012) finds that this kind of reflexivity tends to mediate actions that result in 'structural discontinuities'. While communicative internal conversations aim at maintaining cohesion within the group, the independence implied by autonomous reflexivity is more likely to be disruptive. Archer understands autonomous reflexivity as constituted through purposeful, self-contained and rational deliberation; autonomous reflexives are able to sustain an internal conversation without consultation and are, typically, high achievers in their chosen fields (Archer 2012, p. 34). In the case of the research participants, autonomous reflexivity was characterised, not only by purposeful actions and the attainment of teaching excellence, but by internal forms of motivation. For example, participants did not expect to be rewarded for good teaching – for many it was a matter of personal pride and professionalism. One staff member felt that striving for teaching excellence was more 'beneficial for my own development than for that of the university' (Interviewee 4). Another took on an additional teaching load, as a personal challenge:

> the [pre-first year] group that I've just volunteered for ... I'm just doing it out of my own ... I'm not getting paid for it or anything ... I'm just doing it to explore teaching using technology.
>
> (Interviewee 1)

While staff acknowledged the difficulties of teaching students who were under-prepared for higher education, these difficulties inspired teachers to be innovative:

I think one of the biggest spurts to innovation has been a sense of frustration that I'm not being as effective as I possibly could ... and besides that it's fun to try out new things ... I just find when I have a new idea and I sit down and I start ... hammering it out on the computer I find it so inspiring ... and I often find that the students enjoy being taught in a different way to the regular chalk and talk thing. So that has been a virtuous cycle.

(Interviewee 2)

Many programmes in the institution are accredited or reviewed by professional bodies, and several participants felt that the professional status of the programmes placed expectations on them; as one participant put it: '... keeping up-to-date in the profession in the department is huge' (Interviewee 9).

Meta-reflexivity: making a difference

Archer (2012) understands meta-reflexives to have strong values. In challenging contexts they are likely to experience dissonance between their values and aspirations and the dominant practices and discourses within these contexts. Meta-reflexives therefore problematise the social order as a way of achieving 'the clarification and discursive substantiation of their own values and inclinations towards courses of action that underline their practical reasoning in the social order' (Archer 2012, p. 247).

In an institutional context, where many students are under-prepared for university studies as a result of the policies of the past, the research participants spoke about the importance of good teaching as a way of contributing to students' development beyond simply meeting their immediate needs. For many teachers, the act of teaching was a way of 'giving back' (Interviewee 5), 'making a difference' (Interviewee 7), or bringing 'new young people into my profession' (Interviewee 3). For several participants, good teaching was associated with a journey that teacher and student embark on together. Good teaching is about innovation and doing things differently, particularly if 'doing the same thing' is not effective (Interviewee 8). Good teaching is not about 'going through the motions' (Interviewee 7) or following a set of procedures – it is about inspiring students, challenging them, and making a meaningful difference in their lives. For these reasons, although meta-reflexivity was not a dominant mode across participants, it was an underpinning reflexivity that provided a sustaining vision for what good teaching might achieve.

Participants spoke of their passion for teaching, but were also self-critical, always striving to do better. Critical reflection on one's own teaching practice was understood by all interviewees as a central to development and growth:

It is something that we strive for and in my opinion I will never be perfect ... so I continuously reflect on myself and I continuously try to improve myself.

(Interviewee 5)

I don't think that I've now reached a pinnacle and I'm a good teacher ... I just know that I need to keep improving because I need to keep responding to the students who are different every year and I take student feedback very seriously.

(Interviewee 6)

I don't think I have ever been satisfied ... For me learning means to always improve, reflect. I am satisfied with what I have done at a particular stage in my life but when I reflect on it there are always more opportunities to improve.

(Interviewee 3)

Every time I walk out of the class I think ... well how could I have done that differently? And every morning before I walk into the class ... I'm telling myself today I am going to try and deliver the world's best lecture on this topic and every morning when I walk out of the class I'm thinking that was so not it.

(Interviewee 4)

For the research participants, good teaching was understood as being in service of an ideal – a constantly shifting goal that might be unattainable, but nevertheless pursued with passionate dedication.

Fractured reflexivity: even good teachers have bad days

For a wide range of reasons, the internal conversation of fractured reflexives tends to intensify distress and disorientation rather than clarifying what actions the subject might take. Those whose internal conversation takes this form regularly 'admit to huge difficulties in making decisions, in defining courses of action to be consistently pursued and, above all, in engaging in anything more than the survivalist's day-to-day planning' (Archer 2012, p. 248). The point is not that fractured reflexives are unable to function, but rather that the fractured nature of their reflexivity makes effective action difficult. There was evidence of fractured reflexivity amongst the interviewees, even amongst those striving for teaching excellence, when demands became overwhelming:

because of all the demands ... administrative demands ... we spend most of our time uploading marks ... downloading marks ... checking registrations ... if we can improve our systems and we can give staff more time to focus on teaching and learning ... we as a teaching institution will be much better.

(Interviewee 3)

Structural conditions, such as extremely high workloads that 'are just prohibitive ... workloads and marking ...' (Interviewee 4) can provoke episodes of fractured reflexivity. Participants generally struggled under the burden placed on them by the lack of adequate support services, such as finance, HR, building maintenance and poor IT infrastructure:

> we are so caught up with operational matters that there is never is enough opportunity to speak about the teaching and learning issues.
>
> (Interviewee 3)

Some staff felt that the 'constantly changing regulatory framework in South African higher education', far from creating opportunities for improving teaching, was a barrier and an unnecessary burden:

> Now ... I've been through previous re-curriculation exercises which were a fraction of the bureaucratic technocratic complexity ... there were vast and complex bureaucratic ramifications and a number of forms that have to be filled in ... such that it was hard to think about what's going into the curriculum ... which is what you should be ... rather than which documents that you have fill in ... what are the deadlines and so on ... and your business plan.
>
> (Interviewee 2)

Issues such as the poor state of facilities and building maintenance consumed time and energy that might have been better spent:

> we have very poor facilities and I've been taking this up ... we've been taking it up ... everywhere and anywhere we can ... we have compiled reports ... our facilities are just ... it's poor ... I've taken photos ... we've sent it in ...we've asked for equipment ... and we're hoping ... we're always hoping ... just that environment will go a long way ... I mean we sit with empty cold classrooms with no blinds and no ... some places not even a whiteboard ... I'm not even talking about data projectors and things like that ... we're trying to make do with what we've got ... but there's a big problem with the infrastructure.
>
> (Interviewee 1)

Much energy tends to go into working around the dysfunctionality:

> You know little things ... you want a light replaced in the classroom ... eventually I get a student to climb up on the ladder and put it in you know because ... it's quicker ... so we have to solve problems ... I don't for a moment believe that ... it's reached the stage where it interferes grossly ... I think they're hurdles and we have to overcome them and that's it ... then

we solve it ourselves and you know there are budget limitations there are maintenance limitations and things ... but we have a really nice campus ... it's clean ... it's well maintained ... I am proud of it ... so I think the students have a nice environment to learn in ... I think we have a nice environment to operate in and for that I'm really grateful ... because I think learning in anything less is really hard.

(Interviewee 9)

Several staff felt that there was no point in further developing their practice or trying out new approaches when the resources and facilities to implement innovative practices are lacking:

There's one data projector in a department and even if you do manage to find a data projector, the venues are not such that you can easily use a data projector ... you have to cart it from one venue to the next ... in order to do the kind of developmental work that I am requested to do ... I also need physical facilities and those physical facilities are not forthcoming ... we are in the process of improving our infrastructure ... it takes time but I do not want the quality of my teaching and student learning to be hindered by something like infrastructure ... to the extent that the student can't learn optimally.

(Interviewee 3)

Some participants, who wanted to further develop their teaching, found themselves in a department with colleagues who were not like-minded, often exacerbated by a lack of teaching and learning leadership – creating what one participant called 'a very toxic department'. Clearly in such stressful conditions, teaching excellence (or even basic competence) becomes impossible to achieve:

I think a lot of what one does is determined by the circumstances ... sometimes the circumstances force you into ... or let's say minimises the amount of options that are available to you and sometimes ... yes it is chalk and talk ... because that's all you can do at that moment ... that's all you have available to you at that moment.

(Interviewee 4)

Discussion: choosing teaching

The participants in this study made deliberate choices to engage in teaching above research or other activities that would be more valued by the institution. Constantly improving their practice gave meaning to their identities as university teachers in professional and vocational programmes. Archer's (2012) modes of reflexivity help to explain why the participants made such a strong commitment to teaching and how they attained levels of excellent teaching practice in a challenging environment.

Communicative and autonomous reflexivity emerged as dominant reflexive modes across all the interviews to the extent that it might be appropriate to describe communicative/autonomous reflexivity as a separate reflexive mode (as Porpora and Shumar (2010) do). The participants were engaged in processes of thinking about and enacting teaching by collaborating with like-minded peers and by valuing the engagement and feedback of their students. The participants in this study also made autonomous, professional judgements and acted on these, often against dominant practices and discourses. The attainment of good teaching thus emerges as deeply collegial, but good teaching also emerges as autonomous and independent. The interviews weave communicative and autonomous modes of reflexivity together in different ways. There are several instances in which collaboration and independence were spoken of as parts of the same reflexive process. For example, some participants spoke about learning from a colleague, and then incorporating this into their own repertoire:

> I have had joint classes with the Academic Literacy Lecturer previously on giving them a piece of text background to a topic ... and then I go through the scaffolded reading exercise on it ... that whole notion of scaffolding a concept ... [I have] incorporated it into my own methodologies.
>
> (Interviewee 10)

According to Archer (2012) there are increasingly favourable conditions for the development of autonomous reflexivity, meta-reflexivity and fractured reflexivity, while communicative reflexivity is on the decline in late modernity. In the context of university teaching we see collegial processes becoming eroded through new management practices and thus more difficult to attain. This is likely to have negative consequences for the practice of teaching in contexts where expertise is distributed.

The difficulties of the context meant that there were inevitably signs of fractured reflexivity, of challenges that were too extreme to overcome, and that even good teachers found their actions limited by the resources available to them at any time. These lapses into fractured reflexivity were of temporary duration. They were often told as 'war stories' with switches into more autonomous or communicative modes as the participants explained how these difficulties were tackled and problems addressed.

Committed teachers understood the larger social and material inequalities of the South African higher education sector. Within this larger understanding of higher education, participants recognised that good teaching can make a difference to students' lives. Transformative teaching is thus offered from the position of social justice that develops from meta-reflexivity which, although not dominant, is articulated in a recursive way through communicative and autonomous reflexive capacity. The expanded range of reflexive modes opens up greater opportunities for university teachers to the ways 'in which they can invest themselves such that the accompanying social identity is expressive of who they are as persons in society' (Archer 2000, p. 261). The case study shows the variety of reflexive resources available to university teachers in exercising agency to overcome the constraints of structures and cultures and achieve remarkable and inspirational acts of teaching.

Acknowledgement

The South African National Research Foundation (project leader: Brenda Leibowitz) provided funding for the project titled 'Context, structure and agency' (Grant: 90353).

References

Archer, M. (1995), *Realist social theory: The morphogenetic approach*, Cambridge University Press, Cambridge.

Archer, M. (2000), *Being Human: The problem of agency*, Cambridge University Press, Cambridge.

Archer, M. (2003), *Structure, agency and the internal conversation*, Cambridge University Press, Cambridge.

Archer, M. (2007), *Making our way through the world: Human reflexivity and social mobility*, Cambridge University Press, Cambridge.

Archer, M. (2010), 'The reflexive re-turn', in M. Archer (ed.), *Conversations about reflexivity*, Routledge, London, pp. 1–14.

Archer, M. (2012), *The reflexive imperative in late modernity*, Cambridge University Press, Cambridge.

Ashwin, P. (2008), 'Accounting for structure and agency in "close-up" research on teaching, learning and assessment in higher education', *International Journal of Educational Research*, vol. 47, pp. 151–58.

Badat, S. (2012), 'Redressing the colonial/apartheid legacy: Social equity, redress, and higher education admissions in democratic South Africa', in Z. Hasan & M. Nussbaum (eds), *Equalizing access: Affirmative action in higher education in India, United States, and South Africa*, Oxford University Press, New Delhi, pp. 121–50.

Baloyi, B. & Isaacs, G. (2015), 'South Africa's "fees must fall" protests are about more than tuition costs', CNN/African Voices, available at http://edition.cnn.com/2015/10/27/africa/fees-must-fall-student-protest-south-africa-explainer/

Benade, L. (2015), 'Teachers' critical reflective practice in the context of twenty-first century learning', *Open Review of Educational Research*, vol. 2, no. 1, pp. 42–54.

Boughey, C. (2013), 'The potential to enhance? The use of teaching development grants in South African higher education', paper presented at the 1st International Conference on Enhancement and Innovation in Higher Education, Glasgow, 9–11 June , available at: http://enhancementthemes.ac.uk

Bozalek, V. & Boughey, C. (2012), '(Mis)framing higher education in South Africa', *Social Policy and Administration*, vol. 46, pp. 688–703.

Bryan, L. & Recesso, A. (2006), 'Promoting reflection among science student teachers using a web-based video analysis tool', *Journal of Computing in Teacher Education*, vol. 23, pp. 31–39.

Caetano, A. (2014), 'Defining personal reflexivity: A critical reading of Archer's approach', *European Journal of Social Theory*, vol. 18, no. 1, pp. 1–16.

Case, J. (2015), 'Emergent interactions: Rethinking the relationship between teaching and learning', *Teaching in Higher Education*, vol. 20, pp. 625–35.

Cooper, D. (2015), 'Social justice and South African university student enrolment data by "race", 1998–2012: From "skewed revolution" to "stalled revolution"', *Higher Education Quarterly*, vol. 69, pp. 237–62.

Dewey, J. (1910), *How we think*, D. C. Heath, Lexington, MA.

Elder-Vass, D. (2010), *The causal power of social structures: Emergence, structure and agency*, Cambridge University Press, Cambridge.

Engel-Hills, P., Winberg, C. & Rip, A. (2016), 'Ethics "upfront": Generating an organizational framework for a new university of technology', *Science and Engineering Ethics*, in press, http://link.springer.com/journal/11948

Freire, P. (1985), *The politics of education: Culture, power and liberation*, Macmillan, New York.

Giddens, A. (1984), *The constitution of society: Outline of the theory of structuration*, University of California Press, San Francisco.

Giroux, H. A. (1983), *Theory and resistance in education: A pedagogy for the opposition*, Bergin & Garvey, South Hadley, MA.

Kahn, P. (2009), 'Contexts for teaching and the exercise of agency in early-career academics: Perspectives from realist social theory', *International Journal for Academic Development*, vol. 14, no. 3, pp. 197–207.

Knight, P. (2002), *Being a teacher in higher education*, Society for Research in Higher Education and the Open University Press, Maidenhead.

Leibowitz, B. & Bozalek, V. (2014). 'Access to higher education in South Africa: A social realist account', *Widening Participation and Lifelong Learning*, vol. 16, no. 1, pp. 91–109.

Maxwell, J. (2012), *A realist approach for qualitative research*, Sage, Los Angeles.

Mezirow, J. (2000), *Learning as transformation: Critical perspectives on a theory in progress*, Jossey Bass, San Francisco, CA.

Porpora, D. V. & Shumar, W. (2010), 'Self-talk and self-reflection: A view from the US', in M. Archer (ed.), *Conversations about reflexivity*, pp. 206–220, Routledge, London.

Quinn, L. (2012), 'Enabling and constraining conditions for academic staff development', in L. Quinn (ed.), *Re-imagining academic staff development: Spaces for disruption*, pp. 27–50, Sun Press, Stellenbosch, South Africa.

Scambler, G. (2012), 'Resistance in unjust times: Archer, structured agency and the sociology of health inequalities', *Sociology*, vol. 47, no. 1, pp. 142–56.

Schön, D. A. (1983), *The reflective practitioner: How professionals think in action*, Basic Books, New York.

Schön, D. A. (1987), *Educating the reflective practitioner: Towards a new design for teaching and learning in the professions*, Jossey-Bass, San Francisco, CA.

South African Council on Higher Education (CHE) (2013a), 'A proposal for undergraduate curriculum reform in South Africa: The case for a flexible curriculum structure', available at: www.che.ac.za/media_and_publications/research/proposal-undergraduate-curric ulum-reform-south-africa-case-flexible

South African Council on Higher Education (CHE) (2013b), 'Quality enhancement project: The process', available at: www.che.ac.za/sites/default/files/QEP%20Process %20Framework%20Doc.pdf

South African Department of Higher Education and Training/The Ministerial Oversight Committee on Transformation in South African Public Universities (DHET) (2015), 'The transformation of South African higher education', concept paper prepared for the Second National Higher Education Transformation Summit, Durban, 15–17 October, 2015, available at: www.dhet.gov.za/summit/Docs/2015Docs/Annex%208_TOC_Transformation%20of%20SA%20HE.pdf

Winberg, C. & Garraway, J. (2016), '"It takes a village": Attaining teaching excellence in a challenging context', *South African Journal of Higher Education* (in press).

Part IV

Crossover perspectives

Chapter 12

Researching learning to teach

A narrative on 'crossing over'

Brenda Leibowitz

Prologue

> To what extent are different theoretical approaches genuinely incommensurable views that simply cannot be used interchangeably in education research? Does the choice of framework determine the kind of outcome or implications for practice that the researcher will generate? Are some theoretical perspectives more helpful than others, in contributing to social justice in and through education?

These are variants of questions that I listed in an opening slide of a presentation I made at the Organisational Learning, Culture and Knowledge Conference in July last year. I was midway in a move from one approach, namely critical and social realism, to another, namely practice-based approaches, as these intersect with feminist or new materialisms and posthumanism. This process of crossing from one approach to another has been at times exhilarating, and at times extremely painful. I am sharing this process with the readers of this volume, as a means to reflect on the questions I listed above. The style of this chapter is somewhat untraditional, as it hovers between on the one hand the autobiographical, narrative and introspective, and the other hand, the discursive and analytic.

Getting going

I worked until recently at a Centre for Teaching and Learning where my unit was responsible for supporting academics in learning to teach. A call came out from the South African National Research Foundation for applications for educational research proposals that were based at a minimum of three institutions, of which at least one needed to be rural. A group of colleagues who had been working together on various academic development projects were very excited that at last, research funds were accessible to us as academic developers. We were very committed to our work and were thankful for an opportunity that we believed, would grant credibility and rigour to our deliberations. We were motivated by academic curiosity, but above all, by a desire to enhance our understanding of our work and to improve our professional practice. We planned to focus on our academic development centres' offerings and on the influence of institutional context on academics' willingness to participate in professional development opportunities. Understanding our institutional contexts, we believed, would enhance our professional practice, would consolidate the advice we could give to our senior managers, and finally, inform a more nuanced and contextualised approach to policy on professional development, that we would be able to share with the national Department of Higher Education and Training. Approximately 18 academic developers from across the country came together to finalise a research proposal.

As project leader, I was disposed to launch a study with very little prior clarity on the theoretical underpinning – partly the result of an anti-intellectualism based on my biography of working outside formal academic or faculty positions, and partly because of the short notice we were given before the research grants were due. One influential colleague on the team argued strongly that in order to be scholarly we needed to base our study on a clear theoretical framework, and that the interplay between structure, culture and agency as characterised by Margaret Archer, would be a useful way to study the mechanisms within institutional contexts that influence individuals' engagement with professional development. She maintained that that if one's study was informed by a clear, useful theory, this would grant the research more explanatory power, it would make the research more interesting to readers and it would consequently make it more publishable. Responses amongst team members varied between the following: 'wonderful – a chance to learn about a new theoretical perspective' to 'I am too old to have to learn a new theoretical approach now' to 'that body of literature is dense and impenetrable'. Since nobody posed a strong alternative that found support within the group, the compromise reached was to maintain a broad focus on institutional context, and to utilise a social realist approach, but loosely understood. It was further agreed that those who wished to, should apply additional theoretical lenses to the data later in the process.

Our proposal was successful. The research team of 18 comprised three who were very familiar with social realism, several who immediately set about to read several publications on social realism, and approximately half the group who made their way more hesitantly and slowly into the theory.

Research design and process

The research design was collaborative (O'Sullivan, Stoddard & Kalishman 2010), in the sense that the researchers came together to define the aims and research design, as well as to collect the data and to interpret it together, and thus there was a shared intellectual process. It was participatory, in the sense that the intention was partly for the process to be educational for those involved (Somekh 2005) and in the sense that the researchers were investigating their own contexts (Simons 2005). We were motivated by the desire to enhance teaching and learning at our institutions and across the country. Sub-groups within the larger team designed the various components. The final design was influenced by a critical and social realist paradigm as the team understood it. The structural and cultural conditions influencing academics' intentions to learn to teach and to participate in professional development opportunities at the various universities were investigated at the level of the empirical (Bhaskar 1998), via ascertaining the experience of these conditions by role-players at the eight institutions: senior administrators, heads of academic development units and lecturers. The reflexive responses of these same role-players were sought, in order to understand how they responded to the structural and cultural conditions, thus how they made 'their way in the world' (Archer 2007). The accounts from the role-players were corroborated or counterposed with information obtained from national and institutional policies and other publically available documentation and socio-economic indicators of cultural and structural conditions in the country. Data was gathered according to level, but was also summarised in the form of eight institutional case studies. This allowed for the generation of a large amount of data, which could be analysed according to theme, as well as according to institution.

A summary of the levels, research foci and sources of data is provided in the table below.

Table 12.1 Outline of the data collected in relation to underlying critical and social realist framework

Macro	**National landscape** Data: national policy documents and publically available documents	Eight institutional reports were written on the data collected at each institution
Meso/institutional level	**Structural and cultural conditions at eight universities** Data: reports and policies publically available at eight universities Data: analysis by Directors of Teaching and Learning at eight universities Data: Interviews with Senior Managers (×4) at eight universities	
	Roles of managers in relation to teaching and learning Data: interviews with Senior Managers (×4) at eight universities	
Micro/level of the individual lecturer	Roles of teaching academics, perception of participation and growth and of contextual influences on these	
	Data: audio-taped interviews with teaching academics (minimum ×10) at eight universities Data: online survey sent to academics at eight universities	

At the time of writing this chapter (2016) the project is in its final year, out of six years of funding, and it has been fairly successful. In addition to the number of research outputs, including 18 journal articles, the team is in the process of generating a research report to be published by the South African Council for Higher Education, which will culminate in practical suggestions for senior administrators at university level.

Findings facilitated by the research design

The research design was useful in allowing us to consider how academics made sense of their situations, and allied to this, how they exercised individual agency. One example of this is the chapter by Winberg in this volume. Another is in Leibowitz (2014) where the willingness of lecturers to contribute to the learning of students, despite significant material constraints, was highlighted. A lecturer in that article was quoted as saying, 'Look, it's hard to say the environment is conducive, but I think we have the attitude to make it conducive, we look beyond the potholes' (Leibowitz 2014, p. 63). The focus on the views of role-players at the meso- and micro-levels allowed us to consider issues of perspective and role in more depth (see Bozalek & McMillan, this volume, for one example). The research also allowed us to consider how key contextual factors were understood differently amongst actors. One such factor was that of time. Jawitz and Perez (2015) demonstrated how perceived lack of time to engage in learning to teach was understood as an absolute barrier by some, and not by others, at one research-intensive institution.

An advantage of the multi-site, multiple case research design was that it facilitated comparisons, and for issues to surface that might appear obvious if one is only investigating conditions at one type of university, or one university. An example of a factor in the domain of culture that constrained participation in professional development activities at all eight institutions, – whether research-intensive or not, whether previously advantaged or not – was the consistent valuing of research over teaching. We found this to be shocking, given the varied priorities and conditions at the eight institutions. This matter is being taken up in our final research report with recommendations. An interesting finding, which we had not expected to reach, pertained to the structural condition of being a rural university. This intersected with being 'previously disadvantaged', and appeared to influence professional learning at two of the universities in the study. This is discussed in Leibowitz et al. (2015), where it was mentioned that the lack of facilities such as schools, shopping facilities or libraries discouraged administrators, lecturers and academic developers from staying for many years at the institution. It limits the 'institutional memory' and depth of contextualised expertise and experience academic developers and institutional managers might accumulate. A group of research team members then explored the data pertaining to the theme of rural institutions in contexts of poverty in more depth (Ndebele, Muhuro & Nkonki, in press).

One of the positive spinoffs of the research was that it encouraged us to reconsider some of our basic assumptions. For example, one of the research questions in the original proposal to the funders was, what were the conditions at various institutions, which: 'either encourage or discourage [academics] *to take advantage of professional development opportunities afforded by various institutions?*'. This question implies that academics learn to teach by taking advantage of opportunities provided by others, rather than that they learn from a variety of phenomena in their settings. The data that we collected suggested that less of a role should have been accorded by us to the work of academic developers and professional development programmes, and a greater role should have been accorded by us to the material and social conditions in which academics learn to teach. In van Schalkwyk et al. (2015, p. 7) I and several other colleagues in the project referred to the conditions in which academics learn to teach as 'spaces to flourish'. This realisation stresses the role of the agency of the academics, but it also stresses the role of the environments, and thus the interplay between structure, culture and agency. It also highlights the idea that learning to teach is not a once-off event, occurring at the beginning of one's career or due to a single intervention such as a programme and moving from deficit to maturation (Webster-Wright 2009), which is why in several of our publications we began to use the phrase 'being and becoming' a good teacher rather than 'engaging in professional development opportunities' (Leibowitz et al. 2012).

Limitations

There were also shortcomings in our design, due in part to the manner in which we applied the social realist theories, with the understanding we had of them at the time that we designed the research project. In retrospect, one of the critical shortcomings of the research design is that it was static: it considered the conditions at the various institutions at a particular point in time. The way we conceptualised the multiple case study approach did not facilitate a consideration of the manner in which morphogenesis (change) or morphostasis (no change) occurred at the various institutions, a key contribution of the work of Archer (1995). A further drawback of the research was that the social realist theories are fairly dense and require a fair amount of explanation when one translates them to 'the public'. Some of our findings were fairly straightforward, which led to some delegates at a colloquium we organised on the project to say, 'but why did you need the theory of Margaret Archer to show that?'. A further shortcoming of the research design is that because it was such a loose application of the critical and social realist theories, it has not really contributed to the critical and social realist literature in a significant manner. Only one of the publications actually reflected critically on any aspect of the critical or social realist literature, that of reflexivity (Leibowitz, Garraway & Farmer 2015). This was actually in response to an anonymous review solicited by the journal, which suggested that we should have engaged more critically with the concept of reflexivity and the criticisms thereof.

Thus, evidently the research project, its theoretical underpinnings and research design were able to produce valuable outcomes, including recommendations that we are fine-tuning at the time of writing this chapter. I personally learnt a great deal from the project, about critical and social realism, about academics learning to teach and about collaborative research in large teams. Many of the colleagues in the team reported benefitting similarly. However despite the evident value of the study, I was becoming restless. This was occasioned in part by the shortcomings of our research design, as alluded to above. It was due partly to the fact that critical and social realism are in the first instance a philosophy of social science and in the second instance an account of social change. They are not intended to be theories of learning – and therefore cannot explicate all aspects of professional learning without further development. It is true that there is a significant body of literature on critical and social realism and higher education, but I maintain that the literature is rather more about change in terms of structure, culture or agency, than about learning. Granted it sheds much light on the decisions individuals make about how much to invest in their own learning, but I contend that learning is not always conscious or reflexive. Archer writes about learning that is not conscious as practice, for example about learning to ride a bicycle. This is however where I believed I could learn more, from other sources that paid more attention to issues I was focusing on. I happened to be reading on practice-based approaches to professional learning, and at the same time I participated in a reading group on feminist materialism and posthumanism, led by Karin Murris from the University of Cape Town. I began to wonder how and whether these new approaches could help explain some of the phenomena influencing learning to teach, that I wanted to explain.

The key relationship that I wanted to explore, which I felt was constrained by the critical and social realist approach, was the relation between the material conditions and individual agency. It is very evident from the writing of Archer, as with Marxist and post-Marxist writing, that the material and material resources are regarded as extremely significant. Indeed, the very notion of structure implies distribution of rules and resources (Archer 1995). My fear, however, was that if one treats lack of material resources as a constraint that only the most agential human beings can circumnavigate, this can lead to either forms of determinism, victimhood or the judging of individuals who do not exercise agency, as problematic. This is not to say that critical and social realism inevitably lead to these forms of misrecognition by researchers, but rather, that as theoretical resources, they do not signpost these dangers sufficiently, such that members of our team were alerted to a different way of looking at our data.

New perspectives

The potential of new resources to deepen my understanding of the relationship of institutional contextual factors influencing learning to teach centred on practice-based approaches to professional learning, as this intersects with and is influenced by feminist materialism, new materialiam and sociomaterialism, and posthumanism. I first turned to the work on practice, where I was strongly taken by the accounts of learning portrayed by Gherardi (2012) and the volume edited by Fenwick and Nerland (2014). However through the reading group referred to above, I became aware of how certain strands within practice theory are influenced by and intersect with sociomaterialism and posthumanism, and that I would have to factor the implications of sociomaterialism into my thinking about the data as well.

One of the concepts I found most useful within practice theory is that of situated action, which, from Gherardi, 'means considering the organisation of the action as emerging *in situ* from the dynamic of the interactions', resulting from: 'each participant's understanding of the action of the other or others' (Gherardi 2012, p. 18). The way that situations or practices help shape meaning and subjectivity is important in explaining how lecturers are influenced by their environments in learning to teach. She talks of a 'contingent logic embedded in the situation' (2012, p. 19). This helps to explain how the lecturer's understanding is shaped by the situation, including the use of space, time, technology, and the understandings of the others in the situation. The use of the word 'opportunities' is interesting here. In contexts that have inadequate facilities, are there less opportunities to learn, or are there, rather, opportunities to engage in learning differently? The important point here, is that the lecturer, the students, their understandings, the walls, the microphone are all part of the contingent logic, that further shapes the learning of the students and the professional learning of the lecturer. The context of the practice is itself a 'resource for practical reasoning and action' (Gherardi 2012, p. 28). This does not imply that there is no role for Archer's concept of reflexivity, in that a lecturer might still need to think carefully, whether they are sufficiently concerned to devise strategies to deal with the contingent logic, and to strategise to overcome certain perceived constraints. What I am arguing, however, is that there are significant aspects of the mysteries surrounding learning in institutional contexts, that practice theories are more helpful to resolve.

The idea that subjectivity is shaped by situational dynamics involving all manner of entities became even more challenging and complex when I began to read the work of feminist materialists such as Barad (2007), who have had an influence on practice theories. Barad writes that the discursive and the material are entangled, mutually constitutive, or 'intra-acting'. Neither is ontologically prior, and agency is performed into existence by this entanglement. Thus subjectivity is influenced not only by the culture or the structure, but by all aspects of the material and the discursive simultaneously interpenetrating and influencing each other. Within this intra-action, discourse and discursive practices are dynamic and active. In their entanglement with the material they 'constrain and enable ... what can be said' (Barad 2003, p. 819). They are highly influential, and 'produce, rather than merely describe, the "subjects" and "objects" of knowledge practices' (Barad 2003, p. 819). I find this a useful way to describe the lecturers' accounts of their teaching, their understanding of what teaching implies, and the environment in which they teach. This is an example of such an extract from an interview with a lecturer at a rural and historically disadvantaged university:

> the facilities, like the lecture venues that … don't support a projector, I've actually done a workbook for students. I can actually show you the workbook that I did last year and so I give them lots of notes and stuff that they can follow in class. So, if they can't see the board or they can't hear me, they've still got the notes in front of them. From a classroom management perspective, I've also just become much stricter and because I have problems with voice projection in large classes, I end up circling the lecture venues, so that everybody can get to hear me at some point in time.

In this quote there is a sense that the material and the discursive are not ontologically prior, but they constitute each other and perform particular forms of teaching and learning into existence – a form where learning is about the conveyance of information through language, texts and artefacts – in particular those artefacts that seek to convey knowledge from the expert, via the lecturer, to the student. It is not possible on the basis of this interview, and many others like it, to see either the discursive or the material as prior.

The work of practice-based writers such as Gherardi (2012) or Zukas and Kilminster (2014) show more directly how artefacts function as actors, as the repositories of memory in an organisation, as being constituted by people and in turn constituting them. In the above quote, the lecturer's workbook is an actor, structuring the way the students learn. The lecturer's own subjectivity is constituted by the lack of a microphone as well as the notion that knowledge is a good that can be passed to students.

An important dynamic within practice-based and new materialist approaches are the notion that 'doing and knowing are not separated' (Gherardi 2012, p. 78). This helps to explain the difference between seeing lecturers as developing in formal courses or as imbibing theory by reading, which is more consonant with a social realist approach to knowledge (Maton & Moore 2010, Muller 2014), rather than seeing lecturers as learning relationally, by doing, by interacting with others who practice. The latter would be more akin to a practice orientation. This helps to explain the move in the study, from looking at professional development to professional learning, which was suggested by the data, and which attracted me to practice and new materialist theories.

Ontological and epistemological incompatibilities

Learning about the new paradigms was simultaneously invigorating and frustrating. It was invigorating to learn about a new way of seeing the world. It was frustrating partly because certain forms of sociomaterial writing felt complex and in some instances, esoteric – much the same as writing about critical and social realism, in fact. A second reason why it was frustrating, was that many of the central arguments for a new or feminist materialist approach debunked ideas about reality and truth that are fundamental to western Cartesian enlightenment and humanist ways of thinking (Jackson, Z. 2013). According to Snaza (2015, p. 20), western humanism has come to structure '*the entirety of Western education,* its institutions, its concepts, its practices'. The new ideas felt counter-intuitive, so deeply ingrained are humanist conceptions of the world. However the biggest challenge to trying out new frameworks was that there are significant areas of incommensurability between, in particular social realism, for example ideas on reflexivity, and sociomateriality. Ideas on reflexivity are located within humanist ways of thinking. A humanist ontology is seen by posthumanists as hierarchical, where the human viewpoint predominates (Snaza & Weaver 2015, Bennett 2010) and humans are top of the hierarchy and are central, in taken-for-granted ways. A humanist worldview is more likely to see time as linear, moving from point A to point B (with reference to Archer and morphogenesis one can talk of T1 to T4, and so on), rather than as having neither a future, nor a fixed past (Barad 2015). Importantly from a humanist perspective – certainly the way our research project understood social realism and went about its work – the human is the all-seeing eye that views, interprets, and critiques. In contradistinction to a humanist approach, a new materialist ontology does not see the world in terms of boundaried objects whose identities are fixed and stable. Humans are not above the world of meaning, but within it. Agency does not reside in humans, but within the 'mangle' (Jackson, A. 2013), 'reciprocally engaged in the play of resistance and accommodation' (Jackson, A. 2013, p. 744).

One aspect of the social realist writing of Margaret Archer that is most evidently humanist (see especially Archer 2000, 2007, 2010) is her concern with humans, their reflexivity or internal conversations, that lead them to adopt the life and work trajectories that they do. This is one of the aspects of her research that has fascinated me the most, and that has informed the work I have done on lecturers' motivation to learn to teach, for example a paper I co-wrote on data collected just before beginning this study (Leibowitz et al. 2012) and on biographies, concerns and commitments guiding individuals' behaviour (Leibowitz, Garraway & Farmer 2015). And yet this is the source of possibly the greatest dissonance between social realist and new materialist writing, and a reason why I have had to ask myself whether it is possible to be so influenced by these different ontologies at the same time – let alone to try and write up the research with both approaches in mind. Snaza (2015) for instance, observes the modern humanist ontology as built upon the influences of eighteenth-century philosophers and novelists, who proposed an essentialised view of the human. This is in contrast to a view of humans as inextricably bound up with matter, other life forms and each other, thus a relational ontology rather than seeing individuals as entities in themselves.

Most of the areas of incommensurability pertain to differences between social realism and sociomateriality or posthumanism, although with respect to practice theory, a point of tension is the status of culture and text. In social realist writing culture, text and discourse is given much prominence, yet Fenwick (2014), specifically minimises the importance of text and culture.

Perhaps the greatest area of incommensurability between social realism and sociomaterialism (and posthumanism, which intersects with sociomaterialism) is in terms of research methodology. Posthumanism eschews the notion of the researcher as outside of the world being researched, rather than within it and 'participating in construction' (Springgay 2015, p. 85). The idea that data are passive, for the interpreter or 'knowing human researcher' (Snaza & Weaver 2015, p. 8) to mould, is rejected. From a social justice point of view, post-humanism is 'affirmative' (Braidotti 2013), less likely to adapt a position of critique and more likely to look for opportunities for non-judgement of others (Springgay 2015). Even with regard to data collection methods, there is a degree of incommensurability: within posthumanist thought there is a move away from traditional qualitative methods such as the interview, a practice that could be said to be informed by a representational view of reality, where interviewees can convey world views of intentional humans, through language, to a researcher, who can derive a stable view of reality. Coding, a traditional qualitative research method on which our project relied significantly, is strongly criticised by sociomaterialists and posthumanists (MacLure 2014, St Pierre & Jackson 2014) for imposing categories on deadening data. Similarly, the unit of analysis from a practice perspective shifts from, for example, the document or case to the practice, which Gherardi (2012, p. 2) defines as 'loci – spatial and temporal – in which working, organising, innovating or reproducing occurs'. In our project we did not consider practices as unit of analysis at all. And from a new materialist perspective the unit of analysis shifts from the human, to a coupling of the human and non-human, including materials and technology (Pedersen 2015).

One must not make the mistake of thinking that everything about the two ontologies is in opposition. (I say 'two' because practice approaches straddle humanist and sociomaterialist positions, depending on the author). Far from it. Both refer to 'emergence' and use the word 'contingency'. Both write about the conditions as neither determining nor not determining. Archer writes, for example that constraints with the exception of the most dire can be circumnavigated, but with varying degrees of effort (Archer, 2000). Similarly, Jackson (2013) writes that 'human and material agencies [are] reciprocally engaged in the play of resistance and accommodation' (Jackson, A. 2013, p. 744). Both accept that there is not a predictive relationship between cause and effect because of the infinite number of possible intervening features and relationships between features. Yet where they might differ is in the critical realist notion that there is causality, inherent in the properties of people (Archer 2007) or structural or cultural conditions (Archer 1995) and the new materialist, stronger assertion that 'terminal effects cannot be construed as possibilities that were already latent in some initial moment' (Coole & Frost 2010, p. 14). Both see opportunities for change, transformation or freedom, though in different ways. Furthermore, neither approach is altogether homogenous, as if one can draw a tight boundary around either.

Implications of the differences

For supporting lecturers to learn to teach

Are these incompatibilities merely philosophical, or do they have an effect on the way we understand lecturers and their learning to teach? I would argue that indeed, they do have a significant impact. There is a great difference between attributing agency to lecturers, and seeing agency as distributed within the intra-action. The implications of a practice approach for learning to teach might be that instead of prescribing people's actions with policies and even incentives, administrators might do well to concentrate on creating an enabling environment (Boud & Brew 2013, and this volume), which would include all aspects that comprise practices, including time, space, artefacts, and opportunities for people to learn from each other, and seeing the responsibility to learn to teach, as distributed. An implication of a practice approach is to arrange the environment in which a novice academic works in such a way that s/he will learn over time, with specific apprenticeship mechanisms in place (Fuller & Unwin 2014).

In a critical or social realist view, more emphasis would be placed on intervening in relation to individuals' or groups' reflexivity, as Kahn discusses in Chapter 10. In a critical realist view, as it influenced our research project, there is a fair degree of emphasis on policy discourses and how these influence academics' behaviour. From a new materialist point of view one would not consider beliefs, or discourses of teaching and learning, without considering the materiality in which these beliefs are uttered, negotiated or maintained.

An important aspect of difference is views on predictability. In the case of new materialism there would be no predictability (see Coole & Frost 2010, p. 14) whereas amongst critical realists a case is made for trends or the isolations of explanations for how events turn out how they do (Lawson 1998). A sociomaterial view would make the work of institutional administrators or academic developers who wish to develop strategies for teaching and learning or professional development difficult, as these strategies traditionally consider key factors that are believed to encourage success. In contrast to this, from a new materialist view there is a sense, precisely, that a view of freedom flows from the fact that the natural world always contains a surprise element (Bennett 2010).

Another incommensurability pertains to views of knowledge. If the world consists of stable categories such as what is human, and a strong view of texts as 'real' as does Archer (Archer & Elder-Vass 2012) or Maton and Moore (2010) then there is a limit to the multiplicity of knowledges one can accept as credible, and as worthy of sharing with other students and lecturers. However, if one sees knowledge as dependent on the manner in which it is derived or how the knowledge is traced then a multiplicity of knowledges can co-exist. It becomes possible to teach various competing forms of western science, and alongside this, various indigenous knowledges. Similarly, it becomes possible to adopt western and non-western approaches to teaching and learning.

Thoughts on theory and ontology

So what have I learnt from my transition from one ontological position to another, and how does this square with what others have written on the subject of crossing over? Wenger-Trayner (2013), for instance, argues that one can work with a dominant theory and that a secondary theory can be plugged in to the dominant one. Perhaps this will work when the theories do not clash at an ontological level, as the ones I have cited appear to do, in several important respects. I am not convinced this is the solution for the theories I have referred to.

Ashwin (2009) maintains that all theories are 'simplifications' of reality, and that what one uses is influenced by the questions one is asking. (As an aside: if they are 'simplifications', one wonders why so many need to be so complex and difficult to penetrate! I don't only make this comment out of sympathy for myself, but in thinking about the challenges this poses for collaborative research groups like the one on which this chapter is based, and for any new writing relationship I wish to enter into, with colleagues who have even less time and inclination to do heavy duty reading, due to the work they do, than I do.) Dewey and pragmatists following him have argued (for example Creswell 2003), that the choice depends on the purpose of the research, and thus what is *useful* as an approach. There is value in this argument, but I believe matters are more complex than this position suggests.

In chapter 13 (this volume) Hannon et al. share the value of putting different theories to work on one set of data, despite the ontological differences. Their contribution shows the value of comparison that 'clarifies potential contributions'. It shows that one dataset can be analysed from more than one theoretical and ontological position, and the value of this, but I am not sure this is the same as saying that one entire research project can be approached from different positions, and certainly not two thirds way through the project, as in the case I am discussing. This points to one aspect of the solution, as obvious as it may sound, which is to be clear about the ontological and ethical assumptions informing any of the theories one wishes to use. If these are seen to clash, one should take the time to understand the incompatibilities and to find out where to bridge them, if possible.

Perhaps a more intellectually challenging position to adopt, if one happens to find theories derived from at points incommensurable ideas appealing, is the one that calls for a creative reworking of theories that are in several respects inadequate to a research task. This is more than to plug one into another. It means serious reworking or adding to a theory, such that it might even become a 'new' theory. This is also where researchers can make original contributions to the literature. Another alternative derives from sociomaterialist writers, who argue for the diffraction (Barad 2014 and Bozalek & McMillan, this volume) of one theory through another, reading one theory through the other, troubling the surfaces of either, building on one another, and producing differences that 'matter'. This, too, could lead to the production of original ideas.

The question remains, is crossing over and the trouble it causes, worth the hard work? It is, since there are times when people need to work together across epistemological traditions and disciplines, in order to achieve useful or usable findings. A compelling case for this position is made by Wiklund (2013). She describes the loss and insecurity she has experienced in having to research across the disciplines of physiotherapy, public health and gender studies, and across the differing epistemologies and ontologies associated with these fields. She concludes that this is necessary bridging work in order to achieve 'social robustness' (p. 136) in research, for example if one is to achieve gender-sensitive interventions in youth health services. In theorising learning to teach one is not necessarily crossing disciplines, but one is working across traditions and might be working with academics who teach in different disciplines. Thus being able to reach 'robust' suggestions in education requires us to research together, at the same time.

Closing remarks

I have discovered through the process of trying to understand social realism, practice approaches and sociomaterialism, that the three clusters of theories I have discussed are immensely rich, appealing and extremely complex. To do justice to the similarities, differences and comparative affordances would require far more than this single chapter would allow. What I hope to have achieved in this chapter, however, is to illuminate some of the trials and tribulations of moving from one body of thought to another – partly to write a piece with which other researchers can identify in a cathartic manner, and partly to emphasise the importance for researchers in the field of professional learning, and for academic developers, to be clear about the inherent assumptions on which their research and professional work is based.

Acknowledgements

This chapter is based on a research project, *The Interplay of Structure, Culture and Agency: A Study of Professional Development in Higher Education*, funded by the (South African) National Research Foundation, Grant: 90353.

In addition to comments from the anonymous reviewers and comments from the co-editors, particular thanks for critical and supportive feedback go to Karin Murris and Dirk Postma.

References

Archer, M. (1995), *Realist social theory: The morphogenetic approach*, Cambridge University Press, Cambridge.
Archer, M. (2000), *Being human: The problem of agency*, Cambridge University Press, Cambridge.
Archer, M. (2007), *Making our way through the world: Human reflexivity and social mobility*, Cambridge University Press, Cambridge.

Archer, M. (2010), 'Introduction: The reflexive re-turn', in M. Archer (ed.), *Conversations about reflexivity*, Routledge, London.

Archer, M. S. & Elder-Vass, D. (2012), 'Cultural system or norm circles? An exchange', *European Journal of Social Theory*, vol. 15, no. 1, pp. 93–115. doi:10.1177/13684310 11423592.

Ashwin, P. (2009), *Analysing teaching-learning interactions in higher education: Accounting for structure and agency*, Continuum, London.

Barad, K. (2003), 'Posthumanist performativity: Towards an understanding of how matter comes to matter', *Journal of Women in Culture and Society*, vol. 28, no. 3, pp. 801–31.

Barad, K. (2007), *Meeting the universe half-way*, Duke University Press, Durham, NC.

Barad, K. (2014), 'Diffracting diffraction: Cutting together-apart', *Parallax*, 20, vol. 3, pp. 168–87.

Barad, K. (2015), 'Transmaterialities: Trans*/matter/realities and queer political imaginings', *Journal of Lesbian and Gay Studies*, vol. 21, no. 2-3, pp. 387–422.

Bennett, J. (2010), 'A vitalist stopover on the way to a new materialism', in D. Coole and S. Frost (eds), *New materialisms: Ontology, agency, and politics*, Duke University Press, Durham.

Bhaskar, R. (1998), 'Philosophy and scientific realism', in M. Archer, R. Bhaskar, A. Collier, T. Lawson & A. Norrie (eds), *Critical realism: Essential readings*, Routledge, London.

Boud, D. & Brew, A. (2013), 'Reconceptualising academic work as professional practice: Implications for academic development', *International Journal for Academic Development*, vol. 18, no. 3, pp. 208–21.

Braidotti, R. (2013), *The posthuman*, Polity Press, Cambridge.

Coole, D. and Frost, S. (2010), 'Introducing the new materialisms', in D. Coole and S. Frost (eds), *New materialisms: Ontology, agency, and politics*, pp. 1–46, Duke University Press, Durham.

Creswell, J. (2003), *Research design: Qualitative, quantitative and mixed methods approaches*, Sage, Thousand Oaks.

Fenwick, T. (2014), 'Rethinking professional responsibility: matters of account', in T. Fenwick & M. Nerland (eds), *Reconceptualising professional learning: Sociomaterial knowledges, practices and responsibilities*, Routledge, London.

Fenwick, T. & Nerland, M. (2014) (eds), *Reconceptualising professional learning: Sociomaterial knowledges, practices and responsibilities*, Routledge, London.

Fuller, A. & Unwin, L. (2014), 'Nurturing occupational expertise in the contemporary workplace: An "'apprenticeship turn in professional learning"', in T. Fenwick and M. Nerland (eds), *Reconceptualising professional learning: Sociomaterial knowledges, practices and responsibilities*, Routledge, London.

Gherardi, S. (2012), *How to conduct a practice-based study: Problems and methods*, Edward Elgar, Cheltenham.

Jackson, A. (2013), 'Posthumanist data analysis of mangling practices', *International Journal of Qualitative Studies in Education*, vol. 26, no. 6, pp. 741–48.

Jackson, Z. (2013), 'Animal: New directions in the theorization of race and posthumanism', *Feminist Studies*, vol. 39, no. 3, pp. 669–85.

Jawitz, J. & Perez, T. (2015), 'Investing in teaching development: Navigating risk in a research-intensive institution', *International Journal for Academic Development* (online).

Lawson, T. (1998), 'Economic science without experimentation', in M. Archer, R. Bhaskar, A. Collier, T. Lawson & A. Norrie (eds), *Critical realism: Essential readings*, Routledge, London.

Leibowitz, B. (2014), 'Conducive environments for the promotion of quality teaching in higher education in South Africa', *CRISTAL*, vol. 2, no. 1, pp. 49–73.

Leibowitz, B., Bozalek, V., Winberg, C. & van Schalkwyk, S. (2015), 'Institutional context matters: The professional development of academics as teachers in South African higher education', *Higher Education*, vol. 69, no. 2, pp. 315–30.

Leibowitz, B., Garraway, J. & Farmer, J. (2015), 'Influence of the past on professional lives: A collective commentary', *Mind, Culture and Activity*, vol. 22, pp. 23–26.

Leibowitz, B., van Schalkwyk, S., Ruiters, J., Farmer, J. & Adendorff, H. (2012), '"It's been a wonderful life": Accounts of the interplay between structure and agency by "good" university teachers', *Higher Education*, vol. 63, pp. 353–65.

Maclure, E. (2014), 'The wonder of data', *Cultural Studies – Critical Methodologies*, vol.13, no. 4, pp. 228–32.

Maton, K. & Moore, R. (2010), 'Introduction', in K. Maton & R. Moore (eds), *Social realism, knowledge and the sociology of education*, Continuum, London.

Muller, J. (2014), 'The future of knowledge and skills in science and technology higher education', *Higher Education*, vol. 70, no. 3, pp. 409–16.

Ndebele, C., Muhuro, P. and Nkonki, V. (in press) 'Rurality and the professional development of university teachers', *South African Journal of Higher Education*.

O'Sullivan, P., Stoddard, H. and Kalishman, S. (2010), 'Collaborative research in medical education: A discussion of theory and practice', *Medical Education*, vol. 44, pp. 1175–84.

Pedersen, H. (2015), 'Education policy making for social change', in N. Snaza and J. Weaver (eds), *Posthumanism and educational research*, Routledge, London.

Simons, H. (2005), 'Ethical responsibility in social research: Key concepts', in B. Somekh & C. Lewin, *Research methods in the social sciences*, Sage, Thousand Oaks.

Snaza, N. (2015), 'Towards a genealogy of educational humanism', in N. Snaza & J. Weaver (eds), *Posthumanism and educational research*, Routledge, London.

Snaza, N. & Weaver, J. (2015), 'Introduction: Education and the posthumanist turn', in N. Snaza & J. Weaver (eds), *Posthumanism and educational research*, Routledge, London.

Somekh, B. (2005), 'Educational research', in B. Somekh & C. Lewin (eds), *Research methods in the social sciences*, Sage, Thousand Oaks.

Springgay, S. (2015), '"Approximate-rigorous abstractions": Propositions of activation for posthumanist research in education', in N. Snaza & J. Weaver (eds), *Posthumanism and educational research*, Routledge, London.

St Pierre, E. and Jackson, A. (2014), 'Qualitative data analysis after coding', *Qualitative Inquiry*, vol. 20, no. 6, pp. 715–19.

Van Schalkwyk, S., Herman, N., Leibowitz, B. & Farmer, J. (2015), 'Reflections on professional development in complex spaces', *Studies in Educational Evaluation*, vol. 46, pp. 4–10.

Webster-Wright, A. (2009), 'Reframing professional development through understanding authentic professional learning', *Review of Educational Research*, vol. 79, no. 2, pp. 702–39.

Wenger-Trayner, E. (2013), 'The practice of theory: Confessional of a social learning theorist', in V. Farnsworth & Y. Soloman (eds), *Reframing educational research: Resisting the 'what works' agenda*, Routledge, Abingdon.

Wiklund, M. (2013), 'At the interstices of disciplines: Early career researchers and research collaborations across boundaries', in G. Griffin, K. Hamber & B. Lundgren (eds), *The social politics of research collaboration*, Routledge, Abingdon.

Zukas, M. & Kilminster, S. (2014), 'The doctor and the blue form: Learning professional responsibility', in T. Fenwick and M. Nerland (eds), *Reconceptualising professional learning: Sociomaterial knowledges, practices and responsibilities*, Routledge, London.

Chapter 13

Putting theory to work

Comparing theoretical perspectives on academic practices in teaching and learning change

John Hannon, James Garraway, Tai Peseta and Chris Winberg

Introduction

As research into teaching, learning and professional development has shifted beyond cognitive and individually focused accounts (Fenwick & Edwards this volume (Chapter 1), Peseta et al. 2016), what begins to surface are the negotiations, interdependencies and collectives inherent in academic work environments. These emergent socialities can be analysed by drawing on the rich conceptual resources of sociology that are used to explore complex issues in higher education. Yet sociology encompasses distinct traditions, concepts and methodologies that are rarely brought to comparative analysis in higher education or examined for their relative commensurability. In this chapter we attempt such a comparative endeavour, focusing on academics in a disciplinary collective and the resources they call upon in their professional development as university teachers, and in their response to organisational change.

While descriptions of collective interaction and meso-level accounts of teaching and learning change are receiving greater attention (Roxå, Mårtensson, & Alvetag 2011), in large part due to the important role of disciplines and disciplinary cultures (Trowler 2008) and the scholarship of teaching and learning movement, there are few studies that coalesce around groups of academics who have undergone an in-depth scholarly exploration of teaching and learning together through a post-graduate course in university teaching or equivalent. By focusing our study in this way, we explore *how scholarly expertise, knowledge and institutional know-how for teaching and learning become present and utilised in an academic workgroup*. This study takes the workgroup dynamic as the primary object of analysis, and draws on a specific group of academics as opening up the world of that dynamic.

'Workgroup' is an analytical term used by Trowler (2008, p. 20) to describe the collective activity of academic work, identified as 'the point of social interaction by small groups such as those in the classroom, in university departments, in the curriculum planning team, or in a hundred other task-based teams within the higher education system'. Hence the study departs from impact-based educational literature (Trigwell 2013) in that its focus is not on changes to individual participants' reactions, conceptions and behaviour, although this may appear in the study. The local disciplinary setting of the workgroup, then, is a site for research into the shared negotiation of curriculum, teaching and learning change (Peseta et al. 2016). The insights from the research will extend our understanding about how graduates of formal university teaching programmes from the same workgroup make decisions about negotiating the teaching and learning terrain they work in.

This study is part of a larger international project across five universities, focused on workgroups within which several academics have completed an award programme in university teaching and learning. We bring three theoretical frameworks to bear on a set of interview data from a workgroup: the first, teaching and learning regimes (Trowler 2008), analyses the meanings and social processes that flow through workgroups; second, the social realism of Archer (2000) brings the concepts of structure, culture, and agency to examine the capacity for action in a workgroup context; and third, sociomaterial approaches (Fenwick & Edwards, this volume Chapter 1) explores how connections between people, texts, and materials are assembled, put into practice and enacted into a reality. These frameworks demonstrate distinct methodologies to explore how academic knowledge and practices – material, psychic, and discursive – are negotiated and produced. By bringing these conceptual resources to bear on a single data set, we explore a rich theoretical interplay that allows us to reflect on what is at stake in our own theoretical positioning.

Theoretical crossovers and intersections

In asking how teaching and learning change and practice happen in academic workgroups, a question of theorising arises, and the work that theory does in framing the objects of research. How do we account for abstract concepts like knowledge, learning, change and practice? And how do we conceptualise and follow change – the forms it takes, how it flows, is mobilised, its timeframe and scale that delineate the process? The use of a theoretical lens invites a particular set of concepts, language, and methods to be applied to the world, and Trowler (2012, p. 282) reminds us that making theory explicit will identify and surface what is and is not important in reality, and 'help us to organise apparent chaos'. Yet there are limitations in taking a position: Ashwin (2012, p. 953) notes the limitations of 'single theory' research in conceptualising the object of research and analysing data, for example, if teaching and learning is viewed through the perspective and language of communities of practice, then 'it is completely predictable that my data will offer support for the concepts related to communities of practice' (2012, p. 952). He urges the use of different theories or 'ways of seeing' (2012, p. 753) to build reflexivity and critique to conceptualise research and analysing data.

A further question arises at the intersection of different theoretical approaches: one that has a philosophical cast. When we compare methods by explaining differences in terms of perspectives, can we maintain that perspectives are simply different lenses on reality? Here the question of ontology arises: if the differences are more than perspectival, we need to ask to what extent they share the same account of reality, and how a particular reality is constituted in the language, concepts and explanations of the state of affairs under study. If the theories, on comparison, are incommensurable, what are the implications for comparing different ontologies or 'ways of being' a researcher? Will the contribution of each theory eventually result in a comparative trial of strength?

Crossover studies are uncommon in educational literature, and in comparing theoretical approaches, we are mindful of the adherence of researchers to a favoured theoretical standpoint, and Trowler's (2012, p. 278) caution regarding position-taking: that there is 'the danger that one's professional identity becomes bound up with a particular theoretical approach'. Our aim in this chapter is to *commence* a dialogue across theoretical positions around concepts of change, knowledge, practice, structure and agency in professional learning. Each position has in common a legacy of contributions to higher education research that draw on sociological understandings of social conditions, organisation and networks, and by applying three methodologies to one set of data we aim to heighten the ground for a theoretical crossover. Rather than adopt positions that proclaim and defend a theory, we aim to mobilise each in the service of higher educational pedagogy, testing them out on a common data set.

Setting

This study conducted a comparison of three theoretical lenses to a common data set, and is part of a broader research project on academic workgroups across universities in Australia, England, New Zealand, South Africa and Sweden. The location for the study was a department that specialised in teaching emergency health programmes at a South African university, identified by the pseudonym Emergency Health Care (EHC). The workgroup of six participants all taught the department's clinical health care degree programme, and all had completed a Graduate Certificate in higher education (GCert) qualification. The workgroup included one Head of Department and five early to mid-career academics, two of whom had recently made the transition from practitioner to academic. The study draws on six interview transcripts and one focus group transcript from academics' accounts of their teaching and learning practices in the EHC department, with ethics approval obtained for the project from universities of all contributing authors to this chapter. Participants were asked how they characterised teaching and learning in their department, whether they felt able to share ideas and engender change in the workgroup, and how change was guided and enacted.

Teaching and learning regimes

The notion of teaching and learning regimes is grounded in a socio-cultural practice view of how academic workgroups operate to instantiate particular ideas, practices and norms about university teaching and learning over others (Trowler & Cooper 2002, Trowler 2005). As a heuristic device, the regimes are less attentive to individual behaviour and instead concentrate on how meaning about teaching, learning and curriculum is generated and flows through the social practices and processes of local academic contexts. One of Trowler's (2005, p. 21) goals was to gain a more nuanced grasp on the local – or 'street level' practices – to better appreciate how teaching and learning change, stability, and enhancement actually take hold at points of activity, projects and practice. Teaching and learning regimes are understood then, to comprise a set of cultural moments focused on precisely that ambition. These moments include: the development and attribution of meanings, codes of signification, discursive repertoires, recurrent practices, subjectivities in interaction, the development and sustenance of power relations, tacit assumptions, rules of propriety, and implicit theories (Trowler 2005, pp. 23–26). While the cultural moments encompassing the regimes are plainly much more messy and contain overlapping features in practice, they are made distinct for analytical purposes.

In drawing on teaching and learning regimes as a lens for exploring the set of seven transcripts related to the EHC academic workgroup, the emphasis was on this question: In what ways do local regimes (in this workgroup) accommodate, shift, and change to account for the new *scholarly expertise and institutional knowledge carried by a group of academics who have completed the GCert?* Across the transcripts, five examples of these nine moments are extracted and later drawn together to offer a view of regimes in the EHC academic workgroup.

The cultural moments of teaching and learning regimes

Development and attribution of meanings

At workgroup level, Trowler (2005, p. 23) points out that there are some activities and projects that produce more significant meaning over others in any workgroup setting. It is these meanings, he suggests, which gain 'ontological solidity and the components which compose the project also develop a particular reality'. Invited to comment on the structures and mechanisms that are intended to be spaces for conversation related to teaching and learning, participants point to local processes of assessment moderation. These set of meetings appear to be an important forum for validating assessment standards and processes, arguing about the sequencing of content across the curriculum, and for learning about the variation in how assessment decisions are implemented across the two main programmes.

> So we moderate each other's things across all programmes or at least it's set up that way that we try – everybody needs to be involved almost in

everybody else's programme somewhere. And that's very meaningful because it means that you've got many cross checks in terms of what you're doing and what you're not doing and the motivation behind it.

(Focus group)

These meetings on assessment, then, are activities for consolidating meaning and courses of action in the workgroup.

Recurrent practices

In workgroups, it is often said that there are modes of operating and being which are so ingrained in the fabric of local relations and practices that they come to be seen as natural rather than cultural. Trowler (2005) contends that these recurrent practices typically come to the fore when new staff join a workgroup. Across the transcripts, many staff who were interviewed had completed the GCert bar two who were still in the process of completing. Many could recall fondly what it felt like to be new to the EHC department and feel estranged from a distinctly educational language and conversation that had been circulating among long-standing departmental colleagues:

> you hear all these guys in the meetings saying, 'guys, there needs to be constructive alignment' and you're sitting and you haven't done any formal training and you're wondering what is this constructive alignment that these people are talking about, and taxonomies of learning, you don't understand what they're talking about.
>
> (P2, early career, male)

> one of the other members of our department now [name] ... actually did [the GCert] because he wanted to join the department and one of the things we said to him is that he would be a better application if he had [the GCert] as well.
>
> (P4, mid-career, male)

For these participants, recurrent modes of practice are challenged in the new teaching context of the workgroup, as new ways of doing things, for instance, 'constructive alignment' (Biggs 1999), engender new practices.

Subjectivities in interaction

While academics may arrive new to a workgroup armed with a particular set of identity attachments as a teacher, these investments usually become recalibrated in relation to the workgroup context. In the EHC workgroup, the requirement (by an external professional body) to complete the GCert suggests that the department was demanding a more student-focused approach to teaching

(Prosser & Trigwell 1999) – in essence – they were cultivating a particular set of teaching identities.

> I was very much focused on content, delivery of content and the students being able to you know, become more proficient with the content as opposed to now, where it's much more facilitation based. It's more based on the development of the student overall.
>
> (P4, mid-career, male)

> I wasn't thinking of them [students] as individuals. I was thinking of them as a group of students and that's it. I need to deliver some outcomes, you need to meet them and let's move on.
>
> (P1, early career, female)

The new practices arising from the workgroup context invite fresh reflections not only on what teaching is, there are also renewed teaching identities in play that circulate as subjectivities to be taken up by those in the workgroup.

Rules of propriety

As in many other cultural spheres, appropriateness is tethered to its other – deviancy. In focusing on regimes in academic workgroups, these rules delineate what is normal and what is not. While these rules can take hold in a range of ways, two participants signal frustration that although there is an expectation that the GCert be completed, the responsibility for seeing through the implementation of new/ standard/agreed upon teaching and learning ideas is being shirked by some. In this sense, the ideas from the GCert have become the norm rather than the exception.

> I'm still engaged in things that I've been learning from the [GCert] and that is the biggest challenge that we have is some of them have even gone through a formal higher education diploma but then still default back to ways or practices that don't really meet the students needs or outcomes. I think that's the biggest challenge.
>
> (P1, early career, female)

The 'challenge' here concerns the potential for the new norms to fail to take hold, should the new practices not be shared and adopted in the department.

Implicit theories of teaching and learning

For Trowler and Cooper (2002), workgroup projects and activities contain a hotbed of implicit theories about teaching and learning. Some of these theories are recognisable – constructivism or behaviourism – and others take some investigation to detect. The influence of the GCert course suggests that the EHC staff were not only becoming adept at naming these theories (and their scholarly basis), they were starting to use these theories to understand their own views, to read their colleagues' views, as well as their own workgroup context. Indeed, what the course has provided them with collectively is the capacity to surface implicit theories of teaching and learning.

> The thing that I took home was constructive alignment in terms of aligning the teaching material to the type of assessment you do and that was to align to the outcome that they're being assessed with.
>
> (P1, early career, female)

The practice of 'curriculum alignment' (Biggs 1999), often implicit in institutional procedures, is articulated and made explicit by this participant, and begins to circulate as an important marker of scholarly curriculum design practice.

Surfacing regimes

In the EHC workgroup, one of the effects of expecting all academic staff to complete the GCert course is that it offered a shared set of educational ideas upon which to discuss, critique and argue about teaching, learning and curriculum. This new language provided a foundation for supporting the workgroup to decide on courses of pedagogical action, especially when edicts about teaching and learning change arrive top-down from the institution, or require attention as a result of external drivers such as professional accreditation. In essence, these regimes start to surface as rules of engagement. Yet, there are additional effects and affects evident in the transcripts. GCert courses can have regulatory consequences too. The language of educational frameworks starts to usher in a certain kind of predictability and routineness about teaching, learning and curriculum change, and the ideas themselves can start to dictate the formation of teaching subjectivities – offering the ground for moral judgement – against which teacher's practices and actions are read. While teaching and learning regimes can draw attention to how change emerges and is stabilised in collective academic contexts, they can also highlight the 'unchallenged orthodoxies' (see Chapter 2) that become embedded in schools and departments. Understanding this process may require disentangling teaching practices and identities from institutional demands. The following section takes up the possibilities for change through collective agency and action.

Social realism

A social realist approach to investigating change in society is characterised, firstly, by an understanding that there is a real world 'that exists independently of our perceptions, *theories* and constructions' (Maxwell 2012, p. 5); the approach is thus, as Maxwell suggests, based on a realist ontology. As Archer (1995) outlines, this real world of structural and cultural elements sets up conditions that enable or constrain local actions. However, how individuals and groups come to know about this real world and act within it is dependent on how they reflexively choose to work with these conditions, which are not deterministic though highly influential: 'People choose what they do, but they make their choices from a structurally and culturally generated range of options – which they do not choose' (Carter & New 2004, p. 6).

Thus the identity of actors in the workgroup system is fundamentally relational in that it is a product of the conditioning of the prevailing structural and cultural context and the powers of the actors themselves (Archer 2000). In attempting to understand change in the system these are treated as an analytically separate component both in nature and temporality, the conditions always preceding the actions of actors:

> [the social realist approach] grants the existence of people's emergent properties (PEPs) and also the reality of structural and cultural emergent properties (SEPs and CEPs), and sees the development of agents and actors as relational developments occurring between them.
>
> (Archer 2000, p. 255)

Structure refers to the systems in which the workgroup is situated, and to the formal roles and social relations that people play within it. Structural systems are seen as antecedent to the relations and may condition them. Culture refers to the field of ideas, ideologies and values on the one hand, and the way that social groupings typically interact on the other, with ideas predating social interactions. In analysis the researcher sets out to see if there is complementariness or difference between 'ideas' which may in turn enable system change or morphogenesis (Archer 1995).

Reflexive deliberation is the pivotal point between the objective reality of actors' worlds (structure and culture) and their agency (Archer 2007). Individual agents may have strong influence through positioning in the hierarchy or through access to resources. Where actors act collectively they may exert 'corporate agency'. Corporate agents know what needs to be done to effect change, and to have the right resources to bring to bear on the problem (Archer 1995); they may thus constitute a powerful force for change.

In investigating teaching transformation in the EHC workgroup, three main moves or change cycles can be identified that act sequentially and relationally as the emergent powers of the one serve to enable the development of the other:

1　structural change in the role that EHC practitioners are expected to play, setting up discontinuity between the old and the new;
2　structural discontinuity sets up cultural discontinuity between old and new ways of teaching practitioners;
3　agents with their own emergent properties (gained in part from the GCert) act within the cultural conditions of discontinuity to effect change.

These are now discussed in more detail with reference to the workgroup interviews.

Structural discontinuity

In the first structural move (or more strictly speaking structural morphogenetic cycle), interviewees suggest that the nature of EHC work is changing, from a more procedural skills-based practice to one requiring greater autonomy, responsibility and problem-solving skills. This sets up objective conditions for practitioners to occupy new roles:

> if you wanted to perform any advanced procedure or administer any schedule drugs, you would need to contact a doctor ... but now emergency medical practitioners practiced on their own license and didn't require permission from the doctor anymore. So now we had to move from teaching skills and skills based on training and very procedurally type of you know, information to creating like a reflective practitioner who was able to make a clinical diagnosis and examination of the patient required a little bit more in depth.
>
> (P4, mid-career, male)

Cultural discontinuity

The structural change in roles then sets up the conditions for the emergence of new more critical ways of teaching, or cultural change. This in turn provides enabling conditions for the emergence of new curricular structures, bachelor degrees, where previously practice-based diplomas or short courses existed:

> We have gone from diplomas to degrees but there has also been a lot of change in the profession because they have gone from short courses to degrees.
>
> (Focus group)

So far there appears to be an interaction between the emergent properties of structure and culture which set up the conditions in which change (morphogenesis) may occur. However, whether or not such change, rather than stasis, actually happens depends on the actions of the staff in the workgroup.

The emergence of agency

In vocational fields, departmental cultures are more likely to value competence and efficiency over critical reflection and debate (Hillier & Gregson 2015) in keeping with the interests and values of the field. There would thus be an expectation of morphostasis were these actors to predominate as a corporate agency. However, the corporate agency of the five GCert graduates in the workgroup has enabled the emergence of new ideas within the workgroup. In effecting these emergences, the corporate agents draw on the cultural system of ideas and values that originate from the GCert.

> When I look back to my teaching ... I wasn't thinking about individuals I was teaching. During the GCert I learnt a lot and I could actually differentiate the different learning styles and I could change my teaching.
>
> (P1, early career, female)

These ideas themselves have cultural emergent properties in that they are often in contradistinction to the already existing, more vocationally-orientated ideas about teaching in the workgroup as a whole:

> We essentially knew what needed to change ... OSCE [objective structured clinical examination] assessments where in the past they had to perform skills ... we looked at it in a very step-wise process. But recently we have developed our thinking around what competence means ... we realised that was not a very good approach and so last year we challenged this view, a few of us.
>
> (P4, mid-career, male)

Furthermore, as well as the corporate agency of the GCert group, there are the enabling conditions set up by the Head of Department. He is himself structurally positioned to enable either change or stasis in the teaching practices of the workgroup but exerts his agency towards creating conditions for transformation of practice, as one of the GCert staff observes:

> Well, from my perspective he (the HOD) is a visionary ... he knows what he wants the profession to be ... fortunately for us he is one of the major players nationally.
>
> (Focus group)

The fact that there are five such agents who collectively realise what needs to be done and have the cultural resources to do this (a corporate agency) with the support of a key agent, potentially creates the conditions under which the GCert graduates can effect change in curriculum. However, it is the cultural and structural conditions of the field that provide an enabling environment in which these agents can effect change.

The following approach offers a different framing of the conditions that enable change, in which structures and associated conditions are understood to be part of the arrangements from which change emerges.

A sociomaterial approach to teaching and learning practice

To explore the academic workgroup through a sociomaterialist approach brings an understanding of practice and change as an *effect* of relations between materials and humans, in which the 'actions of humans can be understood to "hang together" through practices and particular material arrangements' (Hager, Lee & Reich 2012, p. 5). In this approach, materials have a dynamic and generative role. Materials are not considered as physical objects or things that have significance in themselves, but through the relations they enact. Latour (2004, p. 237) argues for an understanding of the material as a *thing* that matters, 'highly complex, historically situated, richly diverse'. He draws on the northern European sense of 'thing' as the oldest term for a parliament or *gathering*. 'A thing is, in one sense, an object out there and, in another sense, an *issue* very much *in* there, at any rate, a *gathering*. ... the same word *thing* designates matters of fact and matters of concern' (2004, p. 233, italics in original).

In this double sense, the kinds of things that circulate in the workgroup 'gather' issues: textbooks, digital files, assessments, policies, curriculum, lectures, learning spaces. Things also embody conceptual resources that circulate and are materialised: teaching approaches, techniques, and theoretical frameworks. These become Latour's *matters of concern* by making connections, mobilising practices and producing effects. While qualitative analysis is usually applied to interview data to identify themes or patterns, sociomaterialism applies the method of *tracing* materials through their relations and effects, asking how things are assembled, stay in place and enacted into reality (Fenwick & Edwards, this volume Chapter 1).

Mobilising teaching and learning change

The sense of a 'thing' as a set of social and material relations was conveyed in an account of resuscitation training during the EHC programme, involving a patient simulation: during the training, students' attention tended to be drawn towards the monitoring equipment and away from the critical decision-making the simulation required:

> the challenge we're facing is that we lay the foundations incorrectly, from a first year level as to what these learners need to place value on, and the process that they use to determine what's valuable to make a decision about critical things, about life and death situations.
>
> (P3, mid-career, male)

To re-focus students' attention during the resuscitation training, the participant 'designed a mnemonic to help remember the sequence of events'. With the addition of the mnemonic, the equipment became integrated into a 'cycle' of monitoring life signs and administering critical care. The mnemonic connected the patient (simulated), the equipment and the resuscitation technique into a process that was training, was less equipment-centred (in practice), but more suited to the stressful conditions of emergency care. In this instance, a change in teaching practice for EHC arose in resuscitation training, as the mnemonic became a *thing* or a new gathering of materials and people into a practice that had subsequent effects on learning.

Assembling the EHC educator

Not only were teaching practices assembled through an array of materials and activity: the role of educator in EHC was also accomplished through particular material arrangements. Becoming a professional is often understood in terms of models of distributed cognition or situated learning based on nurturing social connections in a professional setting (Johri 2011). A sociomaterial approach highlights the material ordering in the adaptive and emergent process of assembling the professional educator. The transition from emergency health practitioner to educator was identified by the Head of Department as a key professional development issue for new teaching staff:

> Many of them just recently qualified. So being able to guide them to say this is how education is about, ... as opposed to just ... being very skilled focussed technicians.
>
> (Head)

The challenge in becoming an educator in the EHC was noted, 'there's a big mindset change that has to happen when you go from being a clinician to being a teacher'. But why exactly was a change from the 'mindset' of a clinician to an educator such a challenge? A sociomaterialist approach can trace how practices are embedded in actual time-space configurations: the Head referred to a mix of material arrangements for teaching the EHC programme: in routines, attire, rescue techniques, accreditation requirements, rubrics, adapting skills training to problem solving. This mixture of practices was summarised as a 'culture' that was in tension:

> I think we try to create a culture that is aligned to the profession. So our students are in uniform, they're expected to stand when the lecturer comes into the classroom. You know we have, like rescue is very regimental ... But at the same time we try to say well you know we want the participation, we want your feedback, we want there to be discussion. So ... there's an interplay between those two roles and I think the students initially find this to be challenging.
>
> (Head)

Thus the culture of EHC was unpicked in workgroup discussions, re-working EHC artefacts and processes, reviewing, tinkering and assembling new teaching practices. These discussions reflected efforts to distinguish two roles, and in so doing negotiate a new role and perform a new academic identity. This transition is exemplified in Table 3.1, in which participants contrasted roles.

These descriptions, however, involved more than simply marking role distinctions. They constitute collective 'identity work' (Gherardi 2012, p. 208) that 'consolidates practical knowledge', as the workgroup distinguished the EHC professional from a change in practices, enacting an emerging identity of the university educator. The workgroup drew their shared knowledge from the GCert to articulate and mobilise the change in sociomaterial relations. This challenge in aligning the 'culture' of a university educator to the EHC profession required new arrangements: adapting 'regimental' training regimes with participatory ones; 'practical' assessment with qualitative; being 'practically competent' with being 'theoretically competent'; and aligning professional accreditation with university policies. This transition was marked by adaptations: different classroom arrangements and seating, less reliance on Powerpoint when discussion is warranted, and in particular, changing assessment artefacts to resolve the conflict between regimes of competency and of peer or problem-based learning. In this process, 'things' embody histories and values (Fenwick & Edwards, this volume Chapter 1) that require effort by participants to re-form relations for new practices and identities. Thus the EHC educator is assembled anew from the EHC professional and the university educator.

Table 13.1 Assembling practice – the EHC professional and university educator

Speaker	The EHC professional	The university educator
Head	being very skilled focused technicians	guide them to say this is how education is about
P2, early career, female	the challenge with our practical assessment [is] to get it away from just a tick-boxing exercise	to have qualitative assessment as well as quantitative and then aligning it to theoretical outcomes and goals
P3, mid-career, male	My wife ... introduces me as a paramedic	I say 'excuse me, I'm an educator'
Focus group	[Students] have to be practically competent as well	students have to be theoretically competent, they need to develop intuitive knowledge, problem-solving ability
Focus group	Students are considered either competent or not competent	the university framework is one of continuous assessment

Discussion and conclusion

We organised this chapter to compare three theories to questions about scholarly knowledge, practice and change, in which the authors independently applied one perspective to the same data set. In this endeavour we had two aims: first to bring a set of fresh perspectives to issues of professional development that offer alternatives to institutional narratives of individual progression, through focusing on the collective efforts of academics to articulate conceptual resources for teaching and learning change. Second, to challenge the tendency for theoretical position-taking amongst researchers, and initiate a dialogue across theories that informs research into teaching practices and professional development. In this final section we highlight the contributions from each approach to conceptualising teaching and learning knowledge, practice and change, and discuss the possibility of shared analytical ground at their intersection, and what might be achieved in an exercise in theoretical crossover.

Each approach brought different methods and distinct terminologies to engage with the data. The teaching and learning regimes aimed to make visible and articulate the social processes and the culture that shape how teaching and learning operates in academic workgroups. Culture is viewed as practices that are in a 'mutually-reinforcing stasis' (Trowler 2005, p. 26), but also subject to change, either internally or from external, macro-level factors. The constellation of cultural moments that comprise the regimes suggest helpful lenses for a more micro-level inspection of workgroups that provides ways into an analysis of data. Thus the regimes offer filters for the study of change in social practices. The messiness of working with regimes encourages researchers to bring with them a range of additional conceptual resources to make sense of the local.

Applied to the EHC workgroup, regimes make visible multiple ways in which the GCert had effects on practice and in changes that occurred. Two 'moments' demonstrate the regimes: particular activities are collectively attributed with significance and meaning over others, in this case, moderation of assessment; and in the capability of participants to identify implicit theories of teaching that have hitherto framed their practices.

Yet the boundaries between these cultural moments are not always clear-cut, nor is there any underlying commitment to unearthing causal mechanism. For social realism, culture is bound up with structural elements that set conditions for human action, with causal factors that can be analysed, along with the possibility for change through human agency. The social realist approach highlights the efforts of practitioners to effect change within the structural and cultural discontinuities in their teaching practices. Social realism analyses these changes as the emergence of a 'corporate agency', in which the workgroup acts collectively to draw on cultural ideas from the GCert to enable change by developing new practices.

The sociomaterialist approach shares with teaching and learning regimes the study of messy practices, but where the regimes apply an interpretive analysis in which cultural moments become lenses to describe social practices, sociomaterialism aims to empirically trace particular material and social connections that form relations and have real effects. The EHC workgroup offered many examples of materials that were mobilised for change in teaching practice: artefacts gathered under assessments, peer review rubrics, and 'cross-moderation' meetings became matters of concern beyond their functional role in institutional processes. In these discussions, the participants worked with specific materials to re-assemble and re-order their shared disciplinary practices. Thus sociomaterialism articulated how new practices and identities for the workgroup were reassembled from changing relations with materials, spaces, mindsets, institutional policies in order to arrive at, or enact, the EHC educator.

Theories in crossover

The three approaches intersect in a shared goal of seeking to understand actions and interactions in work settings. All draw on strands of sociology: of teaching, learning and enhancement (Trowler 2005), of social realism (Archer 1995), and of 'associations' (Latour 2005). All contribute to understanding educational change in ways that offer an alternative to educational literature that draws on organisational or management studies, or the individualist focus of cognitive or psychological theories. Yet sociologies allow diverse standpoints for theory and method. We made the following observations from the analyses above.

Culture is treated in different ways. Both the regimes and social realism study change through the interaction of culture and agential action, yet for the regimes, culture is constructed from shared values and attitudes that are articulated through practices, whereas for social realism, cultural and structural elements exist in a real, independently existing world with which individuals must contend. These positions reflect an ontological difference with respect to culture: one constructionist, one objectivist. Yet each approach articulates the possibility of change through agency within system constraints.

Both regimes and sociomaterialism focus on how change takes effect through *practices*. By highlighting practices through the lens of cultural moments, the regimes aim to connect local practices with a systemic view, such that 'social processes flow through and around these moments and they need to be understood as operating simultaneously and holistically rather than individually or in a disaggregated way' (Trowler 2005, p. 24). Sociomaterialism similarly aims to articulate change beyond the local setting, by identifying the nexuses of practice that extend in space and time to form obdurate, stable assemblages. An example of such an extensive assemblage in EHC was the long-standing vocational, competency-based assessment system, yet the embedding of new material connections – changed teaching spaces, new degree level accreditation, different assessment regimes – enabled shifts to a new assemblage.

A significant contrast emerged between social realism and sociomaterialism in the analysis of agency and structure. Social realism analysed change in the workgroup through its collective actions that were located within the prevailing structural and cultural conditions, whereas sociomaterialism sought to trace the particular relations that constituted change, but made no distinctions of scale or level in this process. Thus sociomaterialism challenges understandings of change as structured by forces external to their setting, since, for sociomaterialism, external forces themselves demand explanation, and are implicated in the relations that constitute practice. Where social realism investigates the interplay of agency and structure, sociomaterialism challenges notions of their separateness and the existence of entities prior to the relations formed between them.

There are clear ontological differences between social realism and sociomaterialism in their respective notions of knowledge and change: for social realism these are viewed as objectively real structural entities that set constraints on work contexts, for sociomaterialism, knowledge and change exist as effects or enactments of a set of relations that can be empirically studied. These distinctions are more than perspectival, they offer different accounts of reality in the objects of study.

There are implications for academics, academic developers and those researching learning to teach in the potential dialogue between theories. First, it is important to recognise professional and academic development is not homogenous across institutions and contexts, and Peseta and Barrie in Chapter 7 note a 'shifty nomenclature' that varies with its defined role in an organisation. Second, the application of these theories raises ontological differences in which concepts of change, knowledge and practice are not shared understandings, yet we have shown that incommensurable theories can still share a common endeavour. Through this comparative study, we argue that applying multiple theories to a single data set puts theory to work in a way that sharpens differences and clarifies potential contributions. The three approaches offer quite different theories and methods for researching learning to teach, yet each provides conceptual resources to analyse the forces shaping local contexts, each articulates the competing agendas and interests in the complex configurations of change, and thus each shares the goals of improving teaching practices and building a socially just pedagogy. Finally, comparing theories cautions researchers against forming an identity around one theoretical position, and encourages academics to recognise their capacity for agency, to make visible the process of change through the unfolding of practices, and offer accounts of adapting, tuning and shaping the practices and conditions for teaching and learning change.

Acknowledgement

This paper draws on the research project *The flow of new knowledge practices: an inquiry into teaching, learning and curriculum dynamics in academic workgroups* led by Tai Peseta (University of Sydney) with Kate Thomson (Sydney); Jan McLean & Giedre Kligyte (UNSW); John Hannon (La Trobe); Jan Smith (Durham); John Canning & Gina Wisker (UBrighton); Chris Winberg & James Garraway (CPUT); Brenda Leibowitz (UJohannesburg); Torgny Roxa & Katarina Martenssen (Lund); Sean Sturm (Auckland); and Jeff Jawitz (UCape Town).

References

Archer, M. S. (1995), *Realist social theory: A morphogenetic approach*, Cambridge University Press, Cambridge.

Archer, M. S. (2000), *Being human: The problem of agency*, Cambridge University Press, Cambridge.

Archer, M. S. (2007), *Making our way through the world*, Cambridge University Press, Cambridge.

Ashwin, P. (2012), 'How often are theories developed through empirical research in higher education?', *Studies in Higher Education*, vol. 37, no. 8, pp. 941–55.

Biggs, J. (1999), *Teaching for quality learning at university: What the student does*, Society for Research into Higher Education: Open University Press, Buckingham.

Carter, B. & New, C. (2004), 'Realist social theory and empirical research', paper presented at ESA Social Theory Conference, Paris, 15–17 September.

Gherardi, S. (2012), *How to conduct a practice-based study: Problems and methods*, Edward Elgar, Cheltenham.

Hager, P., Lee, A. & Reich, A. (2012), 'Problematising practice, reconceptualising learning and imagining change', in P. Hager, A. Lee & A. Reich (eds), *Practice, learning and change: Practice-theory perspectives in professional learning*, Springer, Dordrecht.

Hillier, Y. & Gregson, M. (2015), *Reflective teaching in further, adult and vocational Education*, Bloomsbury, New York.

Johri, A. (2011), 'The socio-materiality of learning practices and implications for the field of learning technology', *Research in Learning Technology*, vol. 19, no. 3, pp. 207–17.

Latour, B. (2004), 'Why has critique run out of steam? From matters of fact to matters of concern', *Critical Inquiry*, vol. 30, pp. 225–48.

Latour, B. (2005), *Reassembling the social*, Oxford University Press, Oxford.

Maxwell, J. (2012), *A realist approach for qualitative research*, Sage, London.

Peseta, T., Kligyte, G., McLean, J. & Smith, J. (2016), 'On the conduct of concern: Exploring how university teachers recognise, engage in, and perform "identity" practices within academic workgroups', in J. Smith, J. Rattray, T. Peseta & D. Loads (eds), *Identity work in contemporary higher education*, Sense Publishing, Rotterdam.

Prosser, M. & Trigwell, K. (1999), Understanding learning and teaching: The experience in higher education, SRHE/OUP, Buckingham.

Roxå, T., Mårtensson, K. & Alveteg, M. (2011), 'Understanding and influencing teaching and learning cultures at university – a network approach', *Higher Education*, vol. 62, pp. 99–111.

Trigwell, K. (2013), 'Evaluating the impact of university teaching development programs', in E. Simon & G. Pleschova (eds), *Teacher development in higher education: Existing programs, program impact and future trends*, Routledge, London.

Trowler, P. & Cooper, A. (2002), 'Teaching and learning regimes: Implicit theories and recurrent practices in the enhancement', *Higher Education Research & Development*, vol. 21, no. 3, pp. 221–40.

Trowler, P. (2005), 'A sociology of teaching, learning and enhancement: Improving practices in higher education', *Papers: Revista de Sociologica*, vol. 76, pp. 13–32.

Trowler, P. (2008), *Cultures and change in higher education: Theories and practices*, Palgrave Macmillan, Basingstoke.

Trowler, P. (2012), 'Wicked issues in situating theory in close-up research', *Higher Education Research & Development*, vol. 31, no. 3, pp. 273–84.

Chapter 14

Postscript on theorising learning to teach

Insights, absences and future possibilities

Paul Ashwin

In this concluding chapter of this book, I consider what the preceding contributions, as a collective whole, tell us about theorising learning to teach in higher education. This consideration is set within the context of this book's practical aims of supporting those who are learning to teach and reframing research into learning to teach so that it highlights the importance of educational and social theory and aids the pursuit of social justice.

In doing this I want to move beyond the details of the three approaches of sociomaterialism, social practices, and critical and social realism and particular examples of mixed approaches, to consider what they collectively highlight about learning to teach in higher education. I then consider what they might leave unsaid and, finally, the possibilities for future work that are opened up by the contributions to this book. However, I first want to set out how I understand the meaning of theorising learning to teach in higher education, as this will underpin my argument and analysis. This involves unpacking the meaning of both 'theorising' and the meaning of 'learning to teach'.

The meaning of 'theorising' learning to teach

In theorising learning to teach, how one considers that nature and meaning of 'theory' is crucial. My position is that theories involve simplification. This is based on a realist view of a complex and emergent social world that exceeds our capacity to know it and can only be accessed through simplifying concepts and theories (Ashwin 2009). Thus theories simplify the social world we are engaging with and different theories simplify in different ways (see Sayer 1992, 2000, Law 2004, Mol & Law 2002). So in this sense, theorising 'learning to teach' involves seeing 'learning to teach' in a particular way and not in other ways. One implication of this view is that all particular ways of theorising 'learning to teach' are limited because they all involve a commitment to focus on particular aspects of the situation and not others. The conceptualisations that we use will be dependent on the types of questions that we are interested in asking.

A key distinction here is about how we engage with theories-as-simplifications in research and in our educational practices. In undertaking research we need to have a consistent way of simplifying 'learning to teach' in order to avoid contradictions within the research process. However, as practitioners we can move between different simplifications of 'learning to teach' in order to find the one that best suits the urgencies of our current situation. From this perspective, we need as many different ways of simplifying 'learning to teach' as possible, so that we have a range of choices about how we understand the challenges of practices. Thus in offering and further developing new ways of simplifying 'learning to teach' in higher education, this book offers important resources and alternatives for the development of practices.

The meaning of 'learning to teach'

In order to understand the meaning of 'learning to teach' in higher education, one first needs to be clear what is meant by 'teaching'. This is tricky because, as I have argued before (Ashwin 2015, Ashwin et al. 2015), there are deeply entrenched, powerful and unhelpful myths about the nature of teaching. One of the most powerful and least helpful is that teaching is largely about inspirational individuals engaging in spontaneous performances. This is the view of teaching that is presented by most teaching awards: the vision of the dazzling individual who enchants their students with a brilliant display of erudition, which changes the students' lives forever. This view of teaching supports a view of learning to teach that is simply about developing the performance of individual teachers. The starting point of this book is to challenge this dominant approach to understanding learning to teach. The contributions explore what new insights three particular approaches, sociomaterialism, practice-based approaches, and critical and social realism, can offer for research and practice in academic development.

These new ways of understanding learning to teach are important because the dominant view offers a deeply flawed view of teaching that presents teaching as an individual, personality-driven activity rather than a collective and carefully planned intellectual activity. Teaching is a collective activity in many ways: teachers draw on collective bodies of knowledge to design curricula in discussion with colleagues, professional bodies and students and different aspects of degree programmes are taught by different academics. In order to help students gain access to this knowledge, academics need to design programmes carefully so that students engage in a range of activities that help them to develop personal engagement with this knowledge.

The three approaches explored in this book, despite a number of differences, support such a view of teaching. First, they focus on the collective and material aspects of learning to teach. Whilst they tend to start with everyday interactions, this is with the intention of understanding how interactions are shaped by people, practices and technologies that are stretched way beyond the immediate setting of the interaction. They emphasise how teachers and academic developers are entwined in networks of material, human and conceptual actors. This undoubtedly offers a more complex view of the processes involved in learning to teach but it does not offer a sense of what is meant by teaching. One way of defining teaching that is compatible with this account of these processes is offered by Lee Shulman's (1987) notion of 'pedagogical content knowledge'. This describes the knowledge teachers have of how to make their subjects accessible to diverse groups of students and emphasises that university teachers need to both understand the disciplinary knowledge they teach and to understand how to design their teaching so that all of their students can develop their understanding of this knowledge. This highlights the need for teachers to have expertise of both their discipline or professional field, but also the teaching of that discipline or professional field. It also highlights that teaching is both knowledge- and student-centred: it is about making particular aspects of knowledge accessible to particular groups of students. This makes good teaching particular rather than generic: what is suitable for certain forms of knowledge and particular groups of students will vary.

So if we apply the notion of pedagogical content knowledge to those who support academics who are learning to teach, what do we see? We see a need for academic developers to have a clear sense of the knowledge that they are attempting to give academics access to and a clear sense of how to arrange a set of experiences that give academics the best chance to gain access to this knowledge. This raises three key questions about supporting academics who are learning to teach that the earlier contributions in this book help us to answer:

1   How do we maintain a focus on the collective aspects of learning to teach?
2   How do we understand the impacts of settings on learning to teach?
3   What is the nature of expertise of academic development?

I will consider how the contributions to this book provide answers to these questions before finally considering what is left unsaid about learning to teach in higher education in this book.

How do we maintain a focus on the collective aspects of learning to teach?

The contributions to this book highlight the need for approaches to understanding learning to teach that take account of its collective aspects. In Chapter 10 Peter Kahn argues that such collective approaches are essential for developing creative responses to pressures for change. Given the huge amount of institutional change that teachers and academic developers face, they need to understand the basis on which they can act creatively together in pursuit of sustainable ways of developing effective teaching in higher education.

The challenge of developing collective approaches to understanding learning to teach is that, as I mentioned before, teaching is always particular. This is because changes to either the knowledge that is being focused upon or the students that are engaging with it mean that there will be a need to reconsider whether previous approaches remain the most effective way of developing student understanding.

However, the students and the knowledge are not the only factors that shape teaching. In Chapter 5 David Boud and Angela Brew show how local teaching practices are always positioned in relation to a number of particular contexts, including the spatial, the temporal, the personal, the social and the professional. Similarly, Anne Edwards (Chapter 8) shows how institutional practices help to shape teaching. Edwards also highlights the ways in which teaching is nested within disciplinary and professional practices, which students need to learn to recognise and respond to in an agentic manner. Whilst Edwards foregrounds agency, Lesley Gourlay and Martin Oliver (Chapter 2) emphasise the ways in which students are entangled in networks of human and material actors. These entanglements help to actively create particular forms of agency for students.

In this way the contributions to this book highlight the importance of thinking beyond the individual when considering learning to teach in higher education. There is an urgent need to think about learning to teach in a collective manner that draws strength from our shared commitment to improving the effectiveness of our teaching. This needs to recognise the ways in which teaching is always particular because of the changing configurations of the networks that teachers are engaged with.

How do we understand the impacts of settings on learning to teach?

One of the elements that shapes teaching in particular ways is the setting in which teaching and learning to teach are located. The contributions to this book give a rich sense of the ways in which teaching settings actively shape the nature of teaching.

Marie Manidis and Keiko Yasukawa (Chapter 6) show how the material setting of the physical classroom is a key element of teaching. Rather than being something that teachers respond to passively, they show how the material and the non-material elements of the setting can be actively woven together in order to support students to develop their understanding of knowledge.

However, some elements of the settings may not be under the control of teachers or their impact may not even be fully understood. In Chapter 4 Richard Edwards and Tara Fenwick show how in online settings the algorithms that underpin learning analytics play an active role in shaping how students are positioned as particular kinds of 'learners'. They show how these are more than neutral tools that apply the intentions of teachers. Instead algorithms shape these intentions in particular ways and not others. Unless teachers understand the ways in which these algorithms work then the danger is that they passively accept them rather than question the ways in which they shape the teaching and learning process.

The contributions in this book highlight that rather than simply acting as a container of teaching and learning interactions, the settings in which teaching and learning take place actively shape teachers' and students' engagement with each other and with knowledge. They show that knowledge of the ways in which these settings intertwine with teaching and learning is an essential element of the expertise of academic developers.

What is the nature of expertise of academic development?

Thinking about academic development from the perspective of pedagogical content knowledge also raises questions about the aspects of knowledge that teachers in higher education are given access to by academic developers. In other words what is the nature of expertise that is claimed by academic developers?

In Chapter 9, Sue Clegg outlines how academic development emerged from the 1960s onwards, charged with supporting teacher learning and drawing greater attention to student learning. Clegg highlights how academic developers have been important supporters of research into student learning and the development of the knowledge base about the elements of effective teaching in higher education. She argues strongly that critical realism can provide a productive framework for theorising academic development and so contribute to the further development of expertise in learning to teach in higher education.

Chris Winberg (Chapter 11) emphasises the distributed nature of teaching expertise and shows how the apparent individual expertise of teachers is actually part of collaborative and collective networks. The participants in the interviews in Winberg's chapter highlight the importance of dialogue with supportive peers that support teachers in making professional judgements that go against dominant discourses. The importance of dialogue is also highlighted in the two chapters that examine crossover perspectives. Brenda Leibowitz (Chapter 12) and John Hannon et al. (Chapter 13) both emphasise the power of dialogue between different ways of analysing the same situation. Being able to see the same situation from multiple perspectives can strengthen the agency of academics and support them in developing new practices. Tara Fenwick and Richard Edwards (Chapter 1) persuasively argue that the development of new practices is crucial, that we need to go beyond critique in order to experiment with alternative arrangements and to disrupt dominant practices.

The ways in which alternative ways of seeing can lead to new practices is powerfully illustrated by Vivienne Bozalek and Wendy McMillan (Chapter 3) in their consideration of senior managers' entanglements with learning to teach. Through the analysis of a single interview in which the participant develops new categories in which to understand higher education institutions, they highlight how a critical aspect of the expertise of academic developers is to be able to provide contexts in which teachers can see alternative ways of understanding how to introduce students to powerful knowledge.

However, whilst these chapters give a rich sense of some of the elements of the expertise of academic developers, they do not focus on the sources of knowledge that underpin this expertise. In Chapter 7, Tai Peseta and Simon Barrie argue that the knowledge base we have about effective teaching in higher education needs to be distinguished from our knowledge of how to support teachers in developing their teaching. In other words they highlight the difference between knowledge about teaching and knowledge about how to support others to teach (academic development). They argue that there is far less an organised body of knowledge that underpins academic development, suggesting that it is distributed across a range of sources and contexts. This, added to the variety of paths to becoming an academic developer, leads newcomers to the field to have to learn on the job. They argue that newcomers to the field need to be inducted into an ethic of care for the field, which they argue is captured by the notion of 'stewardship'.

Together the contributions to this book highlight the importance of collective dialogue as an aspect of the expertise of academic development. However, they also highlight the fragmented sense of the sources of knowledge that underpin academic development.

What is left unsaid about learning to teach in higher education?

Clearly any single text can only offer a partial view of learning to teach in higher education. This means that inevitably there are aspects of learning to teach that are not fully considered by the contributions to this book. In this section I consider what is left unsaid about learning to teach before concluding this chapter with a discussion of the possibilities the contributions to this book open up for future work.

The first element that I want to consider is the nature of the underpinning knowledge of the expertise of academic development. As I discussed in the previous section, whilst there is a rich discussion of the knowledge that underpins our understanding of teaching in higher education, there is less discussion of the underpinning knowledge of learning to teach as well as academic development more generally. This is understandable because the focus in many chapters is on how what we know about teaching can inform how we support academics who are learning to teach. Questions about the knowledge that underpins the expertise of academic developers are challenging because academic developers often work with academics, who are doubtful of the rigour and legitimacy of the knowledge that they have to offer. What is highlighted in this book is that this needs to be more than just knowledge about effective teaching and learning in higher education. It also needs to be knowledge about how to help academics to understand the nature of effective teaching. As Keith Trigwell and I have argued (Ashwin & Trigwell 2004), this is about the scholarship of academic development rather than simply the scholarship of teaching.

The second element is that whilst there is a rich consideration of the knowledge that underpins our understanding of teaching, there are interesting absences within the knowledge that is referred to. Particularly interesting is the way that previous approaches to understanding learning to teach in higher education are implicitly critiqued in their absence. It is important to be clear that I am referring to conceptualisations that informed previous research into teaching and learning in higher education rather than the dominant myths that I discussed earlier. Outside of the introductory chapter, there is little discussion of the previous research that chapters are contrasting their approaches with but my understanding is that it is largely the 'approaches to teaching and learning' literature (see for example Marton et al. 1997, Prosser & Trigwell 1999) that contributors have in mind. This approach seeks to understand the ways in which students' and academics' perceptions of their teaching and learning environment lead to particular ways of approaching their learning and teaching and particular kinds of learning outcome. However, this is not the only established approach that does not appear. For example, the academic literacies approach (for example, see Lea & Street 1998, Lillis 2001), which is itself a social practice approach, is similarly absent. Whilst this approach was initially focused on students' writing, it offers important insights about the ways in which students are taught and assessed in higher education. It is important to be clear that in many ways the absence of these literatures is to be expected. The purpose of this book is to explore what these new approaches offer to our understanding of learning to teach in higher education and to explore some of the challenges of how we draw on theories to support our work. Thus the book can be seen as mounting an argument for the relevance of these approaches and seeking to show what they can bring to debates around learning to teach in higher education. However, there are a number of issues that are raised by these absences.

First, as I argued earlier, all approaches simplify the social world in order to engage with it. Thus what these new simplifications offer are not more complex understandings of learning to teach in higher education but *different* understandings. If we are to understand what these new simplifications offer then we need to be able to compare them with the previous simplifications that have been developed, as, for example, Leibowitz (2016) does. Otherwise the danger is that rather than building knowledge we move between different kinds of simplifications without understanding the relations between them (Bernstein 2000).

Second, the danger is that in ignoring these previous approaches we can miss that they were trying to do something different from the approaches discussed in this book. For example, there is no point in criticising the approaches to learning approach for not taking greater account of non-human actors, when the purpose of this approach is to understand the relations between intentions, perceptions, approaches and outcomes of human actors. If we are to build knowledge about learning to teach in higher education, then we need to engage with what the previous research was attempting to do. Clearly, if the previous research does not help us to ask the questions we are interested in then we need to find new approaches and the contributions to this book show how three approaches support the asking of such questions. However, we need to recognise that is driven by a new set of questions rather than because of the failures of previous approaches.

Third, the absence of previous approaches is also a problem because it means we can miss how apparently original insights of new ways of seeing are actually re-descriptions of implications that can equally be drawn from established approaches to learning to teach in higher education. Many, but certainly not all, of the new ways of approaching learning to teach in higher education that are outlined in the earlier contributions are reminiscent of approaches to academic development that were supported by the approaches to learning literature. This is, of course, not to deny that the approaches discussed in this book can help us to design important experiences for academics and can provide powerful insights into their academic practices. However, we do need to be careful not to overplay the apparent newness of what is offered. We can only do this if we establish a productive dialogue between established and new ways of theorising learning to teach in higher education.

The challenge of how we relate old and new ways of understanding learning to teach in higher education is not simply a challenge for this book. It is a challenge about how we build knowledge about learning to teach in higher education. This challenge raises questions about how we can build on what we already know about learning to teach in higher education in order to enrich our research and practices in this area. We need to recognise that this is not an easy thing to do. Yet it is an incredibly important thing to do if we are to develop a richer understanding of learning to teach in higher education.

Conclusion

In conclusion I want to consider the possibilities for future work that are opened up by the contributions to this book. The power of relating different ways of seeing learning to teach in higher education is demonstrated by the crossover perspective chapters in this book. The discipline of moving between different ways of understanding learning to teach can provide greater choice about how to engage with the demanding situations that face academic developers. As is argued in a number of places in this book, the key is not just to see the world in a variety of ways but to use these ways of seeing to develop alternative ways of approaching our practices. It is not enough to simply critique existing practices, we need to use our collective understandings to work together to build alternative ways of learning to teach in higher education. The contributions to this book open up a number of possibilities for developing such alternatives. These will not always be successful and we need to reflect rigorously on our practices in order to understand the ways in which they have succeeded and failed. As the contributions to this book highlight, this will involve the careful consideration of evidence about our practices, a thoughtful examination of theoretical resources and previous research that enable us to make sense of this evidence, and the discussion of the relations between this evidence, theories and research with supportive and critical peers. This is difficult work but it is vital if we are to find ways of working with those who are learning to teach that can support the development of more effective and socially just teaching.

References

Ashwin, P. (2009), *Analysing teaching-learning interactions in higher education: Accounting for structure and agency*, Continuum, London.

Ashwin, P. (2015), 'Seven myths of university teaching', *Times Higher Education*, 25 February,www.timeshighereducation.com/comment/opinion/seven-myths-of-university-teaching/2018719.article

Ashwin, P. & Trigwell, K. (2004), 'Investigating educational development', in D. Baume & P. Kahn (eds), *Enhancing staff and educational development*, Kogan Page, London.

Ashwin, P., Boud, D., Coate, K., Hallett, F., Keane, E., Krause, K-L., Leibowitz, B., MacLaren, I., McArthur, J., McCune, V. & Tooher, M. (2015), *Reflective teaching in higher education*, Bloomsbury Academic, London.

Bernstein, B. (2000), *Pedagogy, symbolic control and identity: Theory, research and critique* (revised edition), Rowman and Littlefield Publishers, Oxford.

Law, J. (2004), *After method: Mess in social science research*, Routledge, London.

Lea, M. & Street, B. (1998), 'Student writing in higher education: An academic literacies approach', *Studies in Higher Education*, vol. 11, pp. 182–99.

Leibowitz, B. (2016), 'The professional development of academics as teachers', in J. Case & J. Huisman (eds) *Researching higher education: International perspectives on theory, policy and practice*, Routledge, London.

Lillis, T. (2001), *Student writing, access, regulation and desire*, Routledge, London.

Marton, F., Hounsell, D. & Entwistle, N. (eds) (1997), *The experience of learning: Implications for teaching and studying in higher education* (second edition), Scottish Academic Press, Edinburgh.

Mol, A. & Law J. (2002), 'Complexities: An introduction', in J. Law & A. Mol (eds), *Complexities: Social studies of knowledge practices*, Duke University Press, Durham, North Carolina.

Prosser, M. & Trigwell, K. (1999), *Understanding learning and teaching: The experience in higher education*, Society for Research into Higher Education and Open University Press, Buckingham.

Sayer, A. (1992), *Method in social science: A realist approach* (second edition), Routledge, London.

Sayer, A. (2000), *Realism and social science*, Sage Publications, London.

Shulman, L. (1987), 'Knowledge and teaching: foundations of the new reform', *Harvard Educational Review*, vol. 57, pp. 1–23.

Index

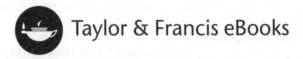